The First and Second Books of the Chronicles

R. J. COGGINS
Lecturer in Old Testament Studies
King's College, London

The Chronicles, divided into two books purely for
convenience, have long suffered from neglect; this is
partly because much of their content can be found
elsewhere in the Old Testament and partly because
their presentation, emphasizing genealogies and
ritual ceremonies, has lacked appeal for modern
man over the last few hundred years. Yet these books,
with their theological interpretation of historical
events, are a valuable source of illumination about
the Judaean community living under Persian rule
about 350 B.C. and its special relationship with
Jerusalem and its temple and with God.

In his introductory section, Mr Coggins discusses
the probable origins and the nature and purpose of
'the Chronicler's' work (whether that of a single
writer or a group) and then examines each book
separately. In the established style of the series the
N.E.B. translation of the text then follows, divided
into brief sections and alternating with passages of
commentary. The results of recent Old Testament
scholarship and modern theological thought are
conveyed in simple language to the student and
layman.

THE CAMBRIDGE BIBLE COMMENTARY

NEW ENGLISH BIBLE

GENERAL EDITORS

P. R. ACKROYD, A. R. C. LEANEY, J. W. PACKER

1 AND 2 CHRONICLES

THE FIRST AND
SECOND BOOKS OF THE

CHRONICLES

COMMENTARY BY

R. J. COGGINS

Lecturer in Old Testament Studies, King's College, London

CAMBRIDGE UNIVERSITY PRESS

CAMBRIDGE

LONDON · NEW YORK · MELBOURNE

Published by the Syndics of the Cambridge University Press
The Pitt Building, Trumpington Street, Cambridge CB2 IRP
Bentley House, 200 Euston Road, London NWI 2DB
32 East 57th Street, New York, NY 10022, USA
296 Beaconsfield Parade, Middle Park, Melbourne 3206, Australia

First published 1976

Printed in Great Britain
at the
University Printing House, Cambridge
(Euan Phillips, University Printer)

Library of Congress Cataloguing in Publication Data

Coggins, R. J. 1929–
The first and second books of the Chronicles. See slip.

(The Cambridge Bible commentary, New English Bible)

Bibliography: p. 310.

Includes index.

1. Bible. O. T. Chronicles – Commentaries. I. Bible. O. T. Chronicles.
English. New English. 1976.   II. Title.   III. Series.

BS 1345.3.C63   222'.6'077   75–17117
ISBN 0 521 08647 7 hard covers
ISBN 0 521 09758 4 paperback

GENERAL EDITORS' PREFACE

The aim of this series is to provide the text of the New English Bible closely linked to a commentary in which the results of modern scholarship are made available to the general reader. Teachers and young people have been especially kept in mind. The commentators have been asked to assume no specialized theological knowledge, and no knowledge of Greek and Hebrew. Bare references to other literature and multiple references to other parts of the Bible have been avoided. Actual quotations have been given as often as possible.

The completion of the New Testament part of the series in 1967 provides a basis upon which the production of the much larger Old Testament and Apocrypha series can be undertaken. The welcome accorded to the series has been an encouragement to the editors to follow the same general pattern, and an attempt has been made to take account of criticisms which have been offered. One necessary change is the inclusion of the translators' footnotes since in the Old Testament these are more extensive, and essential for the understanding of the text.

Within the severe limits imposed by the size and scope of the series, each commentator will attempt to set out the main findings of recent biblical scholarship and to describe the historical background to the text. The main theological issues will also be critically discussed.

Much attention has been given to the form of the volumes. The aim is to produce books each of which will be read consecutively from first to last page. The introductory material leads naturally into the text, which itself leads into the alternating sections of the commentary.

The series is accompanied by three volumes of a more general character. *Understanding the Old Testament* sets out to provide the larger historical and archaeological background, to say something about the life and thought of the people of the Old Testament, and to answer the question 'Why should we study the Old Testament?'. *The Making of the Old Testament* is concerned with the formation of the books of the Old Testament and Apocrypha in the context of the ancient near eastern world, and with the ways in which these books have come down to us in the life of the Jewish and Christian communities. *Old Testament Illustrations* contains maps, diagrams and photographs with an explanatory text. These three volumes are designed to provide material helpful to the understanding of the individual books and their commentaries, but they are also prepared so as to be of use quite independently.

P. R. A.
A. R. C. L.
J. W. P.

CONTENTS

CONTENTS

LIST OF PLANS AND MAP

THE FOOTNOTES TO THE
N.E.B. TEXT

The footnotes to the N.E.B. text are designed to help the reader either to understand particular points of detail – the meaning of a name, the presence of a play upon words – or to give information about the actual text. Where the Hebrew text appears to be erroneous, or there is doubt about its precise meaning, it may be necessary to turn to manuscripts which offer a different wording, or to ancient translations of the text which may suggest a better reading, or to offer a new explanation based upon conjecture. In such cases, the footnotes supply very briefly an indication of the evidence, and whether the solution proposed is one that is regarded as possible or as probable. Various abbreviations are used in the footnotes:

(1) Some abbreviations are simply of terms used in explaining a point: *ch(s)*., chapter(s); *cp*., compare; *lit*., literally; *mng*., meaning; *MS(S)*., manuscript(s), i.e. Hebrew manuscript(s), unless otherwise stated; *om*., omit(s); *or*, indicating an alternative interpretation; *poss*., possible; *prob*., probable; *rdg*., reading; *Vs(s)*., Versions.

(2) Other abbreviations indicate sources of information from which better interpretations or readings may be obtained.

Aq.   Aquila, a Greek translator of the Old Testament (perhaps about A.D. 130) characterized by great literalness.

Aram.   Aramaic – may refer to the text in this language (used in parts of Ezra and Daniel), or to the meaning of an Aramaic word. Aramaic belongs to the same language family as Hebrew, and is known from about 1000 B.C. over a wide area of the Middle East, including Palestine.

Heb.   Hebrew – may refer to the Hebrew text or may indicate the literal meaning of the Hebrew word.

Josephus   Flavius Josephus (A.D. 37/8–about 100), author of the *Jewish Antiquities*, a survey of the whole history of his people, directed partly at least to a non-Jewish audience, and of various other works, notably one on the *Jewish War* (that of A.D. 66–73) and a defence of Judaism (*Against Apion*).

Luc. Sept.   Lucian's recension of the Septuagint, an important edition made in Antioch in Syria about the end of the third century A.D.

Pesh.   Peshitta or Peshitto, the Syriac version of the Old Testament. Syriac is the name given chiefly to a form of Eastern Aramaic used by the Christian community. The translation varies in quality, and is at many points influenced by the Septuagint or the Targums.

Sam. Samaritan Pentateuch – the form of the first five books of the Old Testament as used by the Samaritan community. It is written in Hebrew in a special form of the Old Hebrew script, and preserves an important form of the text, somewhat influenced by Samaritan ideas.

Scroll(s) Scroll(s), commonly called the Dead Sea Scrolls, found at or near Qumran from 1947 onwards. These important manuscripts shed light on the state of the Hebrew text as it was developing in the last centuries B.C. and the first century A.D.

Sept. Septuagint (meaning 'seventy'; often abbreviated as the Roman numeral LXX), the name given to the main Greek version of the Old Testament. According to tradition, the Pentateuch was translated in Egypt in the third century B.C. by 70 (or 72) translators, six from each tribe, but the precise nature of its origin and development is not fully known. It was intended to provide Greek-speaking Jews with a convenient translation. Subsequently it came to be much revered by the Christian community.

Symm. Symmachus, another Greek translator of the Old Testament (beginning of the third century A.D.), who tried to combine literalness with good style. Both Lucian and Jerome viewed his version with favour.

Targ. Targum, a name given to various Aramaic versions of the Old Testament, produced over a long period and eventually standardized, for the use of Aramaic-speaking Jews.

Theod. Theodotion, the author of a revision of the Septuagint (probably second century A.D.), very dependent on the Hebrew text.

Vulg. Vulgate, the most important Latin version of the Old Testament, produced by Jerome about A.D. 400, and the text most used throughout the Middle Ages in western Christianity.

[...] In the text itself square brackets are used to indicate probably late additions to the Hebrew text.

(Fuller discussion of a number of these points may be found in *The Making of the Old Testament* in this series.)

THE FIRST AND SECOND BOOKS
OF THE
CHRONICLES

✳ ✳ ✳ ✳ ✳ ✳ ✳ ✳ ✳ ✳ ✳ ✳ ✳

A NEGLECTED WORK

A simple, though rough and ready, guide to the importance accorded to a religious book is to see how much use is actually made of it within that religion. The books of Chronicles form part of the sacred writings of both Jews and Christians; yet in both communities they are among the least used. In the Jewish canon of Scripture they are to be found among the third division, the Writings, and whereas in our English Bibles we are accustomed to find the books of Chronicles grouped together with the other 'historical' books, in the Hebrew Bible they are the very last books of all – a fact which has suggested to some scholars that it was only at a late stage in the formation of a list of sacred books that Chronicles came to be accepted within it. (For a fuller account of the growth of a canon of Scripture, see *The Making of the Old Testament* in this series, pp. 105–32.)

A similar attitude of relative neglect can be found within the Christian church. For example, when in the sixteenth century the Protestant reformers were insisting on the primacy of scripture, they drew up lectionaries to ensure that all the Bible was heard by the people. In England such a lectionary was devised by Archbishop Cranmer; but though he was most careful to include many parts of the Bible which must have been very unfamiliar, he made no provision for the reading of Chronicles.

There are two obvious reasons for this neglect. The first

I

is that much of the material in Chronicles can be found elsewhere in the Old Testament, parts of 1 Chronicles being based
on Genesis, and substantial parts of both 1 and 2 Chronicles
being based on the books of Samuel and Kings. Already at
the beginning of the Christian era, or perhaps earlier, when
these books were translated into Greek, it seems that this
difficulty was felt, for their Greek title is *ta paralipomena*, 'the
things omitted', that is, from the earlier parts of the Bible.
As we shall see, this attitude, that Chronicles need only be
treated as making up the gaps in our knowledge, is a persistent
one, which has led to frequent failure to appreciate the real
importance of these books.

The second reason for the neglect of the books of Chronicles
is quite simply that their presentation does not appeal to
modern man (and 'modern' in this context is not limited to
the twentieth century, but includes the last 300 or 400 years).
The first nine chapters consist almost exclusively of genealogies (the 'begats' of the Authorized Version), and much of
the later part of the work is taken up with details of the ritual
and ceremonial arrangements of the Jerusalem temple, which
also seem to have little modern relevance. In the last hundred
years or so, a further problem has arisen in connection with
some of the alleged historical details, of battles won and vast
enemy armies put to rout, which our modern scientific and
historical knowledge forces us to consider unhistorical as they
stand.

Both because of the duplication, especially with Samuel
and Kings, and also because of the way modern tastes find the
presentation unattractive, the books of Chronicles have
received much less attention than many other parts of the Old
Testament, and it might seem as if a commentary upon them
could only be justified for the sake of completeness. In fact,
however, there is more than this to be said. The books of
Chronicles may never be the most widely read part of the
Bible; yet they have much to teach us about the way in which
the Judaean community, returned from exile in Babylon,

2

understood its relation with its God, and what it meant to be the people of God. To grasp the significance of these books, it is important to consider them in their own right, and not simply as filling in the gaps in a different presentation; and to accept them as they are presented, 'warts and all', even if what we find is not immediately attractive. To do all this, it is necessary first of all to know something of the background from which they emerged.

THE WORK OF THE CHRONICLER

As with other books which in our English Bibles are divided into two, 1 and 2 Chronicles really form one whole, the division being made simply on grounds of convenience. This is not in dispute. It is less universally agreed that the books of Ezra and Nehemiah should also be seen as part of one complete presentation of God's dealings with Israel. The arguments for this will be set out in greater detail in the volume on Ezra and Nehemiah; for the moment, it will be assumed that 1 and 2 Chronicles, and Ezra and Nehemiah, form one single whole, which we may refer to as the work of the Chronicler. (To refer to 'the Chronicler' in this way does not make any judgement upon the question whether a single writer or a whole group is involved – the latter may seem more likely, but there is no decisive evidence either way.)

From what circumstances did the work of the Chronicler emerge? We need have little doubt that the work was put together in Jerusalem, which is the focus of interest throughout the work. We may narrow this down still further by noting that that interest is largely concentrated on the temple at Jerusalem, both the first temple built by Solomon on a Davidic blueprint, and the second temple of the writer's own time, which was regarded as its true continuation. If we seek to identify the Chronicler, then, it is most likely that we should look to the personnel of the second temple. Probably, though less certainly, the favourable notice of the Levites found throughout the work might suggest that the Chronicler was himself a Levite.

As for date, no certain indications are given in the work itself, but again a reasonable estimate can be reached. There are disputes concerning the date of the latest episodes in the work itself (see the commentary on Ezra and Nehemiah for details), but it is probable that this reaches to the early years of the fourth century B.C., and some of the genealogies may bring us to a slightly later date still. This was the time when Judah was under the control of the Persian Empire, and it is the favourable attitude of the Persian rulers which provides the background for the work of Ezra and Nehemiah. The Persian Empire was overrun by Alexander the Great in 333 B.C. and the immediately following years. Though it has sometimes been argued that the Chronicler's work dates from the time after Alexander, it seems more probable that the favourable attitude to the Persian rulers and the absence of any allusion to Greek rule point to a date around 350 B.C. for the completion of the main body of the work. This is intended only as an approximation; precision in such matters is not possible.

THE CHRONICLER AS HISTORIAN AND AS THEOLOGIAN

More important than an attempt to work out precisely who the Chronicler was, and the exact date of his writing, is to try to understand something of the nature and purpose of that writing. This becomes the more true because it has so often been misunderstood. In particular this is so with the historical framework of the whole.

A characteristic biblical way of expounding and interpreting God's dealings with his people in terms of the requirements of the writer's or speaker's own time is by a survey of the nation's past, stressing those elements which are of particular immediate relevance. New Testament examples may be found in the speech of Stephen before his accusers (Acts 7) or in the catalogue of heroes of faith (Hebrews 11). In the Old

4

Testament, presentations of this kind are even more frequent – several Psalms make their point in this way (e.g. 78; 105; 106); and within the Chronicler's work we shall find such a survey in Neh. 9. But such a presentation might also be undertaken on a more extensive scale – in particular, it is now widely recognized that the books of Joshua, Judges, Samuel and Kings are such a presentation of Israel's past from a point of view very similar to that found in the book of Deuteronomy, and so these works are often collectively known as the Deuteronomic History. It may be that the first four books of the Old Testament, Genesis–Numbers, should be regarded as a similar presentation brought together in what is usually called the Priestly (P) circle.

It is with extended presentations of this kind that the Chronicler's work may best be compared. In each case, the presentation is what we should describe as historical, and indeed much valuable historical information is to be found in these works; but the purpose of the whole is not to write history, and it is anachronistic to expect standards of historical accuracy such as are nowadays regarded as usual. Not 'what actually happened' but 'what is the meaning of this event for the people of God' is the underlying consideration behind the material here presented. From the point of view of historical reliability, therefore, we shall need to treat evidence found only in the work of the Chronicler and unsupported elsewhere with some caution; it should not be dismissed out of hand, as was once customary, but in many cases we shall see that a theological rather than an historical motive lies behind the presentation, and its historical value will accordingly be limited. Such caution will be especially necessary when we come to the books of Ezra and Nehemiah, the events in which are for the most part otherwise unrecorded.

Historical questions certainly cannot and should not be dismissed as of no importance; but it has come increasingly to be recognized in recent years that the Chronicler's presentation, like some of those other historical surveys already alluded to, is basically theological. More important, therefore, than asking questions about historicity, is the attempt to discover the underlying theological purpose of the Chronicler. It is hoped that much of this will emerge in the course of the commentary, but at this point two basic underlying themes may be brought out, which illustrate and add point to many of the smaller details of the work. The first such theme is that of *continuity*. It is clearly the Chronicler's intention to show the continuing favour shown by God to his people, and this underlies a great deal of the work. Thus, the genealogies begin with Adam, and are carried down, probably to the Chronicler's own day. The exile, which in many treatments of the Old Testament period both ancient and modern has come to be regarded as the great divide, is not so regarded by the Chronicler. Instead, he states that the land 'kept the sabbath rest' (2 Chron. 36: 21), and the early chapters of Ezra stress the way in which the rebuilt temple was continuous with the old one – the same site, the same vessels, the same officiants, above all the same Lord there worshipped by the same people. An implication of such a stress is that, in contrast to other works of late Judaism, the Chronicler seems not to look for violent changes or upheavals in the people's fortunes; there is little sign of political interest, the Persian rule is willingly accepted and its benevolence stressed, and the good fortune of Israel rather than its miseries is emphasized.

The second underlying theme which runs throughout the work is the importance of *Jerusalem and its temple*. The genealogies in the early chapters are arranged in such a way as to bring the story to its basic starting-point with David; the material concerning David, though much of it is taken from earlier sources, is rearranged in such a way as to stress David's concern for a proper place of worship rather than the more 'secular' side of his achievement; and the remainder of the story is told so as to show that Jerusalem is the true place of worship in an even more emphatic manner than that of the deuteronomic editor of the books of Kings. This is well illustrated by the fact that reference to the northern kingdom is simply excluded, whereas the earlier work had included much northern material so as to sharpen the condemnation of the north. It has often been argued that part of the Chronicler's purpose was to show how wrong were the contemporary inhabitants of the north, who have been called Samaritans (though this title may be anachronistic, as there is no real evidence that Samaritanism emerged until a later date); but it seems simpler and more natural to suppose that the Chronicler is concerned primarily to uphold the claims of Jerusalem as the true centre for the worship of the Lord by his people, without any one specific rival claim in mind. It is essentially Jerusalem as religious centre, and particularly the temple, which is at the heart of these claims, rather than the political implications of Jerusalem, which have so often been prominent in the different claims made concerning Jerusalem through the centuries.

THE FIRST BOOK OF THE

CHRONICLES

✶ ✶ ✶ ✶ ✶ ✶ ✶ ✶ ✶ ✶ ✶ ✶ ✶

THE CHARACTERISTICS OF I CHRONICLES

All that has been said so far is applicable to the whole work of the Chronicler. In this section we are concerned specifically with 1 Chronicles, which both illustrates those features of the work which are unattractive to modern minds – the lengthy genealogies of chs. 1–9, the portrait of David in so much less 'human' a fashion than is found in 2 Samuel – and also brings out very clearly the basic themes of continuity and the importance of Jerusalem which have just been outlined.

It can readily be seen that the main division of the book is twofold: the genealogies of chs. 1–9, and the account of the reign of David in chs. 11–29. Ch. 10, *The death of Saul*, acts as a link; the account of Saul's rule is limited in effect to a description of his death, and so 'the LORD...transferred the kingdom to David son of Jesse' (1 Chron. 10: 14).

The N.E.B. makes a division within the genealogical section between *Genealogies from Adam to Saul* (chs. 1–8) and *The restored community* (ch. 9). Such a distinction is useful in helping to establish the period being described, provided that the principle of continuity, already referred to, is not forgotten. The 'restored community' of the Chronicler's own time is essentially one with the community of David's time when the Lord's favour had first been shown. It should also be noted that some of the figures mentioned in the genealogies in the earlier chapters were also from a late date, perhaps extending down to the time of the Chronicler; this is especially true in the more extended treatment given to the Davidic line and to the Levites in chs. 3 and 6.

The commentary on these first chapters will show certain places where the expansions and additions to which genealogies are peculiarly prone have probably taken place, but it is not likely, though it has often been alleged, that the genealogies come from a source entirely different from that of the main body of the Chronicler's work. Those who have attempted to establish such a difference have relied largely on inconsistencies between the genealogies and references in the main body of the work, such as the omission from the high-priestly genealogy in ch. 6 of the names of several high priests who are mentioned in 2 Chronicles. Such an objection misunderstands the basic point of the genealogies, which is not a scientific establishment of one's lineage, such as today might be sought in parish registers, but a presentation of the identity of the people of God both in its extension through time (from Adam) and in its extension through space (the twelve tribes). There are numerous signs that the Chronicler's work only gradually reached its final form, and this inevitably means certain minor inconsistencies; but the genealogies should not be separated from the main body of the Chronicler's work.

One other general point needs to be borne in mind in reading the genealogies. Nowadays, with ample documentary evidence available, the custom is to establish the nature of a relationship by setting out the generations involved and so working out that *A* is cousin to *B* or that *C* is great-grand-father to *D*. In the ancient world the procedure might work the other way round, and genealogies would be drawn up (sometimes by professional genealogists) to illustrate the existing social and religious structure. If someone was observed to be in a close association with another, then this would be expressed in terms of a genealogy. Many scholars have held that the twelve tribes of Israel represented such an association, which subsequently came to be expressed in the familiar terms that their founders had been twelve brothers; and in the work of the Chronicler a particularly clear example of this process is found in the case of Samuel (1 Chron. 6: 28),

9

whose priestly status ensures that he is counted among the descendants of Levi, whereas earlier traditions had recognized him as an Ephraimite with no indication of Levitical connections (1 Sam. 1: 1). Other comparable examples will be noted in the commentary.

The second part of the book (chs. 11: 1 – 22: 1) is headed by the N.E.B. *David king over Israel.* To bring out the real significance of this for the Chronicler, it might have been appropriate to extend this title by adding the words 'in Jerusalem'. The special importance of this section, seen by the Chronicler as a real beginning of the life of the community, lies in the fact that it combines the themes of the chosen man and the chosen place. The whole people of God is united under the rule of David, whose status is emphasized in ecclesiastical rather than royal terms; this people is in the place chosen by God for his own dwelling-place. The tradition that Solomon was the actual temple-builder was too strong for the Chronicler to ignore, but in the picture of David given here we see him do everything for the temple except the actual building.

It has often been noted that the Chronicler's picture of David omits those aspects of the material in 2 Samuel which portray him in an unfavourable light. Thus, for example, there is no mention of his adultery with Bathsheba, or of the callous way in which the murder of her husband Uriah was arranged (2 Sam. 11–12). It is perhaps too simple, however, to see such omissions as these as an attempt to whitewash David. It is likely that the editors of 2 Samuel found these stories as part of a longer source which they incorporated as a whole. (It is often called 'the Succession Narrative'; see *2 Samuel* in this series.) But the Chronicler wished to build up his own picture of David, and he was able to use those parts of 2 Samuel that helped his purpose, together with such other material as was available to him, and material of this nature was irrelevant. We should not suspect a deliberate cover-up – after all, the stories in 2 Samuel will have been well enough known to those for whom the Chronicler was writing – but a positive attempt to present a distinct picture of David as seen some 600 years after his death, a picture which we may describe as theological and symbolic rather than personal.

In this connection it is important to recognize that the political and military side of David's role is not greatly emphasized – at least not in the sense of fostering hope of a new military leader like David who would come to restore the former glories of the nation. It is commonly held that at the time of the New Testament many Jews had hopes of a military leader, perhaps a descendant of David, who would rescue them from foreign oppression; and it is likely that such hopes had already been widespread before the Christian era. Such hopes are not prominent in the Chronicler's work. In a way which might be compared to Paul's view of the Roman Empire – 'the existing authorities are instituted by him [God]' (Rom. 13: 1) – the Chronicler appears to have been content with the existing political situation, and to have viewed it as a God-sent opportunity for the people of his own time, centred on Jerusalem and its restored temple, to work out their vocation as God's people. And in that task they had the example of David before them.

✻   ✻   ✻   ✻   ✻   ✻   ✻   ✻   ✻   ✻   ✻   ✻   ✻

Genealogies from Adam to Saul

✻ Whatever may originally have been the purpose of the creation stories in Genesis, it seems very likely that the Chronicler regarded them as telling of the very beginnings of man's life on earth, and so he begins his account of his people with Adam. This first section covers the period to Abraham. The interest is solely in the genealogical links – the dates and ages which form so prominent a part of the Genesis accounts are absent; the N.E.B. footnotes indicate the corresponding passages in Genesis. For the original audience such lists of names, reminding them of their ancestry and privileges, may well have constituted a sermon in themselves. ✻

FROM ADAM TO ABRAHAM

1 1,2,[a] 3 ADAM, SETH, ENOSH, Kenan, Mahalalel, Jared, Enoch,
4 Methuselah, Lamech, Noah.

The sons of Noah:[b] Shem, Ham and Japheth.

5[c] The sons of Japheth: Gomer, Magog, Madai, Javan,[d]
6 Tubal, Meshech and Tiras. The sons of Gomer: Ashkenaz,
7 Diphath[e] and Togarmah. The sons of Javan: Elishah,
Tarshish, Kittim[f] and Rodanim.[g]

8[h] The sons of Ham: Cush, Mizraim,[i] Put and Canaan.
9 The sons of Cush: Seba, Havilah, Sabta, Raama and
10 Sabtecha. The sons of Raama: Sheba and Dedan. Cush was the father of Nimrod, who began to show himself a
11[j] man of might on earth. From Mizraim sprang the
12 Lydians, Anamites, Lehabites, Naphtuhites, Pathrusites, Casluhites, and the Caphtorites,[k] from whom the Philistines were descended.

13 Canaan was the father of Sidon, who was his eldest son,
14 and Heth,[l] the Jebusites, the Amorites, the Girgashites,
15, 16 the Hivites, the Arkites, the Sinites, the Arvadites, the Zemarites, and the Hamathites.

17[m] The sons of Shem: Elam, Asshur, Arphaxad, Lud[n] and

[a] *Verses 2–4: cp. Gen. 5: 9–32.* [b] The sons of Noah: *so Sept.; Heb. om.*
[c] *Verses 5–7: cp. Gen. 10: 2–4.* [d] *Or* Greece. [e] *Or, with many MSS.,* Riphath (*cp. Gen. 10: 3*). [f] *Or* Tarshish of the Kittians.
[g] *Or, with many MSS.,* Dodanim (*cp. Gen. 10: 4*). [h] *Verses 8–10: cp. Gen. 10: 6–8.* [i] *Or* Egypt. [j] *Verses 11–16: cp. Gen. 10: 13–18.*
[k] and the Caphtorites: *transposed from end of verse; cp. Amos 9: 7.*
[l] *Or* the Hittites. [m] *Verses 17–23: cp. Gen. 10: 22–9.* [n] *Or* the Lydians.

Aram. The sons of Aram:*a* Uz, Hul, Gether and Mash.*b*
Arphaxad was the father of Shelah, and Shelah the father 18
of Eber. Eber had two sons: one was named Peleg,*c* 19
because in his time the earth was divided, and his brother's
name was Joktan. Joktan was the father of Almodad, 20
Sheleph, Hazarmoth, Jerah, Hadoram, Uzal, Diklah, 21
Ebal,*d* Abimael, Sheba, Ophir, Havilah and Jobab. All 22,23
these were sons of Joktan.

The line of*e* Shem: Arphaxad, Shelah, Eber, Peleg, 24,*f* 25
Reu, Serug, Nahor, Terah, Abram, also known as 26,27
Abraham, whose sons were Isaac and Ishmael. 28

* I. *Seth:* no mention is here made of Cain or Abel, recorded
in Genesis as the first sons born to Adam. The Chronicler's
interest is in the line that actually survived to become the
chosen people.

5. *The sons of Japheth:* the method usually followed in the
genealogies is to give a brief outline of the less important
figures first, before proceeding to those on whom attention is
concentrated. So Japheth and Ham are dealt with here first;
later in the chapter the line of Ishmael and Abraham's children
by his second wife Keturah will be mentioned before the line
through Isaac, and so similarly with Isaac's family (Esau before
Israel).

6–7. *Diphath...Rodanim:* as the N.E.B. footnotes indicate,
the initial letters of these names are found differently in
Genesis. The Hebrew letters corresponding to 'd' and 'r'
are very similar, and this probably accounts for the confusion.
It may be that the form beginning with 'r' is right in each
case.

[a] The sons of Aram: *so one MS., cp. Gen. 10: 23; others om.* [b] *So
some MSS., cp. Gen. 10: 23; others* Meshech. [c] *That is* Division.
[d] *Or Obal, cp. Gen. 10: 28.* [e] The line of: *prob. rdg.; Heb. om.*
[f] *Verses 24–7: cp. Gen. 11: 10–26.*

8–16. *The sons of Ham* are described in greater detail, with a few comments on some of them, mostly reproduced from Genesis. Gen. 10 is also followed in the way in which the descendants of *Mizraim* (Egypt: see footnote) and *Canaan* are described as nations rather than as individuals.

17–23. *The sons of Shem:* the line on which attention is to be concentrated is dealt with last, and among the sons of Shem, it is through Arphaxad that the significant line descends.

24–8. *Abram (Abraham)* is then reached by following the genealogies of Gen. 11, and his two sons are noted. It is not clear why the usual principle of dealing with the less important first is here abandoned, so that we have Isaac, the inheritor of the promise, dealt with before the first-born Ishmael. *

THE DESCENDANTS OF ABRAHAM AND ISAAC

29[a] The sons of[b] Ishmael in the order of their birth:
30 Nebaioth the eldest, then Kedar, Adbeel, Mibsam, Mish-
31 ma, Dumah, Massa, Hadad,[c] Teman,[d] Jetur, Naphish and
Kedemah. These were Ishmael's sons.

32[e]   The sons of Keturah, Abraham's concubine: she bore
him Zimran, Jokshan, Medan, Midian, Ishbak and Shuah.
33 The sons of Jokshan: Sheba and Dedan. The sons of
Midian: Ephah, Epher, Enoch, Abida and Eldaah. All
these were descendants of Keturah.

34   Abraham was the father of Isaac, and Isaac's sons were
35[f] Esau and Israel. The sons of Esau: Eliphaz, Reuel, Jeush,
36 Jalam and Korah. The sons of Eliphaz: Teman, Omar,
37 Zephi, Gatam, Kenaz, Timna and Amalek. The sons of
Reuel: Nahath, Zerah, Shammah and Mizzah.

[a] *Verses 29–31: cp. Gen. 25: 13–16.*   [b] The sons of: *prob. rdg., cp.
Gen. 25: 13; Heb. om.*   [c] *Or, possibly,* Harar, *cp. Gen. 25: 15.*
[d] *So Sept.; Heb.* Tema.   [e] *Verses 32, 33: cp. Gen. 25: 1–4.*   [f] *Verses
35–7: cp. Gen. 36: 4, 5, 9–13.*

The sons of Seir: Lotan, Shobal, Zibeon, Anah, Dishon, 38[a]
Ezer and Dishan. The sons of Lotan: Hori and Homam; 39
and Lotan had a sister named Timna. The sons of Shobal: 40
Alvan,[b] Manahath, Ebal, Shephi and Onam. The sons of
Zibeon: Aiah and Anah. The son[c] of Anah: Dishon. The 41
sons of Dishon: Amram, Eshban, Ithran and Cheran. The 42
sons of Ezer: Bilhan, Zavan and Akan.[d] The sons of
Dishan: Uz and Aran.

These are the kings who ruled over Edom before there 43[e]
were kings in Israel: Bela son of Beor, whose city was
named Dinhabah. When he died, he was succeeded by 44
Jobab son of Zerah of Bozrah. When Jobab died, he was 45
succeeded by Husham of Teman. When Husham died, he 46
was succeeded by Hadad son of Bedad, who defeated
Midian in Moabite country. His city was named Avith.
When Hadad died, he was succeeded by Samlah of 47
Masrekah. When Samlah died, he was succeeded by Saul 48
of Rehoboth on the River. When Saul died, he was 49
succeeded by Baal-hanan son of Akbor. When Baal- 50
hanan died, he was succeeded by Hadad. His city was
named Pai; his wife's name was Mehetabel daughter of
Matred a woman of Me-zahab.[f]

After Hadad died the chiefs in Edom were: chief Timna, 51
chief Aliah, chief Jetheth, chief Oholibamah, chief Elah, 52
chief Pinon, chief Kenaz, chief Teman, chief Mibzar, 53
chief Magdiel and chief Iram. These were the chiefs of 54
Edom.

[a] *Verses 38–42: cp. Gen. 36: 20–8.* [b] *So many MSS., cp. Gen.
36: 23; others* Alian. [c] *Prob. rdg.; Heb.* sons; *the same correction
is made in several other places in chs. 1–9.* [d] *and Akan: so many MSS.,
cp. Gen. 36: 27; others* Jakan. [e] *Verses 43–54: cp. Gen. 36: 31–43.*
[f] *Or daughter of Mezahab.*

✳ This section takes the genealogy in the chosen line only two generations forward, much of the attention being given to the other descendants of Abraham and Isaac. The choice seems to have been governed partly by the sources in Genesis, partly by the realities of the situation in the Chronicler's own day.

32. *The sons of Jokshan: Sheba and Dedan:* it has often been suggested that Jokshan here is a variant of Joktan (verses 19–23), and that his sons' names are a duplicate of those found in a different context in verse 9. This single example is cited to show how ancient genealogies might embody parallel traditions which were strictly speaking irreconcilable with one another. More detailed study, especially of the genealogies in their earlier form, in Genesis, would show other examples.

34. *Israel:* this name is always used by the Chronicler in preference to his other name Jacob, which is found only in the Psalm quoted in 1 Chron. 16. The reason may have been the desire to stress the Israel theme, and also the reputation for deceit associated with the name Jacob (cp. Gen. 27: 35f.) may have led the Chronicler to prefer the divinely given name Israel (cp. Gen. 32: 28).

35–54. The Edomite genealogies found in Gen. 36 are reproduced in considerable detail. This is unexpected, both because it seems to hinder the Chronicler from his main purpose of setting out the chosen line, and also because most of the other evidence available to us suggests great hostility toward Edom in the later Old Testament period; see Psalm 137 or the book of Obadiah. Perhaps this picture of anti-Edomite feeling was not universal, and certainly it is not supported by the general tone of the Chronicler's work.

36. *Timna:* this name causes some confusion. It is found again in verses 39 and 51, and it is not clear whether variant traditions concerning the same person or different people are here being listed. In addition the corresponding reference in Gen. 36: 12 speaks of Timna as 'concubine to...Eliphaz' rather than his son as here.

38. *Seir:* originally a place-name, meaning 'hairy, shaggy', of a mountain east of the Jordan; the name is used in Gen. 36: 20 of the original inhabitants of the area, and in later Old Testament passages (e.g. Ezek. 35) it came to be an alternative name for the inhabitants of Edom. That appears to be the usage here. The genealogy which follows differs more markedly in minor details from its source in Genesis than the earlier ones in the present chapter. *

JUDAH

* The extended section, 2: 1 – 4: 23, the first of the tribal genealogies, gives details of the families of Judah. Not surprisingly it is the most detailed of all the genealogies, since Judah became dominant in the south, and so, though he was not regarded as the first-born, the traditions of Judah are recorded in great detail, much of which is unknown to us from any other source. *

JUDAH AND ITS CLANS – I

2 These were the sons of Israel: Reuben, Simeon, Levi, 2 Judah, Issachar, Zebulun, Dan, Joseph, Benjamin, Naphtali, Gad and Asher.

3 The sons of Judah: Er, Onan and Shelah; the mother of these three was a Canaanite woman, Bathshua.[a] Er, Judah's eldest son, displeased the LORD and the LORD slew him. 4 Then Tamar, Judah's daughter-in-law, bore him Perez and Zerah, making in all five sons of Judah. 5 The sons of Perez: Hezron and Hamul. 6 The sons of Zerah: Zimri, Ethan, Heman, Calcol and Darda,[b] five in all. 7 The son of Zimri: Carmi.[c] The son of Carmi: Achar, who

[a] Bathshua: *or* daughter of Shua. [b] *So many MSS.; others* Dara.
[c] The son...Carmi: *prob. rdg. (cp. Josh. 7: 1, 18); Heb. om.*

17

8 troubled Israel by his violation of the sacred ban. The son
9 of Ethan: Azariah. The sons of Hezron: Jerahmeel, Ram
10 and Caleb.*a* Ram was the father of Amminadab, Ammina-
11 dab father of Nahshon prince of Judah. Nahshon was the
12 father of Salma, Salma father of Boaz, Boaz father of
13 Obed, Obed father of Jesse. The eldest son of Jesse was
14 Eliab, the second Abinadab, the third Shimea, the fourth
15 Nethaneel, the fifth Raddai, the sixth Ozem, the seventh
16 David; their sisters were Zeruiah and Abigail. The sons
17 of Zeruiah: Abishai, Joab and Asahel, three in all. Abigail
   was the mother of Amasa; his father was Jether the
   Ishmaelite.

18   Caleb son of Hezron had Jerioth by Azubah his wife;*b*
19 these were her sons: Jesher, Shobab and Ardon. When
   Azubah died, Caleb married Ephrath, who bore him
20 Hur. Hur was the father of Uri, and Uri father of Bezalel.
21 Later, Hezron, then sixty years of age, had intercourse
   with the daughter of Machir father of Gilead, having mar-
22 ried her, and she bore Segub. Segub was the father of Jair
23 who had twenty-three cities in Gilead. Geshur and Aram
   took from them Havvoth-jair, and Kenath and its dependent villages, a total of sixty towns. All these were
24 descendants of Machir father of Gilead. After the death of
   Hezron, Caleb had intercourse*c* with Ephrathah*d* and she
   bore him Ashhur the founder*e* of Tekoa.

25   The sons of Jerahmeel eldest son of Hezron by*f* Ahijah
26 were Ram the eldest, Bunah, Oren and Ozem. Jerahmeel
   had another wife, whose name was Atarah; she was the

[a] *So Sept.; Heb.* Celubai.   [b] *his wife: prob. rdg.; Heb.* a woman and.
[c] *Caleb had intercourse: so Sept.; Heb.* in Caleb.   [d] *So Pesh.; Heb.
adds* and Abiah Hezron's wife.   [e] *Lit.* father *and similarly several times
in chs. 2–4.*   [f] *by: prob. rdg.; Heb. om.*

mother of Onam. The sons of Ram eldest son of Jerah- 27
meel: Maaz, Jamin and Eker. The sons of Onam: 28
Shammai and Jada. The sons of Shammai: Nadab and
Abishur. The name of Abishur's wife was Abihail; she 29
bore him Ahban and Molid. The sons of Nadab: Seled 30
and Ephraim;*a* Seled died without children. Ephraim's 31
son was Ishi, Ishi's son Sheshan, Sheshan's son Ahlai. The 32
sons of Jada brother of Shammai: Jether and Jonathan;
Jether died without children. The sons of Jonathan: 33
Peleth and Zaza. These were the descendants of Jerahmeel.

Sheshan had daughters but no sons. He had an Egyptian 34
servant named Jarha; he gave his daughter in marriage to 35
this Jarha, and she bore him Attai. Attai was the father of 36
Nathan, Nathan father of Zabad, Zabad father of Ephlal, 37
Ephlal father of Obed, Obed father of Jehu, Jehu father 38
of Azariah, Azariah father of Helez, Helez father of 39
Elasah, Elasah father of Sisamai, Sisamai father of Shallum, 40
Shallum father of Jekamiah, and Jekamiah father of 41
Elishama.

The sons of Caleb brother of Jerahmeel: Mesha the 42
eldest, founder of Ziph, and*b* Mareshah founder of
Hebron. The sons of Hebron: Korah, Tappuah, Rekem 43
and Shema. Shema was the father of Raham father of 44
Jorkoam, and Rekem was the father of Shammai. The son 45
of Shammai was Maon, and Maon was the founder of
Beth-zur. Ephah, Caleb's concubine, was the mother of 46
Haran, Moza and Gazez; Haran was the father of Gazez.
The sons of Jahdai: Regem, Jotham, Geshan, Pelet, 47

[a] *So one MS.; others* Appaim.
[b] *Prob. rdg.; Heb. adds* the sons of.

48 Ephah and Shaaph. Maacah, Caleb's concubine, was the
49 mother of Sheber and Tirhanah; she bore also Shaaph
founder of Madmannah, and Sheva founder of Mach-
benah and Gibea. Caleb also had a daughter named
Achsah.

50   The descendants of Caleb: the sons*a* of Hur, the eldest
son of Ephrathah: Shobal the founder of Kiriath-jearim,
51 Salma the founder of Bethlehem, and Hareph the founder
52 of Beth-gader. Shobal the founder of Kiriath-jearim was
the father of Reaiah*b* and the ancestor of half the Manahethites.*c*

53   The clans of Kiriath-jearim: Ithrites, Puhites, Shu-
mathites, and Mishraites, from whom were descended the
Zareathites and the Eshtaulites.

54   The descendants of Salma: Bethlehem, the Netophathites, Ataroth, Beth-joab, half the Manahethites, and
the Zorites.

55   The clans of Sophrites*d* living at Jabez: Tirathites,
Shimeathites, and Suchathites. These were Kenites*e* who
were connected by marriage with the ancestor of the
Rechabites.

* 1–2. The names of the twelve *sons of Israel*, pictured here
as the founders of the twelve tribes of Israel, are the same as
those found elsewhere, but the order in which they are given
is peculiar to this section. The six 'Leah-tribes' (i.e. sons of
Israel by his first wife) are given first as in Gen. 35: 23, but
then the two tribes descended from his handmaid Bilhah,
Dan and Naphtali, are separated by the two 'Rachel-tribes',

[a] *So Sept.; Heb.* son.   [b] *Prob. rdg., cp. 4: 2; Heb.* the seer.
[c] *Prob. rdg., cp. verse 54; Heb.* Menuhoth.   [d] *Or* secretaries.
[e] *Lit.* Kinites.

Joseph and Benjamin, with the other handmaid-tribes at the end. Joseph is never treated by the Chronicler as a tribal name; instead, his two sons, Ephraim and Manasseh, are regarded as founders of separate tribes.

3-4. These two verses are condensed from the story in Gen. 38.

6. *Zimri*: this name is found in Josh. 7: 1 in the form 'Zabdi' – it is difficult to decide which form is likely to have been original. The other four names are found in 1 Kings 4: 31, in an account of those whose wisdom is surpassed by that of Solomon. No indication is there given of their families, and the context would suggest that they were not Israelite at all. Probably the Chronicler has introduced them into his genealogy as a deliberate word-play – *Hamul* and *Zerah* here being linked with 'Mahol' and 'Ezrah-ite' in the Kings passage. Though we may find such a word-play artificial, it is not uncommon in the Old Testament, and we shall find further examples of it in the work of the Chronicler. A further reason for the link may be the fact that Ethan and Heman are both found later among the groups of singers (1 Chron. 15: 19).

7. *Achar, who troubled*: another characteristic device of the Chronicler is introduced here. The son of Carmi according to Josh. 7: 1 was 'Achan'. Already in Josh. 7: 24 he is associated with a place called 'Achor', which means 'trouble'. Now his name is slightly changed into a form which means 'one who brings trouble'. It may also be a deliberate allusion by the Chronicler to the same phrase used in the dispute between Ahab and Elijah in 1 Kings 18: 17f.

9. *Jerahmeel...and Caleb*: these were the names of tribes, not originally part of Israel, but of similar semi-nomadic background, who were associated with Judah, and eventually came to be regarded as genuinely Judahite, their ancestors being included in the Judahite genealogy. The other names referred to in this section are found in Ruth 4: 18–22.

13-15. The first three sons of Jesse are named in 1 Sam. 16

(in slightly different forms); the remaining names are not
attested elsewhere. According to I Sam. 16: 10f., David was
the eighth son of Jesse, but here he is *the seventh*, a position
often regarded as being a sign of favour.

18–22. This appears as a distinct section, dealing with the
Calebite group (save for verse 20, which borrows a brief note
from Exod. 31: 2); the origin of this material is obscure, and
some of it appears again in a variant form in verses 50–2.

22. *Jair:* this name provides the opportunity for originally
distinct traditions to be harmonized, for this Jair appears to
be identified with someone of the same name from Transjordan referred to in Deut. 3: 14. In this and many other
cases, too numerous to set out individually, what was originally a place-name appears to have been applied to an individual. (See the N.E.B. footnote concerning the reading of
'founder' for 'father'.)

25–33. The Jerahmeelites are similarly listed, with supplementary information in 34–41. Very little of this material
is found in any other part of the Old Testament, though most
of the individual names are familiar Old Testament ones.

42–9. These lists are followed by further Calebite material,
which suggests either that the Chronicler had access to more
information from this source than from elsewhere, or that a
great many of the families of Judah in his day claimed descent
from Caleb. Again many of the names listed as those of
individuals are really place-names (Hebron, Maon, Beth-zur
are among the best known).

50–5. Finally, a number of other clans, all originating in
the south and all in a close relation with Judah, are listed. It is
widely held that these lists in their geographical arrangement
reflect ancient sources. *

THE FAMILY OF DAVID

These were the sons of David, born at Hebron: the 3₁ᵃ
eldest Amnon, whose mother was Ahinoam of Jezreel;
the second Daniel, whose mother was Abigail of Carmel;
the third Absalom, whose mother was Maacah daughter 2
of Talmai king of Geshur; the fourth Adonijah, whose
mother was Haggith; the fifth Shephatiah, whose mother 3
was Abital; the sixth Ithream, whose mother was David's
wife Eglah. These six were born at Hebron, where David 4
reigned seven years and six months. In Jerusalem he
reigned thirty-three years, and there the following sons 5ᵇ
were born to him: Shimea, Shobab, Nathan and Solomon; these four were sons of Bathshebaᶜ daughter of
Ammiel. There were nine others: Ibhar, Elishama, 6
Eliphelet, Nogah, Nepheg, Japhia, Elishama, Eliada and 7, 8
Eliphelet. These were all the sons of David, with their 9
sister Tamar, in addition to his sons by concubines.

Solomon's son was Rehoboam, his son Abia, his son 10
Asa, his son Jehoshaphat, his son Joram, his son Ahaziah, 11
his son Joash, his son Amaziah, his son Azariah, his son 12
Jotham, his son Ahaz, his son Hezekiah, his son Manasseh, 13
his son Amon, and his son Josiah. The sons of Josiah: the 14, 15
eldest was Johanan, the second Jehoiakim, the third
Zedekiah, the fourth Shallum. The sons of Jehoiakim: 16
Jeconiah and Zedekiah. The sons of Jeconiah, a prisoner:ᵈ 17
Shealtiel,ᵉ Malchiram, Pedaiah, Shenazzar, Jekamiah, 18
Hoshama and Nedabiah. The sons of Pedaiah: Zerubbabel 19

[a] *Verses 1–4: cp. 2 Sam. 3: 2–5.*   [b] *Verses 5–8: cp. 14: 4–7; 2 Sam.*
5: 14–16.   [c] *So Vulg.; Heb.* Bathshua.   [d] Jeconiah, a prisoner:
or Jeconiah: Assir,...   [e] *So Sept.; Heb. adds* his son.

and Shimei. The sons[a] of Zerubbabel: Meshullam and
20 Hananiah; they had a sister, Shelomith. There were five
others: Hashubah, Ohel, Berechiah, Hasadiah and Jushab-
21 hesed. The sons of Hananiah: Pelatiah and Isaiah; his son
was[b] Rephaiah, his son Arnan, his son Obadiah, his son
22 Shecaniah. The sons of Shecaniah: Shemaiah,[c] Hattush,
23 Igeal, Bariah, Neariah and Shaphat, six in all. The sons of
Neariah: Elioenai, Hezekiah and Azrikam, three in all.
24 The sons of Elioenai: Hodaiah, Eliashib, Pelaiah, Akkub,
Johanan, Dalaiah and Anani, seven in all.

✷ 1. Attention now focuses more sharply on David, who is
the principal centre of interest for the Chronicler. The Judahite
line, which had been brought as far as David in the previous
chapter (verse 15), is now carried forward from David, who
lived about 1000 B.C., to the fifth, or perhaps even the
fourth, century. In addition to the references to other biblical
occurrences of these names given in the N.E.B. footnote, the
kings following Solomon are the same as those in 2 Kings and
2 Chronicles (at times with minor variants in the names).
Daniel: in 2 Sam. 3: 3 the corresponding name is 'Chileab'.
A possible explanation for the change is a desire on the
Chronicler's part to link the Davidic house with the famous
folk-hero Daniel, but if this was his intention, some greater
elaboration of the idea would be expected.

    5. *Nathan:* nothing is known of him as an historical figure,
but one form of the genealogy of Jesus (Luke 3: 31) traces his
descent through Nathan rather than through Solomon (as in
Matthew). Later Jewish tradition identified this Nathan with
the prophet of the same name referred to in 2 Sam. 12.
these four were sons of Bathsheba daughter of Ammiel: as the

[a] *So some MSS.; others* son.
[b] his son was: *so Sept., throughout verse; Heb.* the sons of.
[c] *Prob. rdg.; Heb. adds* and the sons of Shemaiah.

N.E.B. footnote indicates, the Hebrew has *Bathshua*, the same name as that of Judah's wife (2: 3). A deliberate link may be intended, and it is not necessary to suppose that the change is due to the intention of omitting any allusion to a story which would reflect badly on David. It is unexpected that Solomon should be listed as her fourth son; the story of his birth in 2 Sam. 12: 24, though not explicitly contradicting this, gives a very different impression.

6–7. Eliphelet, Nogah: these names are lacking in 2 Sam. 5: 15, and have probably been added to the original list in error.

10–14. Some three hundred years are covered by means of this list of the descendants of David who ruled in Judah, a period dealt with in greater detail in 2 Chronicles.

15. Josiah was king over Judah from 640 to 609, and was in effect the last king of Judah with any real claim to independence. From his time, the Davidic dynasty is listed in greater detail. His sons are known from 2 Kings or Jeremiah, with the exception of Johanan, who is otherwise unknown; Shallum is called 'Jehoahaz' in 2 Kings 23: 30–4 – possibly Shallum is a name taken when he became king (cp. Jer. 22: 11).

16. Jeconiah: so-called several times in Jeremiah, known also as 'Coniah' (again in Jeremiah), but more usually as 'Jehoiachin' (so in 2 Kings and in 2 Chron. 36). These minor differences of name suggest that the Chronicler was here using some kind of official source which differed from his sources in 2 Chronicles. The Zedekiah mentioned here is otherwise unknown, unless he has been wrongly identified with the Zedekiah of the previous verse, who was his uncle.

17. a prisoner: it is likely that the text should be followed here, and a reference seen to Jeconiah being taken into exile in Babylon, rather than the footnote, which takes 'Assir' as the name of another son.

Tablets discovered in Babylon which set out the rations provided for captive rulers mentioned Jehoiachin and five sons; presumably the last two of the seven mentioned here were born later. The tablets date from about 590–570 B.C.

19. *The sons of Pedaiah: Zerubbabel:* Zerubbabel plays a prominent part in Haggai, Zechariah and Ezra, and wherever his father's name is mentioned he is described as 'son of Shealtiel'. Rather than elaborate theories to explain this difference, it seems better to note that here again divergent sources are found.

19–24. No certain (or even very probable) reference to any of the other names in this list is found in the Old Testament; curiously, the New Testament genealogies of Jesus, though they both include Zerubbabel, do not mention any of his descendants listed in this chapter.

21. The N.E.B., by modifying the text in the way indicated by the footnote, has allowed for five generations between Hananiah and Shecaniah. Others have disputed whether separate generations are here being referred to.

22. The N.E.B. text makes Shemaiah brother to the five listed after him, so justifying *six in all* at the end of the verse. The Hebrew (followed by N.E.B. footnote and other English versions) makes Hattush and the others 'sons of Shemaiah', and *six* would then be an error for 'five'. Because of these doubts it is not certain how many generations after Jeconiah are listed. This uncertainty, coupled with the notorious unreliability of estimating the length of a generation, makes it difficult to judge the approximate date of the last names in this list. Dates varying from about 400 B.C. to about 300 B.C. for the times of 'the sons of Elioenai' have been proposed.

One feature that may surprise us is the lack of prominence given to these 'Davidic' lists. The naming of so many sons of David may suggest that several families contemporary with the Chronicler were proud of their Davidic descent, but no hopes associated with the restoration of a Davidic king in Jerusalem seem to be implied. The impression is that these names are recorded because of their distinguished ancestor, rather than that there is any expectation of a 'new David' to arise from among them. ✳

JUDAH AND ITS CLANS – II

The sons of Judah: Perez, Hezron, Carmi, Hur and **4**
Shobal. Reaiah son of Shobal was the father of Jahath, 2
Jahath father of Ahumai and Lahad. These were the clans
of the Zorathites.

The sons*a* of Etam: Jezreel, Ishma, Idbash, Penuel the 3–4
founder of Gedor, and Ezer the founder of Hushah; they
had a sister named Hazelelponi. These were the sons of
Hur: Ephrathah the eldest, the founder of Bethlehem.

Ashhur the founder of Tekoa had two wives, Helah and 5
Naarah. Naarah bore him Ahuzam, Hepher, Temeni and 6
Haahashtari.*b* These were the sons of Naarah. The sons of 7
Helah: Zereth, Jezoar, Ethnan and Coz.*c* Coz was the 8
father of Anub and Zobebah and the clans of Aharhel son
of Harum.

Jabez ranked higher than his brothers; his mother called 9
him Jabez because, as she said, she had borne him in pain.
Jabez called upon the God of Israel and said, 'I pray thee, 10
bless me and grant me wide territories. May thy hand be
with me, and do me no harm, I pray thee, and let me be
free from pain'; and God granted his petition.

Kelub brother of Shuah was the father of Mehir the 11
father of Eshton. Eshton was the father of Beth-rapha, 12
Paseah, and Tehinnah father of Ir-nahash. These were the
men of Rechah.

The sons of Kenaz: Othniel and Seraiah. The sons of 13
Othniel: Hathath and Meonothai.*d*

[a] *So Sept.; Heb.* father.   [b] Temeni and Haahashtari: *or* the Temanite
and the Ahashtarite.   [c] and Coz: *so Targ.; Heb. om.*   [d] The sons of
Othniel...Meonothai: *so Vulg.; Heb.* The son of Othniel: Hathath.

14   Meonothai was the father of Ophrah.

Seraiah was the father of Joab founder of Ge-harashim,[a] for they were craftsmen.

15   The sons of Caleb son of Jephunneh: Iru, Elah and Naam. The son of Elah: Kenaz.[b]

16   The sons of Jehaleleel: Ziph and Ziphah, Tiria and Asareel.

17–18   The sons of Ezra: Jether, Mered, Epher and Jalon. These were the sons of Bithiah daughter of Pharaoh, whom Mered had married; she conceived and gave birth to[c] Miriam, Shammai and Ishbah founder of Eshtemoa. His Jewish wife was the mother of Jered founder of Gedor, Heber founder of Soco, and Jekuthiel founder of Zanoah.

19   The sons of his[d] wife Hodiah sister of Naham were Daliah[e] father of Keilah the Garmite, and Eshtemoa the Maacathite.

20   The sons of Shimon: Amnon, Rinnah, Ben-hanan and Tilon.

The sons of Ishi: Zoheth and Ben-zoheth.

21   The sons of Shelah son of Judah: Er founder of Lecah, Laadah founder of Mareshah, the clans of the guild of

22   linen-workers at Ashbea, Jokim, the men of Kozeba, Joash, and Saraph who fell out with Moab and came back

23   to Bethlehem.[f] (The records are ancient.) They were the potters, and those who lived at Netaim and Gederah were there on the king's service.

[a] *Or* the Valley of Craftsmen.
[b] *So some MSS.; others* and Kenaz.
[c] and gave birth to: *prob. rdg.; Heb. om.*
[d] his: *prob. rdg.; Heb. om.*
[e] *So Sept.; Heb. om.*
[f] and came...Bethlehem: *prob. rdg.; Heb. unintelligible.*

✲ 1. Unexpectedly we now return to Judah to trace different descendants. All five names of these *sons of Judah* have appeared at different points in the lists in ch. 2, and this material appears to be supplementary to those lists, and often in contradiction with them. As in ch. 2, the explanation is probably to be sought in the fact that these genealogies really represent the traditions of various clan-groups who together make up what came to be known as the 'tribe of Judah'.

2. *Zorathites:* probably to be identified with the 'Zareathites' of 2: 53, a district rather than a personal name, best known as Samson's family home (Judg. 13: 2). Often in these lists the geographical indications are as important as the genealogical ones as indicative of the extent of the true Israel.

3–12. The lists here are extremely disjointed, and unrelated to any information available to us from elsewhere. They are again a mixture of geographical and genealogical information, originating from different sources. Such an insertion as that in verses 9–10, describing an incident in the family traditions, should not be regarded as extraneous to the genealogies – there is ample evidence from both biblical and non-biblical sources that it was common to insert notes of this kind within ancient genealogies (cp. the notes on Lamech in Gen. 4: 19–24, or on Nimrod in Gen. 10: 8–10). A folk-etymology has linked the word we translate *pain* (Hebrew *'atseb*) with the name *Jabez* (Hebrew *'abets*).

13. *The sons of Kenaz: Othniel:* here we appear once more to have information from a Calebite source, for the other references to Othniel link him with Caleb. He is mentioned in Josh. 15: 17 as having captured Hebron, and in Judg. 3: 9–11 as a judge over Israel.

17–18. The section is remarkable both historically and theologically. It is very unexpected to find an otherwise quite unknown Judahite married to a Pharaoh's daughter and there is no trace here of the criticism of marriage to foreign wives which is so prominent in Ezra and Nehemiah.

21–3. The final section, after the extensive Calebite genealogies, returns to Judah's third son Shelah, whose descendants are not elsewhere listed. Here to an even greater extent than elsewhere, the interest centres on the occupation carried on by different families rather than genealogies as such.

22. *The records are ancient*: there is no need to doubt that the Chronicler is here using ancient material, and this may also account for the extreme difficulty of translating these verses, which (as the N.E.B. footnote indicates) are unintelligible as they stand. ✳

SIMEON

24 The sons of Simeon: Nemuel, Jamin, Jarib, Zerah,
25 Saul, his son Shallum, his son Mibsam and his son
26 Mishma. The sons of Mishma: his son Hamuel, his son
27 Zaccur and his son Shimei. Shimei had sixteen sons and six daughters, but others of his family had fewer children, and the clan as a whole did not increase as much as the
28 tribe of Judah. They lived at Beersheba, Moladah, Hazar-
29, 30 shual, Bilhah, Ezem, Tolad, Bethuel, Hormah, Ziklag,
31 Beth-marcaboth, Hazar-susim, Beth-birei, and Shaaraim. These were their cities until David came to the throne.
32 Their settlements*a* were Etam, Ain, Rimmon, Tochen,
33 and Ashan, five cities in all. They had also hamlets round these cities as far as Baal. These were the places where they lived.

34 The names on their register were: Meshobab, Jamlech,
35 Joshah son of Amaziah, Joel, Jehu son of Josibiah, son of
36 Seraiah, son of Asiel, Elioenai, Jaakobah, Jeshohaiah,
37 Asaiah, Adiel, Jesimiel, Benaiah, Ziza son of Shiphi, son of Allon, son of Jedaiah, son of Shimri, son of Shemaiah,

[a] *Prob. rdg.; Heb.* hamlets.

whose names are recorded as princes in their clans, and 38
their families had greatly increased. They then went from 39
the approaches to Gedor east of the valley in search of
pasture for their flocks. They found rich and good pasture 40
in a wide stretch of open country where everything was
quiet and peaceful; before then it had been occupied by
Hamites. During the reign of Hezekiah king of Judah 41
these whose names are written above came and destroyed
the tribes of Ham[a] and the Meunites whom they found
there. They annihilated them so that no trace of them has
remained to this day; and they occupied the land in their
place, for there was pasture for their flocks. Of their num- 42
ber five hundred Simeonites invaded the hill-country of
Seir, led by Pelatiah, Neariah, Rephaiah, and Uzziel, the
sons of Ishi. They destroyed all who were left of the 43
surviving Amalekites; and they live there still.

* The Simeonite lists are much briefer, both because the
tribe seems historically to have been absorbed into Judah quite
early in Israel's history (perhaps already by the time of David)
and also because the Chronicler's interest focuses on Judah
and Levi. As with much of the Judahite material we find here
a combination of genealogical information, geographical
notes, and miscellaneous scraps of tradition concerning particular individuals.

24. *The sons of Simeon* (and of the other tribes) are listed in
accordance with the census lists in Num. 26, which appear to
have provided an important source for the Chronicler; in
this case some of the names are found also at Gen. 46: 10,
though in variant forms.

27. *the clan as a whole did not increase as much as the tribe of
Judah:* we may take this both as a historical statement,

[a] the tribes of Ham: *prob. rdg., cp. verse 40; Heb.* their tribes.

reflecting Simeon's failure to maintain independent existence, and as a theological appraisal, indicating where God's favour was directed. It may derive from the indication in Num. 26: 14, which shows Simeon as the smallest of the tribes.

28–33. The lists of areas occupied are very similar to those found in Josh. 19: 2–8, and it is disputed whether these are genuine old lists, as the note in verse 31, *These were their cities until David came to the throne*, would lead us to suppose, or whether they are artificial products of a much later period. The problem is for the moment insoluble because many of the place-names, which are for the most part in southern Palestine, cannot be identified with certainty.

33. *Baal:* very unexpected as a place-name, though familiar as the name of the Canaanite god, whose worship much of the Old Testament bitterly opposes; the longer form, 'Baalath-beer', found in Josh. 19: 8, is no doubt correct. The name means 'mistress of the well' and the Joshua passage locates it in the Negeb, i.e. the far south of the land.

34–8. A curiosity in these verses, found in other places in these lists, is that some of the names are given a brief genealogy, others are simply recorded with no further detail. The suggestion has been made that these *princes in their clans* held an office within the tribal structure, the appointment to which was sometimes on hereditary lines, sometimes not, and that it had military connections.

The names listed are not found elsewhere.

39–40. *Gedor:* the name is often emended to the better-known Gerar, south-west of Palestine, which might fit in with the reference to Hamites – these would then be Egyptians (cp. 1: 8 and N.E.B. footnote at that verse). But it is dangerous to identify every unknown place with a well-known one with a similar name, and quite possibly this is another place altogether; the word means 'wall', which is a likely name for a city. Places named Gedor are mentioned also in 4: 4 and 12: 7, and though these are Judahite places, we have already seen that the links between Judah and Simeon were very close.

41-3. This episode, unattested elsewhere, is instructive, both in the way it illustrates the kind of conflict between Israel and the existing inhabitants that must often have taken place, and also in the hatred for the Amalekites which characterizes much of the Old Testament. ✽

THE TRANSJORDANIAN TRIBES

The sons of Reuben, the eldest of Israel's sons. (He was, 5 in fact, the first son born, but because he had committed incest with a wife of his father's the rank of the eldest was transferred to the sons of Joseph, Israel's son, who, however, could not be registered as the eldest son. Judah held 2 the leading place among his brothers because he fathered a ruler, and the rank of the eldest was his, not[a] Joseph's.) The sons of Reuben, the eldest of Israel's sons: Enoch, 3 Pallu, Hezron and Carmi. The sons of Joel: his son 4 Shemaiah, his son Gog, his son Shimei, his son Micah, his 5 son Reaia, his son Baal, his son Beerah, whom Tiglath- 6 pileser[b] king of Assyria carried away into exile; he was a prince of the Reubenites. His kinsmen, family by family, 7 as registered in their tribal lists: Jeiel the chief, Zechariah, Bela son of Azaz, son of Shema, son of Joel. They lived in 8 Aroer, and their lands stretched as far as Nebo and Baal-meon. Eastwards they occupied territory as far as the edge 9 of the desert which stretches from the river Euphrates, for they had large numbers of cattle in Gilead. During Saul's 10 reign they made war on the Hagarites, whom they conquered, occupying their encampments over all the country east of Gilead.

[a] his, not: *prob. rdg.; Heb. om.*
[b] *So Luc. Sept.; Heb.* Tilgath-pilneser.

11   Adjoining them were the Gadites, occupying the dis-
12 trict of Bashan as far as Salcah: Joel the chief; second in
13 rank, Shapham; then Jaanai and Shaphat in Bashan. Their
    fellow-tribesmen belonged to the families of Michael,
    Meshullam, Sheba, Jorai, Jachan, Zia and Heber, seven in
14 all. These were the sons of Abihail son of Huri, son of
    Jaroah, son of Gilead, son of Michael, son of Jeshishai, son
15 of Jahdo, son of Buz. Ahi son of Abdiel, son of Guni, was
16 head of their family; they lived in Gilead, in Bashan and
    its villages, in all the common land of Sharon as far as^a it
17 stretched. These registers were all compiled in the reigns
    of Jotham king of Judah and Jeroboam king of Israel.

18   The sons of Reuben, Gad, and half the tribe of Manas-
    seh: of their fighting men armed with shield and sword,
    their archers and their battle-trained soldiers, forty-four
    thousand seven hundred and sixty were ready for active
19 service. They made war on the Hagarites, Jetur, Nephish,
20 and Nodab. They were given help against them, for they
    cried to their God for help in the battle, and because they
    trusted him he listened to their prayer, and the Hagarites
21 and all their allies surrendered to them.^{b} They drove off
    their cattle, fifty thousand camels, two hundred and fifty
    thousand sheep, and two thousand asses, and they took a
22 hundred thousand captives. Many had been killed, for the
    war was of God's making, and they occupied the land
    instead of them until the exile.

23   Half the tribe of Manasseh lived in the land from Bashan
    to Baal-hermon, Senir, and Mount Hermon, and were

[a] as far as: *so Sept.; Heb.* upon.
[b] They were...surrendered to them: *or* They attacked them boldly,
and the Hagarites and all their allies surrendered to them, for they cried...
to their prayer.

numerous also in Lebanon.[a] The heads of their families 24
were: Epher,[b] Ishi, Eliel, Azriel, Jeremiah, Hodaviah, and
Jahdiel, all men of ability and repute, heads of their
families. But they sinned against the God of their fathers, 25
and turned wantonly to worship the gods of the peoples
whom God had destroyed before them. So the God of 26
Israel stirred up Pul king of Assyria, that is Tiglath-pileser[c]
king of Assyria, and he carried into exile Reuben, Gad,
and half the tribe of Manasseh. He took them to Halah,
Habor, Hara, and the river Gozan, where they are to this
day.

✶ This is an idealized picture of Israel living in the territory
which had been allotted to each of the tribes after their
wandering in the wilderness. In the book of Joshua the
tradition is found that two-and-a-half tribes were settled east
of the Jordan (Josh. 1: 12–18, and other passages), and the
Chronicler draws on that tradition here. Such a tribal division
had long ceased to exist in his day – indeed, it was only for
limited periods that Israel was able to control territory east
of the Jordan – but the picture he is giving is of the ideal
Israel.

1. *the eldest of Israel's sons:* this is an ancient tradition, found
in the stories of the sons of Jacob in Genesis, and perhaps
reflecting a time when Reuben had been a powerful clan.
Yet in historical times its role was insignificant, and this
decline came to be explained by legends such as that related
here, the origin of which probably lies in a passage in Genesis
referring to Reuben's *incest* (Gen. 35: 22), a theme greatly
elaborated in later Jewish writings.

2. To achieve the sense it has given to this verse, the N.E.B.

[a] in Lebanon: *so Sept.; Heb. om.*
[b] *So Sept.; Heb.* and Epher.
[c] *So Pesh.; Heb.* Tilgath-pilneser.

has had to alter the Hebrew text drastically, as the footnote shows. It is probably more satisfactory to follow the other English versions here, and to translate the last clause in some such way as 'yet the rank of the eldest was Joseph's'. The point is of some importance in our evaluation of the Chronicler, for such a version would stress the importance given to all Israel, while the N.E.B. understanding of the text gives greater weight to the primacy of Judah.

3–10. *The sons of Reuben* are the same as those found in other tribal lists, but they are apparently unconnected with the lists that follow. The reference to the *exile* in verse 6 may be a genuine historical record, indicating that the Chronicler had access to ancient lists, but it could equally be an early example of the theory which regarded all the ten northern tribes as being carried away by the Assyrians. The suggestion has been made that these lists from the tribes which had lost their identity at the Chronicler's own time originated as lists of military leaders, and this would account for the prevalence of such details of local wars as that (otherwise unknown) found in verse 10.

11–17. *the Gadites* traditionally occupied the land east of Jordan and immediately north of the territory of Reuben, which was probably merged into that of Gad. The information given in these verses has no parallel elsewhere. The tribe is pictured as having led a pastoral existence in the rich pasture-lands of Gilead and Bashan, east of Jordan.

18–22. A separate note is here provided which relates to all the Transjordanian groups, and pictures them in conflict with the Hagarites, a bedouin tribe from the desert fringes whose conflict with Reuben has already been noted (verse 10). Once again, it appears that many of these lists may have originated as military annals. However this may be, the section is important because it introduces for the first time a theme which will be found all through the work of the Chronicler: his conviction about the nature of war. Verse 20 sets out in a nutshell the Chronicler's distinctive presentation:

the people *cried to their God for help in the battle, and because they trusted him he listened to their prayer.* It is God himself who fights Israel's battles if she is loyal to him. (The exact sense of the verse is not clear, as the N.E.B. footnote indicates, but the general meaning is not in dispute.) *until the exile* (verse 22): presumably the deportation of 587 B.C. is meant, though the word is not found elsewhere in the Chronicler's writings until we reach the book of Ezra, and there it normally refers to the people in Babylon rather than to an event.

23–6. Again what appears to be a list of military origin is given for that part of the tribe of Manasseh which lived east of Jordan. Such pictures of Israel as the holy community prepared for war are comparable with some of the scrolls found at Qumran near the Dead Sea, in which similar ideas are present.

25–6. The exile of these tribes, accounted for by their sin and specifically false worship, is set in contrast with their success when they relied upon their God.

26. *Pul:* this appears to have been the throne-name of the Assyrian ruler generally known as Tiglath-Pileser III. The Chronicler is here drawing on 2 Kings 15: 19 and 29, and it seems likely that he misunderstood his source and regarded Pul and Tiglath-pileser (notice his variant spelling, as given in the footnote) as two separate kings, though the N.E.B. rendering is also possible. The places of exile may also represent a misunderstanding on the Chronicler's part (cp. 2 Kings 17: 6 and 18: 11, where more accurate forms of these Mesopotamian place-names are found). ✶

LEVI

The sons of Levi: Gershon,[a] Kohath and Merari. The **6** 1,[b] 2 sons of Kohath: Amram, Izhar, Hebron and Uzziel. The 3 children of Amram: Aaron, Moses and Miriam. The sons

[a] Gershom *in verses 16 and 17.*   [b] 5: 27 *in Heb.*

37

4^a of Aaron: Nadab, Abihu, Eleazar and Ithamar. Eleazar
was the father of Phinehas, Phinehas father of Abishua,
5, 6 Abishua father of Bukki, Bukki father of Uzzi, Uzzi
7 father of Zerahiah, Zerahiah father of Meraioth, Meraioth
8 father of Amariah, Amariah father of Ahitub, Ahitub
9 father of Zadok, Zadok father of Ahimaaz, Ahimaaz
10 father of Azariah, Azariah father of Johanan, and Johanan
father of Azariah, the priest who officiated in the LORD's
11 house which Solomon built at Jerusalem. Azariah was the
12 father of Amariah, Amariah father of Ahitub, Ahitub
13 father of Zadok, Zadok father of Shallum, Shallum father
14 of Hilkiah, Hilkiah father of Azariah, Azariah father of
15 Seraiah, and Seraiah father of Jehozadak. Jehozadak went
into exile when the LORD sent Judah and Jerusalem into
exile under Nebuchadnezzar.

16,^{b c}17   The sons of Levi: Gershom, Kohath and Merari. The
18 sons of Gershom: Libni and Shimei. The sons of Kohath:
19 Amram, Izhar, Hebron and Uzziel. The sons of Merari:
Mahli and Mushi. The clans of Levi, family by family:
20^d Gershom: his son Libni, his son Jahath, his son Zimmah,
21 his son Joah, his son Iddo, his son Zerah, his son Jeaterai.
22^e The sons of Kohath: his son Amminadab, his son Korah,
23 his son Assir, his son Elkanah, his son Ebiasaph, his son
24 Assir, his son Tahath, his son Uriel, his son Uzziah, his son
25, 26 Saul. The sons of Elkanah: Amasai and Ahimoth, his son
27 Elkanah,^f his son Zophai, his son Nahath, his son Eliab,
28 his son Jeroham, his son Elkanah. The sons of Samuel:

[a] *Verses 4–8: cp. verses 50–3.*   [b] *6: 1 in Heb.*
[c] *Verses 16–19: cp. Exod. 6: 16–19.*
[d] *Verses 20, 21: cp. verses 41–3.*
[e] *Verses 22–8: cp. verses 33–8.*
[f] his son Elkanah: *so Sept.; Heb.* Elkanah, the sons of Elkanah.

Joel the eldest and Abiah the second.[a] The sons of Merari: 29
his son[b] Mahli, his son Libni, his son Shimei, his son Uzza,
his son Shimea, his son Haggiah, his son Asaiah.   30

These are the men whom David appointed to take 31
charge of the music in the house of the LORD when the
Ark should be deposited there. They performed their 32
musical duties before the Tent of the Presence until Solomon built the house of the LORD in Jerusalem, and took
their regular turns of duty there. The following, with 33
their descendants, took this duty. Of the line of Kohath:
Heman the musician, son of Joel, son of Samuel, son of 34
Elkanah, son of Jeroham, son of Eliel, son of Toah, son 35
of Zuph, son of Elkanah, son of Mahath, son of Amasai,
son of Elkanah, son of Joel, son of Azariah, son of Zepha- 36
niah, son of Tahath, son of Assir, son of Ebiasaph, son of 37
Korah, son of Izhar, son of Kohath, son of Levi, son of 38
Israel. Heman's colleague Asaph stood at his right hand. 39
He was the son of Berachiah, son of Shimea, son of 40
Michael, son of Baaseiah, son of Malchiah, son of Ethni, 41[c]
son of Zerah, son of Adaiah, son of Ethan, son of Zim- 42
mah, son of Shimei, son of Jahath, son of Gershom, son 43
of Levi. On their left stood their colleague of the line of 44
Merari: Ethan son of Kishi, son of Abdi, son of Malluch,
son of Hashabiah, son of Amaziah, son of Hilkiah, son of 45, 46
Amzi, son of Bani, son of Shamer, son of Mahli, son of 47
Mushi, son of Merari, son of Levi. Their kinsmen the 48
Levites were dedicated to all the service of the Tabernacle,
the house of God.

But it was Aaron and his descendants who burnt the 49

[a] Joel...the second: *so Luc. Sept.; Heb.* the eldest Vashni and Abiah.
[b] his son: *so Pesh.; Heb. om.*   [c] *Verses 41–3: cp. verses 20, 21.*

sacrifices on the altar of whole-offering and the altar of incense, in fulfilment of all the duties connected with the most sacred gifts, and to make expiation for Israel, exactly as Moses the servant of God had commanded.

50[a] The sons of Aaron: his son Eleazar, his son Phinehas, his
51 son Abishua, his son Bukki, his son Uzzi, his son Zera-
52 hiah, his son Meraioth, his son Amariah, his son Ahitub,
53 his son Zadok, his son Ahimaaz.

54   These are their settlements in encampments in the districts assigned to the descendants of Aaron, to the clan of
55 Kohath, for it was to them that the lot had fallen: they gave them Hebron in Judah, with the common land round it,
56 but they assigned to Caleb son of Jephunneh the open country belonging to the town and its hamlets.
57[b] They gave to the sons of Aaron: Hebron the city[c] of
58, 59 refuge, Libnah, Jattir, Eshtemoa, Hilen,[d] Debir, Ashan,
60 and Beth-shemesh, each with its common land. And from the tribe of Benjamin: Geba, Alemeth, and Anathoth, each with its common land, making thirteen cities in all by their clans.

61   They gave to the remaining clans of the sons of Kohath
62 ten cities by lot from the half tribe[e] of Manasseh. To the sons of Gershom according to their clans they gave thirteen cities from the tribes of Issachar, Asher, Naphtali,
63 and Manasseh in Bashan. To the sons of Merari according to their clans they gave by lot twelve cities from the tribes
64 of Reuben, Gad, and Zebulun. Israel gave these cities,
65 each with its common land, to the Levites. (The cities

[a] *Verses 50–3: cp. verses 4–8.*   [b] *Verses 57–81: cp. Josh. 21: 13–39.*
[c] *Prob. rdg., cp. Josh. 21: 13; Heb.* cities.
[d] *So many MSS.; others* Hilez.   [e] *So Vulg.; Heb. adds* half.

mentioned above, from the tribes of Judah, Simeon, and
Benjamin, were assigned by lot.)

Some of the clans of Kohath had cities allotted[a] to them. 66
They gave them the city[b] of refuge, Shechem in the hill- 67
country of Ephraim, Gezer, Jokmeam, Beth-horon, 68
Aijalon, and Gath-rimmon, each with its common land. 69
From the half tribe of Manasseh, Aner and Bileam, each 70
with its common land, were given to the rest of the clans
of Kohath.

To the sons of Gershom they gave from the half tribe 71
of Manasseh: Golan in Bashan, and Ashtaroth, each with
its common land. From the tribe of Issachar: Kedesh, 72
Daberath, Ramoth, and Anem, each with its common 73
land. From the tribe of Asher: Mashal, Abdon, Hukok, 74, 75
and Rehob, each with its common land. From the tribe of 76
Naphtali: Kedesh in Galilee, Hammon, and Kiriathaim,
each with its common land.

To the rest of the sons of Merari they gave from the 77
tribe of Zebulun: Rimmon[c] and Tabor, each with its
common land. On the east of Jordan, opposite Jericho, 78
from the tribe of Reuben: Bezer-in-the-wilderness, Jah-
zah, Kedemoth, and Mephaath, each with its common 79
land. From the tribe of Gad: Ramoth in Gilead, Maha- 80
naim, Heshbon, and Jazer, each with its common land. 81

* The material concerning Levi is second in detail only to
that concerning Judah, and this double emphasis reflects the
two concerns of the author – the establishment of the people
at Jerusalem under the chosen ruler from the line of Judah,

[a] allotted: *prob. rdg., cp. Josh. 21: 20; Heb.* of their frontier.
[b] *Prob. rdg., cp. Josh. 21: 21; Heb.* cities.
[c] *So Sept.; Heb.* his Rimmon.

and then the part played in their worship by the priestly families of Levi. A particularly important theme in this chapter is the establishment of those who could claim descent from Levi and so be allowed to minister in the temple, for this was an important element in maintaining the right relation of the people to their God.

1–3*a*. The information in these verses is based on Exod. 6, where the same spelling *Gershon* (cp. N.E.B. footnote) is found.

3*b*. *Nadab, Abihu*: a story in Lev. 10 tells of the death of these two sons of Aaron for their presumption in priestly matters, and the priestly lines therefore are traced through Eleazar and Ithamar. Conflicts between groups claiming to be descended from one or other of these played a prominent part in Judaism well into the Christian era.

4–15. The genealogy here changes from a 'family tree' type, in which all known descendants are listed, to a 'linear' type, which simply lists a series of successors, without any indication of precise relationships. Part of this list is repeated in verses 50–3, and a different part in 9: 11. A shortened form is found in Ezra 7: 1–5, where Ezra's own place in this line is affirmed, but some of the names are not found elsewhere in the Old Testament. A good deal of confusion and controversy existed concerning these priestly lists, and sometimes there are apparent contradictions even within the work of the Chronicler himself. Thus, for example, there appear to be discrepancies between this list and the variant of it in 9: 11, where several of the same names are found in a different order.

8. *Ahitub...Zadok...Ahimaaz: Ahitub* is referred to in 1 Sam. 22 as the father of Ahimelech, and in the Hebrew text of 2 Sam. 8: 17 he is called father of Zadok. But this last identification is almost universally regarded as mistaken (see the N.E.B., which places it in a footnote), though it provides the Chronicler's source of information here. Zadok's parentage is in fact unknown, and it is widely held that he was not of Israelite descent at all, but was the existing priest (and

perhaps also king) of Jerusalem at the time of the city's capture by David. But it is important for the Chronicler to show that all those who had exercised priestly functions with apparent divine approval should be shown to be descended from Aaron. That *Ahimaaz* was the son of Zadok is not disputed – he plays a prominent part in 2 Samuel.

9–13. A good deal of confusion is exhibited by these verses. It is certainly not impossible that the degree of repetition of names as found here could have a basis in reality, but it is much more likely that some expansion has taken place – the list in Ezra 7 may be a more original form. The purpose may be connected with the note in verse 10 concerning the building of Solomon's temple. Even here some confusion exists, for it seems more likely that this note should refer to the first Azariah (verse 9), both because of the chronology, and also because this would give twelve generations from Aaron to Solomon's temple, and a further twelve generations until the exile. Such a scheme may be a forerunner of the arrangement into series of fourteen generations found in the genealogy of Jesus in Matt. 1.

12–14. The names in these verses are virtually identical with, and may be based upon, the brief list in 9: 11, found also in Neh. 11: 11. The period covered is that of the monarchy, but curiously no mention is found here of several high priests who are mentioned during this period in 2 Chronicles (e.g. Jehoiada, in 2 Chron. 22: 11). The artificial nature of this list is again clear.

15. *Jehozadak:* probably to be identified with the 'Jozadak' (a variant form of the same name) of Ezra 3: 2, and mentioned here to bring out the theme of continuity between the temples built before and after the exile, and their ministers. A characteristic theme of the Chronicler is that the exile was brought about by God himself, using Nebuchadnezzar the king of Babylon as his instrument.

16–30. A great deal of repetition exists within this section, which has probably been compiled at different times. The

43

first four verses follow Exod. 6: 16–19, as indicated in the
N.E.B. footnote, and give apparently full details of Levi's
sons and grandsons. The Gershomite list in verses 20–1 is a
fragment of that found in an extended form, with some
differences of detail and proceeding back to the founder, in
verses 41–3; we have no means of deciding which list is the
more reliable. There is a similar situation with regard to the
Kohathite list which follows: it is found also in verses 32–8,
though the differences here both in the names themselves and
in the order in which they appear, are considerable. Particularly striking is the introduction of Samuel in verse 28.
He is clearly to be identified with the central figure of the
first book of Samuel (his father is Elkanah, his sons Joel and
Abiah), but in the earlier traditions he is described as an
Ephraimite (1 Sam. 1: 1). Again we observe that one of the
Chronicler's purposes was to legitimate all those who had
served the Lord faithfully, rather than to give what we would
consider an historically accurate genealogy. Finally, the
Merarite line is given in a form which is clearly independent
of the other list of the same family in verses 44–7.

31. *to take charge of the music:* at this point we are introduced
to one of the Chronicler's dominant interests – the musical
worship of the Jerusalem temple. It has often been suggested
that the Chronicler himself was associated with one of the
musical guilds, so important a role does he ascribe to them.
However this may be, we shall find all through his work great
emphasis on the choice of proper persons for this task, and the
significance of the proper performance of the music. Unfortunately, we know very little of the details of its execution.
It is noteworthy here, and throughout the description of the
building of the temple, that all the arrangements are ascribed
to David; only the building itself was left for Solomon to
carry out, so that David's arrangements could then be put
into effect, whereas in the account in 1 Kings, preparation and
execution of the work are both ascribed to Solomon.

33. *Heman:* his name occurs frequently in the books of

Chronicles as leader of one of the musical groups in the temple. The tradition may originate with the wise man referred to in 1 Kings 4: 31, though this tradition has already been used in a different way by the Chronicler at 2: 6. In any case Heman is here given a genealogy which leads back through the Kohathite line to Levi, in a form which, as we have already noted, is related to that in verses 22–8.

39. *Asaph: Heman's colleague* was the leader of another major musical group, about which we have rather greater information, since, in addition to numerous references in Chronicles, a number of psalms are attributed to Asaph in their titles. Unfortunately the N.E.B. translation has omitted these titles, but reference to Asaph should appear in Pss. 50 and 73–83. Here once again a Levite genealogy is provided, on this occasion going back through Gershom; as we have already noted, this list bears resemblances to that in verses 20–1.

44–7. *Ethan:* this is the third of the musical groups, about which some uncertainty exists, since elsewhere in Chronicles it is given the name 'Jeduthun' (e.g. 1 Chron. 25: 1). It is noteworthy also that an Ethan is found in the genealogical table of Asaph which has no equivalent in the earlier corresponding list. The genealogy leading back through Merari is not found elsewhere, save that Mahli is elsewhere (e.g. verse 19) said to have been the brother of Mushi.

48. Another frequent theme of the Chronicler is here introduced – the important role played by the Levites in *all the service of the Tabernacle, the house of God.* Though the role of the Levites is inferior to that of the priests, there is frequent stress on the loyalty with which they carried out their functions.

49–53. The specifically priestly duties are now set out, with stress upon the fact that they were confined to *Aaron and his descendants.* In the times before the exile the priests had had a wide range of responsibilities, but by the Chronicler's day the characteristically priestly functions were those associated with the offering of sacrifice, itself conceived primarily as making *expiation for Israel,* and this state of affairs

45

is here set out as though it had been the case even in earliest times. There follows an Aaronite genealogy virtually identical with that in verses 4–8, but terminating with the name of Ahimaaz, the contemporary of David.

54–81. The other ancient tradition concerning the tribe of Levi was that they did not receive a part of the promised land as an inheritance; instead they were given specific areas within the other tribal territories. This allocation is now described, in terms based largely on the description of this allocation in Josh. 21. The lists here are not simply copied verbatim from Joshua, but are a new composition based upon that source or one akin to it, with a number of minor differences in detail. Since it was only in the time of David that Israel gained control of all of Palestine, these lists can scarcely be earlier than the monarchy. It has been argued that they must date from the time before the older structures were destroyed by the division of the kingdom, but others have regarded this whole description of the division of the land as utopian – a description of what might and should have been, rather than of a precise historical reality. ✷

THE NORTHERN TRIBES

7₁ [a] The sons of [b] Issachar: Tola, Pua, Jashub and Shimron, 2 four. The sons of Tola: Uzzi, Rephaiah, Jeriel, Jahmai, Jibsam, and Samuel, all able men and heads of families by paternal descent from Tola according to their tribal lists; their number in David's time was twenty-two thousand 3 six hundred. The son of Uzzi: Izrahiah. The sons of Izrahiah: Michael, Obadiah, Joel and Isshiah, making a 4 total of five, all of them chiefs. In addition there were bands of fighting men recorded by families according to

[a] *Verses 1, 6, 13, 30 and 8: 1–5: cp. Gen. 46: 13, 17, 21–4.*
[b] *So Pesh.; Heb.* To the sons of.

the tribal lists to the number of thirty-six thousand, for
they had many wives and children. Their fellow-tribes- 5
men in all the clans of Issachar were able men, eighty-
seven thousand; every one of them was registered.

The sons of[a] Benjamin: Bela, Becher and Jediael, three. 6
The sons of Bela: Ezbon, Uzzi, Uzziel, Jerimoth and Iri, 7
five. They were heads of their families and able men; the
number registered was twenty-two thousand and thirty-
four. The sons of Becher: Zemira, Joash, Eliezer, Elioenai, 8
Omri, Jeremoth, Abiah, Anathoth and Alemeth; all these
were sons of Becher according to their tribal lists, heads 9
of their families and able men; and the number registered
was twenty thousand two hundred. The son of Jediael: 10
Bilhan. The sons of Bilhan: Jeush, Benjamin, Ehud,
Kenaanah, Zethan, Tarshish and Ahishahar. All these 11
were descendants of Jediael, heads of[b] families and able
men. The number was seventeen thousand two hundred
men, fit for active service in war.

The sons of Dan:[c] Hushim and the sons of Aher.[d] 12

The sons of Naphtali: Jahziel, Guni, Jezer, Shallum. 13
These were sons of Bilhah.

The sons of Manasseh,[e] born of his concubine, an 14[f]
Aramaean: Machir father of Gilead. Machir married a 15
woman whose name was[g] Maacah. The second son was
named Zelophehad, and Zelophehad had daughters.[h]
Maacah wife of Machir had a son whom she named 16

[a] The sons of: *so some MSS.; others om.*   [b] *Prob. rdg.; Heb.* to the
heads of.   [c] The sons of Dan: *prob. rdg., cp. Gen. 46: 23; Heb.* And
Shuppim and Huppim, the sons of Ir.   [d] *Or* another.   [e] *Prob.
rdg.; Heb. adds* Asriel.   [f] *Verses 14–19: cp. Num. 26: 29–33.*   [g] whose
name was: *prob. rdg.; Heb.* to Huppim and Shuppim, and his sister's
name was...   [h] The second...daughters: *possibly to be transposed to
follow* Gilead *at the end of verse 14.*

Peresh. His brother's name was Sheresh, and his sons were
17 Ulam and Rakem. The son of Ulam: Bedan. These were
18 the sons of Gilead son of Machir, son of Manasseh. His
sister Hammoleketh was the mother of Ishhod, Abiezer
19 and Mahalah. The sons of Shemida: Ahian, Shechem,
Likhi and Aniam.

20   The sons of Ephraim: Shuthelah, his son Bered, his son
21 Tahath, his son Eladah, his son Tahath, his son Zabad, his
son Shuthelah. Ephraim's other sons Ezer and Elead were
killed by the native Gittites when they came down to lift
22 their cattle. Their father Ephraim long mourned for them,
23 and his kinsmen came to comfort him. Then he had intercourse with his wife; she conceived and had a son whom
he named Beriah (because disaster[a] had come on his
24 family). He had a daughter named Sherah; she built
25 Lower and Upper Beth-horon and Uzzen-sherah. He also
had a son named Rephah; his son was[b] Resheph, his son
26 Telah, his son Tahan, his son Laadan, his son Ammihud,
27 his son Elishama, his son Nun, his son Joshua.

28   Their lands and settlements were: Bethel and its dependent villages, to the east Naaran, to the west Gezer,
29 Shechem, and Gaza,[c] with their villages. In the possession
of Manasseh were Beth-shean, Taanach, Megiddo, and
Dor, with their villages. In all of these lived the descendants of Joseph the son of Israel.

30   The sons of Asher: Imnah, Ishvah, Ishvi and Beriah,
31 together with their sister Serah. The sons of Beriah: Heber
32 and Malchiel father of Birzavith. Heber was the father of

[a] *Heb.* beraah.
[b] his son was: *so Luc. Sept.; Heb. om.*
[c] *So some MSS.; others* Aiah.

Japhlet, Shomer, Hotham, and their sister Shua. The sons 33
of Japhlet: Pasach, Bimhal and Ashvath. These were the
sons of Japhlet. The sons of Shomer: Ahi, Rohgah, 34
Jehubbah and Aram. The sons of his brother Hotham:*a* 35
Zophah, Imna, Shelesh and Amal. The sons of Zophah: 36
Suah, Harnepher, Shual, Beri, Imrah, Bezer, Hod, 37
Shamma, Shilshah, Ithran and Beera. The sons of Jether: 38
Jephunneh, Pispah and Ara. The sons of Ulla: Arah, 39
Haniel and Rezia. All these were descendants of Asher, 40
heads of families, picked men of ability, leading princes.
They were enrolled among the fighting troops; the total
number was twenty-six thousand men.

* The setting-out of the tribal genealogies continues, though
it will at once be seen that the material available for some
tribes was markedly less than for others. No mention at all
is made of Zebulun, and the N.E.B. only includes Dan by
emending the Hebrew text (see footnote to 7: 12). Nevertheless, if this emendation is correct, twelve tribes are listed, the
two sons of Joseph counting as two tribes, as in many of the
lists.

1–5. *The sons of Issachar* are found listed also in Gen. 46: 13
and Num. 26: 23–5, but the remaining names do not occur
elsewhere. They are not to be pictured as immediate sons of
Tola, as the latter part of verse 2 makes clear; instead this may
be a fragment of a military list, in view of the emphasis
revealed by such phrases as *able men* and *bands of fighting men*.
Whether or not such lists originally date from the time of
David, that is clearly the period of greatest interest for the
author. The concluding phrase *every one of them was registered*
probably also refers to some form of military muster, and
this may also account for the numbers that are given, a feature
not found in all the tribal lists.

[a] *Prob. rdg., cp. verse 32; Heb.* Helem.

49

6–11. This last point may account for the otherwise somewhat surprising inclusion of Benjamite details at this point. Not only is Benjamin dealt with in greater detail in ch. 8, but its inclusion here comes in the middle of an account otherwise devoted to the Galilean tribes. But the same references to military leaders, and the same type of numerical information, suggest that the source of the Benjamite record was the same as that just used for Issachar. As a comparison with ch. 8 will show, the tradition about the names of the Benjamite clans is a varied one: the names here are similar for the first generation to those in Gen. 46: 21, but they differ from other lists, both in Numbers and in 1 Chronicles. Only Bela, the first-born, appears in all lists.

8. *Anathoth:* it is a little unexpected to find this as a personal name, for the name is best known as a settlement north of Jerusalem, the birthplace of the prophet Jeremiah. It may be that it was in an individual or group from this place, which is in Benjamite territory, that the reference here originated.

12. As the N.E.B. footnote indicates, the Hebrew text of this verse contains no reference to Dan, but only some unexpected and unexplained additional Benjamite names. The name *Hushim*, listed in Gen. 46: 23 as 'son of Dan', together with the lack of any reference to the tribe of Dan in these lists, has led to many scholars making an emendation along these lines, though not all would agree that the names 'Huppim and Shuppim', which refer to known Benjamite clans, should be omitted.

13. The names of the *sons of Naphtali* are found also in Gen. 46: 24 and Num. 26: 48–50. As with Dan, it would appear that no further information concerning these tribes, settled in the far north, was available to the Chronicler.

These were sons of Bilhah: this adds further support to the suggested emendation in verse 12, since Dan and Naphtali were the two sons of Rachel's handmaid Bilhah according to the Genesis traditions.

14–19. The information concerning Manasseh is likewise

partially based on earlier sources; but many of the names are found in a different relationship, and some scholars have argued that these changes were deliberate – Manasseh was a major northern tribe, and the Chronicler, being hostile to the north, deliberately rearranged the genealogy in a way that would be understood as insulting. Such a view is not impossible, but we have insufficient evidence to regard it as established.

20–7. It will be seen at once that the material devoted to 'the sons of Ephraim', the other Josephite tribe, is of a different character. Shuthelah (verse 21) and Tahan (verse 25) are mentioned in Num. 26: 35, but the names are not otherwise found in Ephraimite lists. After the first genealogy we find a fragment of tribal lore of a type similar to that already noted in the Simeonite lists (4: 39–43), but this time giving a word-play on the sound of the word 'Beriah', which was associated by a popular etymology with the word *beraah* meaning 'disaster'; word-plays of this kind are very characteristic of Hebrew.

26–7. *Ammihud...Elishama...Nun...Joshua:* a fragment of a different Ephraimite tradition is preserved here. 'Elishama son of Ammihud' is mentioned several times in Numbers (1: 10, etc.), but nowhere else are these names linked with those that precede them here or with the better-known Nun and Joshua. Since Moses is consistently represented as being four generations after Jacob, it is a little surprising to find that Joshua is here represented as coming eleven generations after Jacob. It is noteworthy also that Joshua is mentioned nowhere else in the Chronicler's work save for an allusion at Neh. 8: 17; for the Chronicler it was to David that the land was given, and the earlier conquest was passed over in silence.

28–9. These two verses draw the *descendants of Joseph* together in the description of their territory, by a brief summary of the description in Josh. 16 and 17; all the names are found there except *Gaza*, an emendation of the best Hebrew manuscripts already found in the Authorized Version, but nevertheless unlikely. The reference is probably to an unknown place 'Aiah' (see N.E.B. footnote), which later scribes modified to the better-known Gaza, one of the five Philistine cities. It is noteworthy that another link with the Philistine area is found at verse 21, where 'Gittites' refers to the inhabitants of Gath.

30–40. *The sons of Asher* are the last of the far northern tribes to be listed. Once again the first names (as far as Malchiel) are found in earlier lists (Gen. 46: 17–18 and Num. 26: 44–6); the later names, which again have marked military features (notice especially *enrolled among the fighting troops* (verse 40)) and seem not in every instance to be related to one another, are unattested elsewhere. ✳

BENJAMIN

8 The sons of Benjamin were: the eldest Bela, the second
2 Ashbel, the third Aharah, the fourth Nohah and the fifth
3 Rapha. The sons of Bela: Addar, Gera father of Ehud,[a]
4, 5 Abishua, Naaman, Ahoah, Gera, Shephuphan and
6 Huram. These were the sons of Ehud, heads of families
7 living in Geba, who were removed to Manahath: Naaman, Ahiah, and Gera – he it was who removed them.
8 He was the father of Uzza and Ahihud. Shaharaim had sons born to him in Moabite country, after putting away
9 his wives Mahasham[b] and Baara. By his wife Hodesh he
10 had Jobab, Zibia, Mesha, Malcham, Jeuz, Shachia and
11 Mirmah. These were his sons, heads of families. By
12 Mahasham[c] he had had Abitub and Elpaal. The sons of Elpaal: Eber, Misham, Shamed who built Ono and Lod

[a] father of Ehud: *prob. rdg., cp. Judg. 3: 15; Heb.* Abihud.
[b] Mahasham: *prob. rdg., cp. Luc. Sept. in verse 11; Heb.* Hushim.
[c] Mahasham: *prob. rdg., cp. Luc. Sept.; Heb.* Hushim.

with its villages, also Beriah and Shema who were heads of 13
families living in Aijalon, having expelled the inhabitants of
Gath. Ahio, Shashak, Jeremoth, Zebadiah, Arad, Ader, 14, 15
Michael, Ispah, and Joha were sons of Beriah; Zebadiah, 16, 17
Meshullam, Hezeki, Heber, Ishmerai, Jezliah, and Jobab 18
were sons of Elpaal; Jakim, Zichri, Zabdi, Elienai, Zilthai, 19, 20
Eliel, Adaiah, Beraiah, and Shimrath were sons of Shimei; 21
Ishpan, Heber, Eliel, Abdon, Zichri, Hanan, Hananiah, 22, 23, 24
Elam, Antothiah, Iphedeiah, and Penuel were sons of Sha- 25
shak; Shamsherai, Shehariah, Athaliah, Jaresiah, Eliah, and 26, 27
Zichri were sons of Jeroham. These were enrolled in the 28
tribal lists as heads of families, chiefs living in Jerusalem.

Jehiel*a* founder of Gibeon lived at Gibeon; his wife's 29*b*
name was Maacah. His eldest son was Abdon, followed by 30
Zur, Kish, Baal, Nadab, Gedor, Ahio, Zacher and Mik- 31
loth.*c* Mikloth was the father of Shimeah; they lived 32
alongside their kinsmen in Jerusalem.*d*

Ner was the father of Kish, Kish father of Saul, Saul 33
father of Jonathan, Malchishua, Abinadab and Eshbaal.
Jonathan's son was Meribbaal, and he was the father of 34
Micah. The sons of Micah: Pithon, Melech, Tarea and 35
Ahaz. Ahaz was the father of Jehoaddah, Jehoaddah father 36
of Alemeth, Azmoth and Zimri. Zimri was the father of 37
Moza, and Moza father of Binea; his son was Raphah,
his son Elasah, and his son Azel. Azel had six sons, whose 38
names were Azrikam, Bocheru, Ishmael, Sheariah,
Obadiah and Hanan. All these were sons of Azel. The 39
sons of his brother Eshek: the eldest Ulam, the second

[a] *So Luc. Sept., cp. 9: 35; Heb. om.*
[b] *Verses 29–38: cp. 9: 35–44.*
[c] and Mikloth: *so Sept., cp. 9: 37; Heb. om.*
[d] *So Pesh.; Heb. adds* with their kinsmen.

40 Jeush, the third Eliphelet. The sons of Ulam were able men, archers, and had many sons and grandsons, a hundred and fifty. All these were descendants of Benjamin.

* A second Benjamite list is here found, and more details are given than for any tribe except Judah and Levi. The reason for this is probably the tradition that Benjamin remained loyal to the house of David at the division of the kingdom after the death of Solomon (1 Kings 11: 35).

1–5. The names in these verses seem to be derived from the same earlier lists as we have noted for other tribes (Gen. 46: 21–2 and Num. 26: 38–41), though on this occasion the variations are too great to suppose that a simple copying from such sources is implied.

6–27. Of the names given here, together with isolated scraps of tradition, nothing further is known.

28. *chiefs living in Jerusalem*: this provides a further reason for the prominence of Benjamite material. *Jerusalem* was never properly absorbed into Judah, as the many references to 'Judah and Jerusalem' as distinct areas show, and Judg. 1 refers to attempts to control the city being made by both Judah and Benjamin (verses 8 and 21). The city lay on the boundary between the two tribal areas, and hence considerable Benjamite material will presumably have been available to the Chronicler.

29–38. A separate list of Benjamite leaders is given here, in a form substantially identical with 9: 35–44 (the N.E.B. footnotes indicate places where the translators have modified one list by comparison with the other). Again the origin of this material 'in Jerusalem' is indicated, and it acquires particular interest and significance because of the references to the family of Saul.

30. This Gibeonite family list (Gibeon is now identified with virtual certainty as modern el-Jib, 8 miles (nearly 13 km) north of Jerusalem) includes among its members the names

Kish (presumably not to be identified with Saul's father) and Baal: the name by itself is unusual, but many forms compounded with the name of the great Canaanite god are found in these lists.

33. *Ner:* here presented as father of Kish and so grandfather of Saul; elsewhere he appears to be Kish's brother (9: 36; 1 Sam. 14: 51). *Jonathan, Malchishua, Abinadab and Eshbaal:* of the sons of Saul, Jonathan is well known from the stories in 1 Samuel, where Malchishua and Abinadab are also referred to (1 Sam. 31: 2). But in the books of Samuel Eshbaal is never called by that name – he is called 'Ishyo' (man of Yahweh) in 1 Sam. 14: 49, and 'Ishbosheth' (man of shame) in 2 Sam. 2: 8. Most probably Eshbaal was his actual name, but this was suppressed because of its associations with the worship of the Canaanite god Baal. Such associations were no longer regarded with the same dread in the Chronicler's day. Similarly we today might use an expression such as 'By jove', which for an early Christian would have been tantamount to idolatry.

34. *Meribbaal:* 'Mephibosheth' in 2 Samuel, for the same reason as prompted the change to 'Ishbosheth'.

35–40. In Samuel the descendants of Saul are not listed beyond Micah (2 Sam. 9: 12, 'Mica'); here a further nine (perhaps more – the relationships are not all quite clear) generations of the family of Saul are listed. An outline sketch of the history of Israel normally gives the impression that the significance of the family of Saul virtually ended with his own death, and certainly did not survive the attempt of his son to rule in Transjordan (2 Sam. 3). This list shows that the family continued to be remembered and presumably remained prominent at least in the territory of Benjamin. It further suggests that the Chronicler's view of Saul may not have been wholly negative. His kingship was certainly only a prelude to the greater rule of David – but it nevertheless had its part to play in the unfolding drama of God's salvation of his people. *

The restored community

9 So all israel were registered and recorded in the book of the kings of Israel; but Judah for their sins
2*a* were carried away to exile in Babylon. The first to occupy their ancestral land in their cities were lay Israelites,
3 priests, Levites, and temple-servitors.*b* Jerusalem was occupied partly by Judahites, partly by Benjamites, and
4 partly by men of Ephraim and Manasseh. Judahites:*c* Uthai son of Ammihud, son of Omri, son of Imri, son of
5 Bani, a descendant of Perez son of Judah. Shelanites:
6 Asaiah the eldest and his sons. The sons of Zerah: Jeuel
7 and six hundred and ninety of their kinsmen. Benjamites: Sallu son of Meshullam, son of Hodaviah, son of Hasse-
8 nuah, Ibneiah son of Jeroham, Elah son of Uzzi, son of Micri, Meshullam son of Shephatiah, son of Reuel, son of
9 Ibniah, and their recorded kinsmen numbering nine hundred and fifty-six, all heads of families.
10, 11   Priests: Jedaiah, Jehoiarib, Jachin, Azariah son of Hilkiah, son of Meshullam, son of Zadok, son of Meraioth, son of Ahitub, the officer in charge of the house of God,
12 Adaiah son of Jeroham, son of Pashhur, son of Malchiah, Maasai son of Adiel, son of Jahzerah, son of Meshullam,
13 son of Meshillemith, son of Immer, and their colleagues, heads of families numbering one thousand seven hundred and sixty, men of substance and fit for the work connected with the service of the house of God.

[a] *Verses 2–22: cp. Neh. 11: 3–22.*
[b] *Heb.* Nethinim.   [c] *Prob. rdg.; Heb. om.*

Levites: Shemaiah son of Hasshub, son of Azrikam, son 14
of Hashabiah, a descendant of Merari, Bakbakkar, 15
Heresh, Galal, Mattaniah son of Mica, son of Zichri, son
of Asaph, Obadiah son of Shemaiah, son of Galal, son of 16
Jeduthun, and Berechiah son of Asa, son of Elkanah, who
lived in the hamlets of the Netophathites.

The door-keepers were Shallum, Akkub, Talmon, and 17
Ahiman; their brother Shallum was the chief. Until then 18
they had all been door-keepers in the quarters of the
Levites at the king's gate, on the east. Shallum son of 19
Kore, son of Ebiasaph, son of Korah, and his kinsmen of
the Korahite family were responsible for service as guards
of the thresholds of the Tabernacle;^a their ancestors had
performed the duty of guarding the entrances to the camp
of the LORD. Phinehas son of Eleazar had been their over- 20
seer in the past – the LORD be with him! Zechariah son of 21
Meshelemiah was the door-keeper of the Tent of the
Presence. Those picked to be door-keepers numbered^b 22
two hundred and twelve in all, registered in their hamlets.
David and Samuel the seer had installed them because
they were trustworthy. They and their sons had charge, 23
by watches, of the gates of the house, the tent-dwelling of
the LORD. The door-keepers were to be on four sides, 24
east, west, north, and south. Their kinsmen from their 25
hamlets had to come on duty with them for seven days at
a time in turn. The four principal door-keepers were 26
chosen for their trustworthiness; they were Levites and
had charge of the rooms and the stores in the house of
God. They always slept in the precincts of the house of 27
God (for the watch was their duty) and they had charge of

[a] *Lit.* Tent.   [b] numbered: *so Pesh.; Heb.* at the thresholds.

28 the key for opening the gates every morning. Some of
them had charge of the vessels used in the service of the
temple, keeping count of them as they were brought in
29 and taken out. Some of them were detailed to take charge
of the furniture and all the sacred vessels, the flour, the
wine, the oil, the incense, and the spices.

30 Some of the priests compounded the ointment for the
31 spices. Mattithiah the Levite, the eldest son of Shallum the
Korahite, was in charge of the preparation of the wafers
32 because he was trustworthy. Some of their Kohathite
kinsmen were in charge of setting out the rows of the
Bread of the Presence every sabbath.

33 These, the musicians, heads of Levite families, were
lodged in rooms set apart for them, because they were
liable for duty by day and by night.

34 These are the heads of Levite families, chiefs according
to their tribal lists, living in Jerusalem.

* One of the dominant concerns of the Chronicler is to
demonstrate the continuity between the ancient tribal lists and
the community of his own day; and this he does in many
ways. So here the theme of continuity is brought out by the
unexpected inclusion of a list of those who returned from
exile in Babylon to establish Israel in the promised land once
more. The theme is thus more important than what would to
us seem the logical order, for in ch. 10 the Chronicler returns
to an account of the establishment of David's kingdom.

1. Two somewhat contrasting themes are here brought out.
On the one hand is the stress on *all Israel*, whose ancestors
have now been listed. *the book of the kings of Israel* may refer
to the annals from which the genealogies were drawn, or
may be a metaphorical way of speaking, with no real book
involved. In any case, not just one or two tribes, but the

whole community, are to be seen as God's favoured people. But the note of failure is also found. Even Judah, the most favoured of all, had failed to live up to its privileges, and was therefore *carried away to exile in Babylon.*

2–34. The whole of this section (and not just verses 2–22, as indicated in the N.E.B. footnote) should be compared with Neh. 11. The exact relationship between the two lists is not easy to determine, as there are many differences in detail, but it is commonly held that the form in Nehemiah represents an earlier stage of transmission. Some of the differences may well arise from the different purposes to which the material was put, the emphasis here being on the promptitude with which the people returned, from their enforced exile to 'their ancestral land in their cities' (verse 2), the occupation here referred to being the re-occupation of the land after the exile in Babylon.

2. *temple-servitors:* the Hebrew word thus translated is *nethinim,* literally 'given ones'. The term is found only in the writings of the Chronicler, and its exact meaning is uncertain – our only clear clue is that many of their names suggest that they were ultimately of foreign extraction.

3. *Judahites...Benjamites...men of Ephraim and Manasseh:* particularly noteworthy here is the inclusion of representatives of the two northern tribes, the more so because the parallel form of the list in Nehemiah refers to Judah and Benjamin only. The Chronicler's stress upon 'all Israel' is thus maintained, and we shall see all through his work that, though Judah was the tribe who responded most loyally to its opportunities, the way for a return to covenant faithfulness was always open to members of other tribes.

5. *Shelanites:* the Hebrew text here has 'Shilonites', i.e. men of Shiloh, the sanctuary often mentioned in 1 Sam., but the emendation is a very probable one, and would provide one of several links with the Judahite lists of ch. 2.

10. *Jehoiarib:* it was from this family that the Maccabees,

the Jewish heroes of the wars of liberation in the second century B.C., were descended (1 Macc. 2: 1).

11. *Azariah...Ahitub:* this is a fragment of the genealogy already found in 6: 12–13, with the addition of a different name, Meraioth: the same form is found in Neh. 11: 11, save that there the form 'Seraiah' is found instead of Azariah. (In ch. 6 both names are found.) These variant traditions show the great interest in the priestly line, and this particular point is related to the ancestry of Ezra who is described as 'son of Seraiah' (Ezra 7: 1). *officer in charge of the house of God:* precisely what function is here involved remains unknown. A near approximation to the phrase is found in Jer. 20: 1 (N.E.B. 'chief officer in the house of the LORD'), and it is noteworthy that the person there so described is 'Pashhur son of Immer', names that feature in the following list, while Jer. 21: 1 has a 'Pashhur son of Malchiah'. No doubt part of the Chronicler's technique was to work in names that would be familiar to his readers.

13. *men of substance:* the exact meaning of this phrase is not always clear. It has already occurred several times in the tribal lists, usually in reference to military ability. So in 5: 24 it was translated 'men of ability', and that may be the sense here (cp. the Revised Standard Version 'very able men'), or alternatively there may be an implication of wealth and a particular social standing.

14–16. The names of the Levites are not known from elsewhere, save for the parallel in Neh. 11: 15–18. As is usually the case in the lists provided by the Chronicler, the numbers of Levites are markedly smaller than those of priests.

16. *the hamlets of the Netophathites:* the village of Netophah seems to have been associated with David in his rise to power – two of his 'valiant heroes' came from there (11: 30) – and also with the community after the exile, since it is mentioned both here as a Levite settlement and among the lists of returning exiles in Ezra 2: 22. It was apparently situated near Bethlehem, and was one of a number of villages near

Jerusalem which were designated as settlements for Levite families.

17. *door-keepers:* though such an office must have existed in the times before the exile, it is only with the Chronicler that we find it elaborated, with very large numbers being involved. Their task of guarding the sanctuary from any form of defilement gave their office a religious importance.

19-20. *the Korahite family:* this section links the 'door-keepers' both with the groups of singers, as is indicated by the reference to the Korahites as singers in 2 Chron. 20: 19 and in the headings to some Psalms (44-9 and others), and also, as the *guards of the thresholds of the Tabernacle,* with the ancient wilderness-wandering tradition. This link is made explicit with the reference to Phinehas, already mentioned in 6: 4, and a prominent figure in the Pentateuch (Num. 25: 6-18). All this shows how the 'door-keepers' were in no sense to be regarded as merely carrying out menial tasks.

22. *David and Samuel:* again we have an indication of the attribution to David of all the temple-arrangements, but only here is Samuel associated with him – this may be an allusion to the fact that Samuel had been a temple-minister at Shiloh (1 Sam. 2).

23-33. It is probable that the arrangements described here were those familiar to the author from his own time.　✵

THE FAMILY OF SAUL

Jehiel founder of Gibeon lived at Gibeon; his wife's 35[a] name was Maacah, and his sons were Abdon the eldest, 36 Zur, Kish, Baal, Ner, Nadab, Gedor, Ahio, Zechariah and 37 Mikloth. Mikloth was the father of Shimeam; they lived 38 alongside their kinsmen in Jerusalem.[b] Ner was the father 39 of Kish, Kish father of Saul, Saul father of Jonathan,

[a] Verses 35-44: cp. 8: 29-38.
[b] Prob. rdg.; Heb. adds with their kinsmen.

40 Malchishua, Abinadab and Eshbaal. The son of Jonathan was Meribbaal, and Meribbaal was the father of Micah.
41 The sons of Micah: Pithon, Melech, Tahrea and Ahaz.*a*
42 Ahaz was the father of Jarah, Jarah father of Alemeth,
43 Azmoth, and Zimri; Zimri father of Moza, and Moza father of Binea; his son was Rephaiah, his son Elasah, his
44 son Azel. Azel had six sons, whose names were Azrikam, Bocheru, Ishmael, Sheariah, Obadiah and Hanan. These were the sons of Azel.

* This list of Benjamites is found in substantially similar form in 8: 29–38, and its repetition here (whatever its original purpose) serves to emphasize the importance of the Saul episode, which is otherwise somewhat obscured by the fact that only his death is described. *

The death of Saul

10 *1b* THE PHILISTINES fought a battle against Israel, and the men of Israel were routed, leaving their dead on
2 Mount Gilboa. The Philistines hotly pursued Saul and his sons and killed the three sons, Jonathan, Abinadab and
3 Malchishua. The battle went hard for Saul, for some
4 archers came upon him and he was wounded by them. So he said to his armour-bearer, 'Draw your sword and run me through, so that these uncircumcised brutes may not come and make sport of me.' But the armour-bearer refused, he dared not; whereupon Saul took his own

[a] and Ahaz: *so Luc. Sept., cp. 8: 35; Heb. om.*
[b] *Verses 1–12: cp. 1 Sam. 31: 1–13.*

sword and fell on it. When the armour-bearer saw that 5
Saul was dead, he too fell on his sword and died. Thus 6
Saul died and his three sons; his whole house perished at
one and the same time. And all the Israelites in the Vale, 7
when they saw that their army had fled and that Saul and
his sons had perished, fled likewise, abandoning their
cities, and the Philistines went in and occupied them.

Next day, when the Philistines came to strip the slain, 8
they found Saul and his sons lying dead on Mount Gilboa.
They stripped him, cut off his head and took away his 9
armour; then they sent messengers through the length
and breadth of their land to take the good news to idols
and people alike. They deposited his armour in the temple 10
of their god,[a] and nailed up his skull in the temple of
Dagon. When the people of Jabesh-gilead heard all that 11
the Philistines had done to Saul, the bravest of them set 12
out together to recover the bodies of Saul and his sons;
they brought them back to Jabesh and buried their bones
under the oak-tree there, and fasted for seven days. Thus 13
Saul paid with his life for his unfaithfulness: he had dis-
obeyed the word of the LORD and had resorted to ghosts
for guidance. He had not sought guidance of the LORD, 14
who therefore destroyed him and transferred the kingdom
to David son of Jesse.

* From this point on, much of the material will be found to
overlap with that in the books of Samuel and Kings. Though
it is hoped that sufficient comment will be provided here to
make the sense clear and to bring out the distinctive viewpoint
of the Chronicler, it is inevitable that on some issues

[a] Or gods.

63

it is impossible to repeat comments made in the volumes on those books, which should also be consulted where possible.

The extent of Saul's genealogy shows that the Chronicler's verdict on him is not wholly negative. In some ways his story is a paradigm of that of Israel as a whole – a story of refusal to live up to the great role for which God had prepared him. In neither case was the rejection final, for the restoration of Judah from exile has its counterpart in the continuing history of the family of Saul.

1. The opening of the narrative account seems very abrupt, but the author will have reckoned that his readers were familiar with the source from which it was taken (1 Sam. 31: 1–13); the previous verses will have prepared them for a reference to Saul.

6. *his whole house perished at one and the same time:* this note is unexpected, the more so as it does not appear in 1 Samuel, and may therefore have been an addition by the Chronicler which points in a different direction from the list indicating the continuance of Saul's family. The stress here seems rather to be on the collapse of Saul's house as the agents of God's rule in Israel.

13–14. These verses have no equivalent in 1 Samuel. For the final compiler of the book of Samuel (the present division into 1 and 2 Samuel only came much later) the story of Saul was not yet complete – an alternative version of his death, and David's lament over Saul and Jonathan, have still to be included. For the Chronicler, however, the kingdom of Saul is over, and in a much more direct way than in Samuel, this is seen as the work of the LORD, *who ... destroyed him and transferred the kingdom to David.* Brief allusion is made to Saul's sins of disobedience and of failure to seek guidance from the LORD – both allusions which would be picked up by readers familiar with 1 Sam. 15 and 28 – and now David is presented as ready to fulfil his role, with none of the stories of his rise to power which play so prominent a part in 1 Samuel. He is as it were produced instantly as the acceptable agent of God's purpose. ✢

David king over Israel

DAVID BECOMES KING

THEN ALL ISRAEL assembled at Hebron to wait upon 11 1*a* David. 'We are your own flesh and blood', they said. 'In the past, while Saul was still king, you led the 2 forces of Israel to war, and you brought them home again. And the LORD your God said to you, "You shall be shepherd of my people Israel, you shall be their prince."' All the elders of Israel came to the king at Hebron; there 3 David made a covenant with them before the LORD, and they anointed David king over Israel, as the LORD had said through the lips of Samuel.

Then David and all Israel went to Jerusalem (that is 4 Jebus, where the Jebusites, the inhabitants of the land, lived). The people of Jebus said to David, 'Never shall 5 you come in here'; none the less David did capture the stronghold of Zion, and it is now known as the City of David. David said, 'The first man to kill a Jebusite shall 6 become a commander or an officer', and the first man to go up was Joab son of Zeruiah; so he was given the command.

David took up his residence in the stronghold: that is 7 why they called it the City of David. He built the city 8 round it, starting at the Millo and including its neigh-

[a] *Verses 1–9: cp. 2 Sam. 5: 1–3, 6–10.*

bourhood, while Joab reconstructed the rest of the city.
9 So David steadily grew stronger, for the LORD of Hosts
was with him.

* Though the material in this section originates from 2 Sam.
5, the presentation differs markedly, and again a very strong
impression is created of the direct intervention of the LORD
on behalf of David. To a greater extent than in 2 Samuel, the
historical circumstances are merely incidental.

1. *all Israel assembled at Hebron:* the account in Samuel
shows how David had established his power around Hebron,
in the far south, while Saul was still king (1 Sam. 30: 31),
and had been 'anointed king over the house of Judah' there
(2 Sam. 2: 4). All this is omitted by the Chronicler, who
stresses the direct divine intervention by which the rule
passes immediately from Saul to David.

3. *as the LORD had said through the lips of Samuel:* the
reference is probably to the story of David's anointing by
Samuel in 1 Sam. 16, though no specific word is attributed
to Samuel there.

4. *Jebus:* this form is not common in earlier sources, though
there are many references to the Jebusites, from whom the
name may derive. The ancient name was probably Jerusalem.

5–6. The account of the capture of Jerusalem is a simplified
version of that in 2 Sam. 5; it may be that some of the details
of that story were already obscure by the Chronicler's day.
Noteworthy here is the stress on the role of Joab (cp. also
verse 8), who is not mentioned at this point in 2 Samuel.

8. *the Millo:* the significance of this term (which is apparently related to the Hebrew word meaning 'to fill') has been
greatly disputed. The most probable suggestion is that it
refers to the dwellings built on the steeply sloping eastern
wall of the city, traces of which have been revealed by recent
archaeological investigations.

9. *So David steadily grew stronger, for the LORD of Hosts*

was with him: the purposes of the Chronicler and of the editor of Samuel were substantially similar, as is well illustrated by this verse, found already as 2 Sam. 5: 10, and characteristic of the Chronicler's theme. ✻

DAVID'S HEROES

Of David's heroes these were the chief, men who lent 10[a] their full strength to his government and, with all Israel, joined in making him king; such was the LORD's decree for Israel. First came Jashoboam[b] the Hachmonite, chief 11 of the three;[c] he it was who brandished his spear over three hundred, all slain at one time. Next to him was 12 Eleazar son of Dodo the Ahohite, one of the heroic three. He was with David at Pas-dammim where the Philistines 13 had gathered for battle in a field carrying a good crop of barley; and when the people had fled from the Philistines he stood his ground[d] in the field, saved it[e] and defeated 14 them. So the LORD brought about a great victory.

Three of the thirty chiefs went down to the rock to 15 join David at the cave of Adullam, while the Philistines were encamped in the Vale of Rephaim. At that time 16 David was in the stronghold, and a Philistine garrison held Bethlehem. One day a longing came over David, 17 and he exclaimed, 'If only I could have a drink of water from the well[f] by the gate of Bethlehem!' At this the 18 three made their way through the Philistine lines and drew water from the well by the gate of Bethlehem, and

[a] *Verses 10–41: cp. 2 Sam. 23: 8–39.*
[b] *Some Sept. MSS. have* Ishbaal.
[c] *So Luc. Sept.; Heb.* thirty *or* lieutenants.
[d] *So Sept., cp. 2 Sam. 23: 12; Heb.* they stood their ground.
[e] saved it: *or* cleared it of the Philistines.   [f] *Or* cistern.

brought it to David. But David refused to drink it; he
19 poured it out to the LORD and said, 'God forbid that I
should do such a thing! Can I drink the blood of these
men*a*? They have brought it at the risk of their lives.' So
he would not drink it. Such were the exploits of the
heroic three.

20 Abishai the brother of Joab was chief of the thirty.*b* He
once brandished his spear over three hundred dead, and
21 he was famous among the thirty.*b* He held higher rank
than the rest of the thirty*b* and became their captain, but
22 he did not rival the three. Benaiah son of Jehoiada, from
Kabzeel, was*c* a hero of many exploits. It was he who
smote the two champions of Moab, and who went down
23 into a pit and killed a lion on a snowy day. It was he who
also killed the Egyptian, a giant seven and a half feet*d*
high armed with a spear as big as the beam of a loom; he
went to meet him with a club, snatched the spear out of
the Egyptian's hand and killed him with his own weapon.
24 Such were the exploits of Benaiah son of Jehoiada,
25 famous among the heroic thirty.*e* He was more famous
than the rest of the thirty, but did not rival the three.
David appointed him to his household.

26 These were his valiant heroes: Asahel the brother of
27 Joab, and Elhanan son of Dodo from Bethlehem; Shamm-
moth from Harod,*f* and Helez from a place unknown;
28 Ira son of Ikkesh from Tekoa, and Abiezer from Ana-
29 thoth; Sibbecai from Hushah, and Ilai the Ahohite;
30 Maharai from Netophah, and Heled son of Baanah from

[a] *So Vulg.; Heb. adds* at the risk of their lives.
[b] *So Pesh.; Heb.* three.   [c] *So Pesh.; Heb. adds* the son of.
[d] *Lit.* five cubits.   [e] *Prob. rdg.; Heb.* three.
[f] *Prob. rdg., cp. 2 Sam. 23: 25; Heb.* Haror.

Netophah; Ithai son of Ribai from Gibeah of Benjamin, 31
and Benaiah from Pirathon; Hurai from the ravines of 32
Gaash, and Abiel from Beth-arabah; Azmoth from 33
Bahurim, and Eliahba from Shaalbon; Hashem[a] the 34
Gizonite, and Jonathan son of Shage the Hararite; Ahiam 35
son of Sacar the Hararite, and Eliphal son of Ur; Hepher 36
from Mecherah, and Ahijah from a place unknown;
Hezro from Carmel, and Naarai son of Ezbai; Joel the 37,38
brother of Nathan, and Mibhar the son of Haggeri; Zelek 39
the Ammonite, and Naharai from Beeroth, armour-
bearer to Joab son of Zeruiah; Ira the Ithrite, and Gareb 40
the Ithrite; Uriah the Hittite, and Zabad son of Ahlai. 41
Adina son of Shiza the Reubenite, a chief of the Reu- 42
benites, was over these thirty.[b] Also Hanan son of 43
Maacah, and Joshaphat the Mithnite; Uzzia from Ash- 44
taroth, Shama and Jeiel the sons of Hotham from Aroer;
Jediael son of Shimri, and Joha his brother, the Tizite; 45
Eliel the Mahavite, and Jeribai and Joshaviah sons of 46
Elnaam, and Ithmah the Moabite; Eliel, Obed, and Jasiel, 47
from Zobah.[c]

---

* It is not always clear upon what principle the Chronicler
rearranged the order of the material he took over from
2 Samuel, but it may be that here he wishes to follow the
account of the heroic deed of Joab with a fuller picture of the
followers of David and their exploits. The most striking feature
of this list in comparison with that in 2 Sam. 23 is the fact
that in 2 Samuel the last name is that of 'Uriah the Hittite',
whom David had had killed so that he could marry his wife

[a] *So some Sept. MSS., cp. 2 Sam. 23: 32; Heb.* the sons of Hashem.
[b] was over these thirty: *so Pesh.; Heb.* had thirty over him.
[c] from Zobah: *prob. rdg.; Heb. obscure.*

Bathsheba; by contrast the Chronicler adds further names. It is possible that he had access to the original form of the list, and that the editor of Samuel had cut it short for dramatic effect, though some scholars have argued that the last names in the Chronicler's version are a later and secondary addition.

10. *men who lent their full strength to his government and, with all Israel, joined in making him king:* this introduction, which has no counterpart in Samuel, is required partly by the placing of this material early in the story, in association with David becoming king; but it also well illustrates the Chronicler's stress on *all Israel* as the subject of David's kingship and the complete supremacy of David – these heroes only *lent their full strength* to him rather than playing any independent role. The verse also stresses the loyalty of the people and its acceptance: *such was the LORD's decree for Israel.*

11. *the three:* the Hebrew has 'thirty', but the words for 'three' and 'thirty' are similar, and the emendation is a likely one. Both terms appear to have acquired a technical sense, perhaps borrowed from Egyptian usage, which meant that more than the precise number might be involved.

17–19. This incident, taken over without significant change from 2 Sam. 23, provides a vivid picture both of the way in which the water so bravely obtained came to be regarded as the blood of the warriors and therefore might not be drunk, and also of the way in which David commanded the loyalty of his servants, a basic stress of the Chronicler in this section of his work.

20–1. *the thirty:* again an emendation of the Hebrew text by N.E.B. illustrates the confusion that could be caused in the transmission of similar terms (cp. the details in the footnotes). The earlier names in this list are not otherwise known, but Abishai is found also in 2 Samuel, where he is regularly called 'son of Zeruiah', who was his mother.

26–47. In addition to the fact that the Chronicler's list extends beyond that in 2 Samuel, there are a few, mostly minor, changes in the names. We have no means of being

certain whether this implies that the Chronicler had independent access to old material, or whether the text of 2 Samuel
which he was using differed slightly from the one known to
us; such variants in texts in the days before printing are
perfectly possible. ✳

FURTHER SUPPORT FOR DAVID

These are the men who joined David at Ziklag while **12**
he was banned from the presence of Saul son of Kish.
They ranked among the warriors valiant in battle. They 2
carried bows and could sling stones or shoot arrows with
the left hand or the right; they were Benjamites, kinsmen
of Saul. The foremost were Ahiezer and Joash, the sons 3
of Shemaah the Gibeathite; Jeziel and Pelet, men of
Beth-azmoth;*a* Berachah and Jehu of Anathoth; Ish- 4*b*
maiah the Gibeonite, a hero among the thirty and a chief
among them; Jeremiah, Jahaziel, Johanan, and Josabad of
Gederah; Eluzai, Jerimoth, Bealiah, Shemariah, and 5*c*
Shephatiah the Haruphite; Elkanah, Isshiah, Azareel, 6
Joezer, Jashobeam, the Korahites; and Joelah and Zeba- 7
diah sons of Jeroham, of Gedor.

Some Gadites also joined David at the stronghold in 8
the wilderness, valiant men trained for war, who could
handle the heavy shield and spear, grim as lions and swift
as gazelles on the hills. Ezer was their chief, Obadiah the 9
second, Eliab the third; Mishmannah the fourth and 10
Jeremiah the fifth; Attai the sixth and Eliel the seventh; 11
Johanan the eighth and Elzabad the ninth; Jeremiah the 12,13
tenth and Machbanai the eleventh. These were chiefs of 14

[a] men of Beth-azmoth: *lit.* sons of Azmoth.
[b] *Verses 4 and 5 in Heb.*   [c] *Verse 6 in Heb.*

the Gadites in the army, the least of them a match for a
15 hundred, the greatest a match for a thousand. These were
the men who in the first month crossed the Jordan, which
was in full flood in all its reaches, and wrought havoc in
the valleys, east and west.

16   Some men of Benjamin and Judah came to David at
17 the stronghold. David went out to them and said, 'If you
come as friends to help me, join me and welcome; but if
you come to betray me to my enemies, innocent though
I am of any crime of violence, may the God of our fathers
18 see and judge.' At that a spirit took possession of[a] Amasai,
the chief of the thirty, and he said:[b]

> We are on your side, David!
> We are with you, son of Jesse!
> Greetings, greetings to you
> and greetings to your ally!
> For your God is your ally.

So David welcomed them and attached them to the
columns of his raiding parties.

19   Some men of Manasseh had deserted to David when he
went with the Philistines to war against Saul, though he
did not, in fact, fight on the side of the Philistines. Their
princes brusquely dismissed him, saying to themselves
that he would desert them for his master Saul, and that
20 would cost them their heads. The men of Manasseh who
deserted to him when he went to Ziklag were these:
Adnah, Jozabad, Jediael, Michael, Jozabad, Elihu, and
21 Zilthai, each commanding his thousand in Manasseh. It
was they who stood valiantly by David against the raiders,

[a] took possession of: *lit.* clothed itself with.
[b] and he said: *so Sept.; Heb. om.*

for they were all good fighters, and they were given
commands in his forces. From day to day men came in to 22
help David, until he had gathered an immense army.[a]

These are the numbers of the armed bands which 23
joined David at Hebron to transfer Saul's sovereignty to
him, as the LORD had said: men of Judah, bearing heavy 24
shield and spear, six thousand eight hundred, drafted for
active service; of Simeon, fighting men drafted for active 25
service, seven thousand one hundred; of Levi, four thou- 26
sand six hundred, together with Jehoiada prince of the 27
house of Aaron and three thousand seven hundred men,
and Zadok a valiant fighter, with twenty-two officers of[b] 28
his own clan; of Benjamin, Saul's kinsmen, three thou- 29
sand, though most of them had hitherto remained loyal
to the house of Saul; of Ephraim, twenty thousand eight 30
hundred, fighting men, famous in their own clans; of the 31
half tribe of Manasseh, eighteen thousand, who had been
nominated to come and make David king; of Issachar, 32
whose tribesmen were skilled in reading the signs of the
times to discover what course Israel should follow, two
hundred chiefs, with all their kinsmen under their command; of Zebulun, fifty thousand troops well-drilled for 33
battle, armed with every kind of weapon, bold and single-
minded; of Naphtali, a thousand officers with thirty- 34
seven thousand men bearing heavy shield and spear; of 35
the Danites, twenty-eight thousand six hundred well-
drilled for battle; of Asher, forty thousand troops well- 36
drilled for battle; of the Reubenites and the Gadites and 37
the half tribe of Manasseh east of Jordan, a hundred

[a] an immense army: *lit.* a great army like the army of God.
[b] of: *so Sept.; Heb. om.*

73

and twenty thousand, armed with every kind of weapon.

38 All these warriors, bold men in battle, came to Hebron, loyally determined to make David king over the whole of Israel; the rest of Israel, too, had but one thought, to make

39 him king. They spent three days there with David, eating and drinking, for their kinsmen made provision for them.

40 Their neighbours also round about, as far away as Issachar, Zebulun, and Naphtali, brought food on asses and camels, on mules and oxen, supplies of meal, fig-cakes, raisin-cakes, wine and oil, oxen and sheep, in plenty; for there was rejoicing in Israel.

✶ The particular significance of these further lists, which are for the most part without parallel elsewhere, seems to be that they show how support came for David from all the tribes, not simply from his own fellow-Judahites. Once again, the 'all Israel' theme is here underlined.

1. *at Ziklag while he was banned from the presence of Saul:* the reference is to the story in 1 Sam. 27, which tells of David being granted Ziklag (an unknown locality in the south) as a Philistine fief; that element in the story is not mentioned here, but it is assumed that the readers will be familiar with 1 Samuel. The exact meaning of the word translated here *banned* is not clear; it may be a reference to David's exclusion from Saul's court (so the N.E.B. translation), or it may refer to the limitations upon David's movements at this time.

2. *with the left hand:* there are several other references to 'left-handed' Benjamite warriors. See for example the story of the judge Ehud in Judg. 3: 15–29.

8. *Gadites:* the names that follow are apparently from a form of military muster analagous to those which provide the basis of some of the tribal lists in chs. 2–8. The description

74

of their qualities in this introductory verse is clearly of a stereotyped nature. *the stronghold in the wilderness:* if this is also a reference to David's fugitive days, as in verse 1, it is more surprising, since Gad was one of the most northerly tribes, and the *stronghold in the wilderness,* though its exact site is unknown, was certainly in the south.

17. *if you come to betray me:* again seems to reflect David's precarious position in the wilderness, where what from one point of view could be called betrayal could from another angle be regarded as loyalty to the king, Saul.

18. *took possession of:* the Hebrew literally has 'clothed itself with' (see the N.E.B. footnote), an expression frequently used to denote a powerful burst of inspiration. Elsewhere, what follows is some dramatic action (e.g. Gideon's slaughter of the Midianites in Judg. 6: 34–40); here Amasai is inspired to utter the poetic oath of loyalty to David which follows. If Amasai here is the same as 'Amasa' of 2 Sam. 17: 25, it is ironic that he in fact deserted David at the time of Absalom's rebellion. The oath itself forms a counterpoint to the rejection of David and his descendants found at 2 Chron. 10: 16, and emphasizes that some remained loyal.

19. *Some men of Manasseh:* again it is unexpected to find men from a northern tribe involved in the far south, and no mention of such a group is made in 1 Sam. 29. *though he did not, in fact, fight on the side of the Philistines:* the Hebrew text here actually reads 'they did not...', but the N.E.B. follows the Greek – probably rightly seeing this as part of the Chronicler's concern to stress that David had never fought against his own people. The suspicions of the Philistine princes are referred to in 1 Sam. 29: 4.

23–37. This section refers once again to David at Hebron, rather than to his time in the wilderness, and its style marks it as coming from a different source from the previous verses. Here the emphasis is on the way in which all Israel rallied to David's support. The numbers, particularly from the remote northern and Transjordanian tribes (verses 33–7), are astonishingly large, but we have no means of knowing on what basis the Chronicler was working here.

28. *Zadok a valiant fighter:* the reference is presumably to the same Zadok as is mentioned frequently as David's priest. The Levites play an important part in the various descriptions of war in the books of Chronicles, but it is unusual to have them described individually in the terms here used.

29. *Saul's kinsmen, three thousand:* the point is presumably that Saul was of the tribe of Benjamin, rather than that all these were his actual kinsmen. Once again, the implication of loyalty to Saul is noteworthy.

38-40. *determined to make David king:* the climax of this episode is reached, with all Israel from *as far away as Issachar, Zebulun, and Naphtali* in the far north, united in the common purpose of proclaiming David as king, an achievement which gave cause for *rejoicing in Israel.* ✼

THE BRINGING OF THE ARK

13 David consulted the officers over units of a thousand and
2 a hundred on every matter brought forward. Then he said to the whole assembly of Israel, 'If you approve, and if the LORD our God opens a way, let us*a* send to our kinsmen who have stayed behind, in all the districts of Israel, and also to the priests and Levites in the cities where they have common lands, bidding them join us.
3 Let us fetch the Ark of our God, for while Saul lived we
4 never resorted to it.' The whole assembly resolved to do this; the entire nation approved it.

5 So David assembled all Israel from the Shihor in Egypt to Lebo-hamath, in order to fetch the Ark of God from
6*b* Kiriath-jearim. Then David and all Israel went up to

[a] and if...let us: *or* and if it is from the LORD our God, let us seize the opportunity and...   [b] *Verses 6-14: cp. 2 Sam. 6: 2-11.*

Baalah, to Kiriath-jearim, which belonged to Judah, to
fetch the Ark of God, the LORD enthroned upon the
cherubim, the Ark which bore his name.[a] And they con- 7
veyed the Ark of God on a new cart from the house of
Abinadab, with Uzza and Ahio guiding the cart. David 8
and all Israel danced for joy before God without restraint
to the sound of singing, of harps and lutes, of tambourines,
and cymbals and trumpets. But when they came to the 9
threshing-floor of Kidon, the oxen stumbled, and Uzza
put out his hand to hold the Ark. The LORD was angry 10
with Uzza and struck him down because he had put out
his hand to the Ark. So he died there before God. David 11
was vexed because the LORD's anger had broken out upon
Uzza, and he called the place Perez-uzza,[b] the name it
still bears. David was afraid of God that day and said, 12
'How can I harbour the Ark of God after this?' So he did 13
not take the Ark with him into the City of David, but
turned aside and carried it to the house of Obed-edom the
Gittite. Thus the Ark of God remained beside the house 14
of Obed-edom, in its tent,[c] for three months, and the
LORD blessed the family of Obed-edom and all that he
had

⁂ This story, which has its continuation in ch. 15, is based
on the account in 2 Sam. 6, but the introductory verses (1–4)
provide a different setting for the ancient story. They stress
that the removal of the Ark to Jerusalem was a religious
decision reached by 'the whole assembly' and 'the entire
nation' (verse 4), dependent upon the will of God (verse 2)

[a] which bore his name: *prob. rdg.; Heb. obscure.*
[b] *That is* Outbreak on Uzza.
[c] *Or* in his tent.

and without the political implications of the story in 2 Samuel.
It is also set in marked contrast to Saul's failure (verse 3).
In this way some of the more puzzling aspects of the story
that follows are explained in advance.

3. *while Saul lived we never resorted to it:* there is in fact
a reference to Saul calling for the Ark of God to be brought
to him in 1 Sam. 14: 18, but there is some suggestion that
references to Saul's use of the Ark have been mainly edited out
of the text. (See the N.E.B. translation of that text, and the
footnote, together with the commentary on 1 Samuel in this
series.)

4. *the entire nation:* in the reduced circumstances of the
Israel of the Chronicler's own day, such a decision could more
easily be envisaged than in David's time. The Chronicler
seems to envisage a unanimous decision by the whole nation.

5. *assembled all Israel:* the picture in the previous verse is
continued, in terms of the gathering together of the disper-
sion. A recurring theme in this work is the centrality of the
worship of God in Jerusalem against the claims of any other
sanctuary. *the Shihor in Egypt:* this is several times mentioned
in the Old Testament as a boundary. It was a body of water
in Egypt whose exact location remains disputed. *Lebo-hamath:*
another boundary point, this time in the far north. The terms
used are one of several pairs whereby the Old Testament
characterizes the completeness of the land, 'from Dan to
Beersheba' being the most common such pair. *Kiriath-jearim:*
the account of how the Ark came to be there is found in
1 Sam. 6, a story which the Chronicler assumes would be
familiar to his readers.

6. *the Ark of God, the LORD enthroned upon the cherubim,
the Ark which bore his name:* this compound phrase has some
curious features. The phrase describing the cherubim (mytho-
logical winged bull-like monsters, not at all to be confused
with the usual present-day idea of cherubs) came to be a
regular part of the description of Yahweh, invisible upon his
throne. The last phrase makes no sense in the Hebrew text

as it stands and some emendation such as that in the N.E.B. is necessary. The important point is that the Chronicler is here picking up an idea characteristic of the deuteronomic writers, who regularly spoke of the *name* of God as dwelling among his people.

9. *threshing-floor of Kidon:* the word *Kidon* is peculiar to this passage, and it is not known whether it is intended as a place- or a personal name. In the corresponding passage in 2 Sam. 6: 6, there is also a doubt, where the 'threshing-floor of Nacon' has sometimes been interpreted as 'a certain threshing-floor' (so the N.E.B.). Threshing-floors were often associated with the sites of sanctuaries, and that may have been significant in the earlier form of the story, but it is likely that here the Chronicler is simply following his source.

10–14. The remainder of the story follows 2 Sam. 6: 7–11 with only minor changes, and again it seems as if the Chronicler was content to let his source speak for itself. For the modern reader the story of the death of Uzza raises acute problems (see the commentary on 2 Samuel for some suggestions about the significance of this story in its earlier form); for the Chronicler it was already regarded as what we should call 'holy Scripture' and was treated accordingly.

14. *beside the house of Obed-edom:* not in it, but *in its* own *tent* (so the N.E.B. text, probably rightly). ✻

DAVID'S POWER

Hiram king of Tyre sent an embassy to David; he sent **14**[a] cedar logs, and masons and carpenters with them to build him a house. David knew by now that the LORD had 2 confirmed him as king over Israel and[b] had made his royal power stand higher for the sake of his people Israel.

David married more wives in Jerusalem, and more sons 3

[a] *Verses 1–16: cp. 2 Sam. 5: 11–25.*
[b] *and: so Targ., cp. 2 Sam. 5: 12; Heb. om.*

4[a] and daughters were born to him. These are the names of
the children born to him in Jerusalem: Shammua, Sho-
5,6 bab, Nathan, Solomon, Ibhar, Elishua, Elpelet, Nogah,
7 Nepheg, Japhia, Elishama, Beeliada and Eliphelet.

8   When the Philistines learnt that David had been
anointed king over the whole of Israel, they came up in
force to seek him out. David, hearing of this, went out to
9 face them. Now the Philistines had come and raided the
10 Vale of Rephaim. So David inquired of God, 'If I attack
the Philistines, wilt thou deliver them into my hands?'
And the LORD answered, 'Go; I will deliver them into
11 your hands.' So he[b] went up and attacked them at Baal-
perazim and defeated them there. 'God has used me to
break through my enemies' lines,' David said, 'as a river
breaks its banks'; that is why the place was named
12 Baal-perazim.[c] The Philistines left their gods behind them
there, and by David's orders these were burnt.

13,14   The Philistines made another raid on the Vale. Again
David inquired of God, and God said to him, 'No, you
must go up towards their rear; wheel round without
making contact and[d] come upon them opposite the
15 aspens. Then, as soon as you hear a rustling sound in the
tree-tops, you shall give battle, for God will have gone
16 out before you to defeat the Philistine army.' David did
as God commanded, and they drove the Philistine army
17 in flight all the way from Gibeon to Gezer. So David's
fame spread through every land, and the LORD inspired
all nations with dread of him.

[a] *Verses 4–7: cp. 3: 5–8.*   [b] *So Sept., cp. 2 Sam. 5: 20; Heb.* they.
[c] *That is* Baal of Break-through.
[d] No...contact and: *or* Do not go up to the attack; withdraw from
them and then...

* The three months' sojourn of the Ark at the house of Obed-edom (13: 14) provides an opportunity for the Chronicler to insert at this point other material relating to David's greatness. It is not always possible to discern the principles on which the material has been arranged, but much of that which relates to David's secular power is placed first, before his preparation for the building of the temple is described. The Chronicler himself would probably not have made the kind of distinction between sacred and secular power that is usual for us.

1. *Hiram king of Tyre:* he plays a prominent part in all the traditions relating to the temple-building, though here his role is quite secondary.

3. *David married more wives:* 2 Sam. 5: 13 also has a reference to 'concubines' which is omitted here; it may be that what had been regarded earlier as perfectly normal royal practice was by the Chronicler's time no longer acceptable.

4–7. David's *children:* Elpelet and Nogah are not included in the list in 2 Sam. 5, possibly because of a scribal error there; they appear in the other form of this list, in 1 Chron. 3: 5–8. The other noteworthy feature is the name Beeliada ('Eliada' in the other lists). This provides an indication that it was possible for David, like Saul, to give his sons names compounded with Baal, a practice which had been offensive to earlier editors of this list.

8–16. These two stories of successful warfare against the Philistines are substantially taken over from 2 Sam. 5, but the overall picture is somewhat different. In 2 Samuel the stories form part of an extended account of the way in which David established himself as king independent of the Philistines; here these two stories simply illustrate the general idea of David's reliance on God in all his battles and the success which this brought him. This may account for the omission of the note in 2 Sam. 5: 17 that 'David...took refuge in the stronghold', and for the reducing of references to the Philistines' 'overrunning' the country to mere raids and attacks (verses 10 and 13).

12. *these were burnt:* a more appropriate end for the Philistine *gods* than being carried off, apparently as booty, as in 2 Sam. 5.

17. This verse provides the Chronicler's appropriate context for the Philistine warfare – a means of increasing *David's fame*, and perhaps even more significant, an indication that in all his battles the LORD was on his side, reducing all his enemies to panic. ✳

THE PROCESSION OF THE ARK CONTINUED

15 David built himself quarters in the City of David, and prepared a place for the Ark of God and pitched a tent for
2 it. Then he decreed that only Levites should carry the Ark of God, since they had been chosen by the LORD to carry
3 it and to serve him[a] for ever. Next David assembled all Israel at Jerusalem, to bring up the Ark of the LORD to the
4 place he had prepared for it. He gathered together the
5 sons of Aaron and the Levites: of the sons of Kohath, Uriel the chief with a hundred and twenty of his kinsmen;
6 of the sons of Merari, Asaiah the chief with two hundred
7 and twenty of his kinsmen; of the sons of Gershom, Joel
8 the chief with a hundred and thirty of his kinsmen; of the sons of Elizaphan, Shemaiah the chief with two hundred
9 of his kinsmen; of the sons of Hebron, Eliel the chief with
10 eighty of his kinsmen; of the sons of Uzziel, Amminadab
11 the chief with a hundred and twelve of his kinsmen. And David summoned Zadok and Abiathar the priests, together with the Levites, Uriel, Asaiah, Joel, Shemaiah,

[a] *Or* it.

Eliel, and Amminadab, and said to them, 'You who are 12
heads of families of the Levites, hallow yourselves, you
and your kinsmen, and bring up the Ark of the LORD the
God of Israel to the place which I have prepared for it. It 13
was because you were not present the first time, that the
LORD our God broke out upon us. For we had not sought
his guidance as we should have done.' So the priests and 14
the Levites hallowed themselves to bring up the Ark of
the LORD the God of Israel, and the Levites carried the 15
Ark of God, bearing it on their shoulders with poles as
Moses had prescribed at the command of the LORD.

David also ordered the chiefs of the Levites to install as 16
musicians those of their kinsmen who were players skilled
in making joyful music on their instruments, lutes and
harps and cymbals. So the Levites installed Heman son of 17
Joel and, from his kinsmen, Asaph son of Berechiah; and
from their kinsmen the Merarites, Ethan son of Kushaiah,
together with their kinsmen of the second degree, 18
Zechariah,*a* Jaaziel, Shemiramoth, Jehiel, Unni, Eliab,
Benaiah, Maaseiah, Mattithiah, Eliphelehu, and Mikneiah,
and the door-keepers Obed-edom and Jeiel. They installed 19
the musicians Heman, Asaph, and Ethan to sound the
cymbals of bronze; Zechariah, Jaaziel, Shemiramoth, 20
Jehiel, Unni, Eliab, Maaseiah, and Benaiah to play on
lutes;*b* Mattithiah, Eliphelehu, Mikneiah, Obed-edom, 21
Jeiel, and Azaziah to play on harps.*c* Kenaniah, officer of 22
the Levites, was precentor in charge of the music because
of his proficiency. Berechiah and Elkanah were door- 23

[a] *So some MSS., cp. verse 20; others add* a son.
[b] *Prob. rdg.; Heb. adds* al alamoth, *possibly a musical term.*
[c] *Prob. rdg.; Heb. adds* al hashsheminith lenasseah, *possibly musical terms.*

24 keepers for the Ark, while the priests Shebaniah, Jehoshaphat, Nethaneel, Amasai, Zechariah, Benaiah, and Eliezer
sounded the trumpets before the Ark of God; and Obed-
edom and Jehiah also were door-keepers for the Ark.

25[a] Then David and the elders of Israel and the captains of
units of a thousand went to bring up the Ark of the
Covenant of the LORD with much rejoicing from the
26 house of Obed-edom. Because God had helped the Levites
who carried the Ark of the Covenant of the LORD, they
sacrificed seven bulls and seven rams.

27 Now David and all the Levites who carried the Ark,
and the musicians, and Kenaniah the precentor,[b] were
arrayed in robes of fine linen; and David had on a linen
28 ephod. All Israel escorted the Ark of the Covenant of the
LORD with shouts of acclamation, blowing on horns and
trumpets, clashing cymbals and playing on lutes and harps.
29 But as the Ark of the Covenant of the LORD was entering
the city of David, Saul's daughter Michal looked down
through a window and saw King David dancing and
making merry, and she despised him in her heart.

* The story of the bringing of the Ark to Jerusalem, begun in
ch. 13, is now taken up again. Though 2 Sam. 6 provides a
recognizable source for some parts of this chapter, there is
much additional material here, almost certainly from the
Chronicler's own hand. Chs. 15 and 16 represent the first
great climax in his description of the establishment of David's
kingdom, and he naturally describes the ceremonies in terms
that would be appropriate and understandable in the light
of the religious customs of his own day.

[a] *Verses 25–9: cp. 2 Sam. 6: 12–16.*
[b] the precentor: *prob. rdg.; Heb. obscure.*

1. *and pitched a tent for it:* according to the Pentateuch (cp. Exod. 40: 1–3) the Ark had been housed in a tent before the building of a permanent sanctuary, and the Chronicler here associates David with that custom.

2. *only Levites should carry the Ark of God:* not only is this in line with the practice and theology of the Chronicler's own day, it also provides an explanation of the fate of the unfortunate Uzza in ch. 13, a point made more explicitly at verse 13.

3. *Next David assembled all Israel:* once again the *all Israel* theme is repeated, as an integral element of the religious significance of David's kingship.

4–15. The arrangements for carrying the Ark are in accord with the law *as Moses had prescribed it* (verse 15). A number of the names listed here also occur in the Levite genealogies in ch. 6, but it is possible that the Chronicler was here using different sources of information.

16. *musicians:* another prominent interest of the Chronicler, and, no doubt, of the temple-worship of his own day, is next described, again with an allusion back to the genealogies in 6: 31–48. *lutes and harps and cymbals:* sufficient archaeological and literary evidence is available from the ancient world to enable us to have a clear idea of at least the families of musical instruments referred to here and elsewhere (see *Old Testament Illustrations* in this series, pp. 130f.); unfortunately insufficient is known about the details of the chant for any kind of precise reconstruction of the music of the services to be built up. This is particularly limiting in our appreciation of the Psalms and of the Chronicler's work.

18. *Obed-edom:* it is noteworthy that two men of this name are mentioned, a *door-keeper* here, and a harpist at verse 21. No specific identification with 'Obed-edom the Gittite', beside whose house the Ark had been left, is made; but it is probable that the Chronicler introduces the name deliberately to show the propriety of what had been done.

20–1 (footnotes): the reference to *alamoth*, which as the

footnote in N.E.B. indicates is probably a musical term, is found also in the title to Ps. 46 (not included in N.E.B.). Similarly with the additions to the next verse: *hashsheminith* is found in the title of Ps. 6, and a form akin to *lenasseah* in several psalm-titles.

26. *they sacrificed seven bulls and seven rams:* this section is based on 2 Sam. 6, but there are important modifications. In particular, in the earlier story David had performed the sacrifices, which are now in the hands of the Levites, and are multiplied sevenfold, to emphasize the solemnity of the occasion.

27–9. Again some of the details come from 2 Sam. 6, but whereas that chapter conveys to us a very ancient picture of festivities of a type probably akin to Canaanite practice, here the picture is of a solemn religious procession. The episode of Michal, an important part of the earlier story, is here noted without further comment, and is inserted before the account of the installation of the Ark, which precedes it in 2 Samuel. ✳

THE INSTALLATION OF THE ARK

16 1*ᵃ* When they had brought in the Ark of God, they put it inside the tent that David had pitched for it, and they offered whole-offerings and shared-offerings before God.
2 After David had completed these sacrifices, he blessed the
3 people in the name of the LORD and gave food, a loaf of bread, a portion of meat,*ᵇ* and a cake of raisins, to each
4 Israelite, man or woman. He appointed certain Levites to serve before the Ark of the LORD, to repeat the Name, to
5 confess and to praise the LORD the God of Israel. Their leader was Asaph; second to him was Zechariah; then

[a] *Verses 1–3: cp. 2 Sam. 6: 17–19.*
[b] portion of meat: *mng. of Heb. word uncertain.*

came Jaaziel,[a] Shemiramoth, Jehiel, Mattithiah, Eliab,
Benaiah, Obed-edom, and Jeiel, with lutes and harps,
Asaph, who sounded the cymbals; and Benaiah and 6
Jahaziel the priests, who blew the trumpets before the
Ark of the Covenant of God continuously throughout 7
that day. It was then that David first ordained the offering
of thanks to the LORD by Asaph and his kinsmen:

Give the LORD thanks and invoke him by name,   8[b]
  make his deeds known in the world around.
Pay him honour with song and psalm   9
  and think upon all his wonders.
Exult in his hallowed name;   10
  let those who seek the LORD be joyful in heart.
  Turn to the LORD, your strength,[c]   11
seek his presence always.
  Remember the wonders that he has wrought,   12
    his portents and the judgements he has given,
O offspring of Israel his servants, O chosen sons of Jacob. 13

He is the LORD our God;   14
  his judgements fill the earth.
He called to mind[d] his covenant from long ago,[e]   15
the promise he extended to a thousand generations –
  the covenant made with Abraham,   16
    his oath given to Isaac,
the decree by which he bound himself for Jacob,   17
his everlasting covenant with Israel:

[a] *Prob. rdg., cp. 15: 18, 20; Heb.* Jeiel.
[b] *Verses 8–22: cp. Ps. 105: 1–15.*
[c] your strength: *or* the symbol of his strength; *lit.* and his strength.
[d] He called to mind: *so some Sept. MSS., cp. Ps. 105: 8; Heb.* Call to
mind.
[e] from long ago: *or* for ever.

18   'I will give you the land of Canaan', he said,
       'to be your possession, your patrimony.'

19   A small company it was,^a
    few in number, strangers in that land,

20   roaming from nation to nation,
    from one kingdom to another;

21   but he let no man ill-treat them,
    for their sake he admonished kings:

22   'Touch not my anointed servants,
     do my prophets no harm.'

23^b   Sing to the LORD, all men on earth,
     proclaim his triumph day by day.

24   Declare his glory among the nations,
     his marvellous deeds among all peoples.

25 Great is the LORD and worthy of all praise;
    he is more to be feared than all gods.

26   For the gods of the nations are idols every one;
    but the LORD made the heavens.

27   Majesty and splendour attend him,
     might and joy are in his dwelling.

28   Ascribe to the LORD, you families of nations,
    ascribe to the LORD glory and might;

29   ascribe to the LORD the glory due to his name,
    bring a gift and come before him.
     Bow down to the LORD in the splendour of holiness,^c

30   and dance in his honour, all men on earth.
     He has fixed the earth firm, immovable.

[a] it was: so *some MSS.*, cp. Ps. *105: 12; others* you were.
[b] *Verses 23–33: cp. Ps. 96: 1–13.*
[c] *Or* in holy vestments.

Let the heavens rejoice and the earth exult,   31
let men declare among the nations, 'The LORD is king.'
> Let the sea roar and all the creatures in it,   32
> let the fields exult and all that is in them;
>> then let the trees of the forest shout for joy   33
>> before the LORD when he comes to judge the earth.

Blessed be the LORD the God of Israel   36
> from everlasting to everlasting.

It is good to give thanks to the LORD,   34 [a]
> for his love endures for ever.
Cry, 'Deliver us, O God our saviour,   35 [b]
gather us in and save us from the nations
> that we may give thanks to thy holy name
> and make thy praise our pride.'

Blessed be the LORD the God of Israel   36
> from everlasting to everlasting.

And all the people said 'Amen' and 'Praise the LORD.'

David left Asaph and his kinsmen there before the Ark 37
of the Covenant of the LORD, to perform regular service
before the Ark as each day's duty required; as door- 38
keepers he left Obed-edom son of Jeduthun, and Hosah.
(Obed-edom and his[c] kinsmen were sixty-eight in number.) He left Zadok the priest and his kinsmen the priests 39
before the Tabernacle of the LORD at the hill-shrine in
Gibeon, to make offerings there to the LORD upon the 40
altar of whole-offering regularly morning and evening,
exactly as it is written in the law enjoined by the LORD
upon Israel. With them he left Heman and Jeduthun and 41
the other men chosen and nominated to give thanks to
the LORD, 'for his love endures for ever.' They[d] had 42

[a] *Verse 34: cp. Ps. 107: 1.*   [b] *Verses 35, 36: cp. Ps. 106: 47, 48.*
[c] *So Sept.; Heb.* their.   [d] *So Sept.; Heb. adds* Heman and Jeduthun.

trumpets and cymbals for the players, and the instruments used for sacred song. The sons of Jeduthun kept the gate.

43   So all the people went home, and David returned to greet his household.

* The central part of this chapter consists of an extended quotation of the psalm used at the installation-ceremony, again probably reflecting the liturgical usage of the Chronicler's own day. This substantial insertion into the material derived from 2 Samuel gives an indication of the freedom with which the Chronicler was able to use his source. While the earlier material was clearly highly revered, it was in no sense regarded as sacrosanct in its textual detail, and modification and extended comment upon it were perfectly legitimate, a practice described as 'midrashic' (cp. the comment on 2 Chron. 13: 22).

1–3. These verses substantially follow the account of the installation of the Ark in 2 Sam. 6: 17–19, which fits in well with the Chronicler's own picture.

4. *to repeat the Name:* this translation is uncertain. The basic idea of the word so rendered is 'call to remembrance', and its exact force here is doubtful. If the N.E.B. rendering is correct, what is described may be some kind of liturgical response such as is found in Ps. 136, with its verse-by-verse repetition of 'for his love endures for ever'.

5. The names are for the most part repeated from those in 15: 17–21, though in a different order. Probably we may see here more than one layer of tradition in the account of this most important occasion.

7. *the offering of thanks to the LORD by Asaph:* this introduction to the extended psalm-quotation which follows suggests both that psalms played an important part in services of thanksgiving in the second temple, and that a leading role in their performance was played by the guild of musicians

here described as *Asaph and his kinsmen*. They are mentioned in the titles to Pss. 73–83.

8–22. As indicated in the N.E.B. footnote, there follows a quotation of the first fifteen verses of the long historical Psalm 105. The quotation ends before the detailed description of Israel's descent into Egypt begins, which may make it more appropriate as a general ascription of praise such as is offered here. In particular the emphasis of this part of the Psalm is on the promise of the land to Abraham, which makes an especially appropriate theme for the occasion. We may regard it as likely that this use of psalms and parts of psalms was a regular feature of worship in the second temple, and some scholars have regarded this as forming our first piece of evidence for the Psalms being regarded as Holy Scripture. Evidence of use and evidence of canonization are not, however, necessarily the same thing, and this may be no more than a pointer to the aptness of the description, 'the hymnbook of the second temple' as appropriate for one stage in the development of the Psalter. (For fuller commentary on this and the other psalm(s) in this chapter, see the commentaries on Psalms.)

23–33. Immediately added to the extract from Ps. 105 follows one from Ps. 96. On this occasion virtually the whole Psalm is quoted. As in other quotations from earlier works, it is unwise either to suppose that minor differences involve textual corruption, or that the Chronicler has deliberately changed the text that was in front of him; once again we are reminded of the possible diversity within textual traditions. In its original form this psalm is widely held to date from before the exile, and to be associated with the worship of the first temple. The Chronicler, probably reflecting the usage of his own day, places it here as an appropriate hymn to the greatness of the Lord as creator.

34. The N.E.B. footnote calls attention to Ps. 107: 1, which is identical with this verse; but the wording is so common in the Psalter (and, no doubt, in liturgical usage generally) that we need not suppose a deliberate quotation here.

35-6. Again these two verses have close affinity with a section of a psalm (Ps. 106: 47-8), but it is likely that the Chronicler is deliberately using language of a type associated with psalms rather than quoting a specific passage; the pattern of the service of worship, rather than a detailed breakdown into sources, should be our primary concern here.

36. *all the people said 'Amen' and 'Praise the LORD'*: if this is intended as an affirmation by the assembled congregation of their unity with the praise that has just been offered, then we have here one of the first examples of the use of *Amen* in the sense of 'truly it is so', in the way that has been usual within the Christian church throughout its history.

37-42. In 2 Sam. 6 the bringing of the Ark to Jerusalem is presented as if it were a once-for-all event, without any surrounding context, though it bears close similarities to the apparently liturgical rite described in Ps. 132. The Chronicler is anxious to emphasize that a regular liturgical pattern had now been established, and so he gives appropriate details. Asaph and Obed-edom have already played a prominent part in the ceremonies; Hosah has not previously been mentioned, but he will be given his genealogy among the doorkeepers in 26: 10-12.

39. *Zadok the priest...at the hill-shrine in Gibeon:* the Jerusalem temple is not yet built, so the priests are pictured as exercising their ministry at Gibeon, which prepares the way for the greater sanctuary, just as Saul, whose family is associated with Gibeon (8: 29), prepares the way for David. The allusion to the practice of worship there will be picked up again in 2 Chron. 1.

43. The last verse of the account is related to 2 Sam. 6: 19-20, but there it is followed by the Michal incident, which the Chronicler has already used (15: 29); here it serves as a link to the next chapter (the words translated *household* here and 'house' in 17: 1 are the same, and the idea of a 'house' will be a key theme in the next section). *

THE PROMISE OF A HOUSE

As soon as David was established in his house, he said to **17**₁[a]
Nathan the prophet, 'Here I live in a house of cedar,
while the Ark of the Covenant of the LORD is housed in
curtains.' Nathan answered David, 'Do whatever you 2
have in mind, for God is with you.' But that night the 3
word of God came to Nathan: 'Go and say to David my 4
servant, "This is the word of the LORD: It is not you
who shall build me a house to dwell in. Down to this day 5
I have never dwelt in a house since I brought Israel up
from Egypt; I lived in a tent and a tabernacle.[b] Wherever 6
I journeyed with Israel, did I ever ask any of the judges
whom I appointed shepherds of my people why they
had not built me a house of cedar?" Then say this to my 7
servant David: "This is the word of the LORD of Hosts:
I took you from the pastures, and from following the
sheep, to be prince over my people Israel. I have been 8
with you wherever you have gone, and have destroyed
all the enemies in your path. I will make you as famous as
the great ones of the earth. I will assign a place for my 9
people Israel; there I will plant them, and they shall dwell
in their own land. They shall be disturbed no more, never
again shall wicked men wear them down as they did from 10
the time when I first appointed judges over Israel my
people, and I will subdue all your enemies. But I will
make you great and the LORD shall build up your royal
house. When your life ends and you go to join your fore- 11

[a] *Verses 1–27: cp. 2 Sam. 7: 1–29.*
[b] I lived...tabernacle: *prob. rdg.; Heb.* I have been from tent to tent
and from a tabernacle.

fathers, I will set up one of your family, one of your own
12 sons, to succeed you, and I will establish his kingdom. It is
he shall build me a house, and I will establish his throne
13 for all time. I will be his father, and he shall be my son. I
will never withdraw my love from him as I withdrew it
14 from your predecessor. But I will give him a sure place in
my house and kingdom for all time, and his throne shall
be established for ever."'

* The word 'house' in English can be used both of a building
and of a dynasty or family, and the corresponding Hebrew
word has the same double sense, which is an important theme
of this chapter, with its twofold concern: building a house
(temple) for God, and his promise of establishing the house
(dynasty) of David. The chapter follows its source in 2 Sam. 7
very closely, for here the Chronicler's concerns seem to be
very akin to those of the deuteronomic editors of the earlier
work.

5. The curious Hebrew phrase here ('from tent to tent and
from a tabernacle': see N.E.B. footnote) has been corrected
by the N.E.B. to correspond more closely with 2 Sam. 7.
But it may be that the point being made is somewhat different
– not so much the dwelling in a tent, as the preliminary nature
of that state of affairs, before the time of David, the chosen
agent of a more permanent arrangement.

10. *the LORD shall build up your royal house:* the first part
of the promise is that of God himself, who assures David of
the establishment of his family.

12. *he shall build me a house:* the second part of the promise
will be fulfilled by Solomon. The tradition linking him with
the building of the first temple was too strong to be changed,
though David makes all possible preparations. It is noteworthy
that the Chronicler omits the reference, found at this point
in 2 Samuel, to the inevitable wrong-doing of Solomon, and

this provides an important clue to his understanding of the break-up of the kingdom at Solomon's death. *for all time:* the use of phrases like this, and much of the content of the remainder of this chapter, raises the question whether the Chronicler looked forward to the re-establishment of the Davidic kingship, living as he did at a time when Israel was under foreign domination. Such expectations, often called 'messianic' because they looked forward to an anointed one (messiah), seem to play little part in the Chronicler's own thought. There are few traces of political nationalism in his work. For him, rather, the promises were being fulfilled in the theocratic community of his own day. ✳

DAVID'S PRAYER

Nathan recounted to David all that had been said to 15 him and all that had been revealed. Then King David 16 went into the presence of the LORD and took his place there and said, 'What am I, LORD God, and what is my family, that thou hast brought me thus far? It was a small 17 thing in thy sight, O God, to have planned for thy servant's house in days long past, and now thou lookest upon me as a man already embarked on a high career, O LORD God. What more can David say to thee of the honour 18 thou hast done thy servant, well though thou knowest him? For the sake of thy servant, LORD, and according to 19 thy purpose, thou hast brought me to all this greatness.*a* O LORD, we have never heard of one like thee; there is no 20 god but thee. And thy people Israel, to whom can they 21 be compared? Is there any other*b* nation on earth whom God has gone out to redeem from slavery, to make them

[a] *So Sept.; Heb. adds* by making known all the great things.
[b] any other: *so Sept.; Heb.* one.

95

his people? Thou hast won a name for thyself by great
and terrible deeds, driving out nations before thy people
22 whom thou didst redeem from Egypt. Thou hast made
thy people Israel thy own for ever, and thou, O LORD,
23 hast become their God. But now, LORD, let what thou
hast promised for thy servant and his house stand fast for
24 all time; make good what thou hast said. Let it stand fast,
that thy fame may be great for ever, and let men say,
"The LORD of Hosts, the God of Israel, is Israel's God."
So shall the house of thy servant David be established
25 before thee. Thou, my God, hast shown me thy purpose
to build up thy servant's house; therefore I have been able
26 to pray before thee. Thou, O LORD, art God, and thou
27 hast made these noble promises to thy servant; thou hast
been pleased to bless thy servant's house, that it may
continue always before thee; thou it is who hast blessed it,
and it shall be blessed for ever.'

* Again the Chronicler follows 2 Sam. 7, and again in both
contexts the prayer plays an important part in the way it
stresses the overall divine initiative in establishing the Davidic
rule, the significance of David's own role, and the way in
which this is worked out in Israel's history.

21. This verse affords an excellent illustration of the way in
which the Chronicler both accepted the older interpretation of
the people's history and also added a new dimension. He
accepted the reference to the first deliverance, the exodus
from Egypt, which, though not prominent in the Chronicler's
work, is not to be regarded as being ignored altogether. But
to the readers of his own day the idea that God had *gone out
to redeem* them *from slavery* would refer even more appropriately to the deliverance from exile in Babylon.

27. The blessings of the Davidic house appear in this

context to be the religious achievement of David rather than his own political successes or those of any hoped for 'new David'. ✻

DAVID'S WARS

After this David defeated the Philistines and conquered **18** 1[a] them, and took from them Gath with its villages; he 2 defeated the Moabites, and they became subject to him and paid him tribute. He also defeated Hadadezer king of 3 Zobah-hamath, who was on his way to set up a monument of victory by the river Euphrates. From him David 4 captured a thousand chariots, seven thousand horsemen and twenty thousand foot; he hamstrung all the chariot-horses, except a hundred which he retained. When the 5 Aramaeans of Damascus came to the help of Hadadezer king of Zobah, David destroyed twenty-two thousand of them, and established garrisons among these Aramaeans; 6 they became subject to him and paid him tribute. Thus the LORD gave David victory wherever he went. David 7 took the gold quivers borne by Hadadezer's servants and brought them to Jerusalem. He also took a great quantity 8 of bronze[b] from Hadadezer's cities, Tibhath and Kun; from this Solomon made the Sea of bronze,[b] the pillars, and the bronze[b] vessels.

When Tou king of Hamath heard that David had 9 defeated the entire army of Hadadezer king of Zobah, he 10 sent his son Hadoram to King David to greet him and to congratulate him on defeating Hadadezer in battle (for Hadadezer had been at war with Tou); and he brought

[a] *Verses 1–13: cp. 2 Sam. 8: 1–14.*
[b] *Or copper.*

11 with him[a] vessels[b] of gold, silver, and copper, which King David dedicated to the LORD. He dedicated also the silver and the gold which he had carried away from all the other nations, from Edom and Moab, from the Ammonites and the Philistines, and from Amalek.

12 Edom was defeated by Abishai son of Zeruiah, who destroyed eighteen thousand of them in the Valley of Salt

13 and stationed garrisons in the country. All the Edomites now became subject to David. Thus the LORD gave victory to David wherever he went.

14[c] David ruled over the whole of Israel and maintained

15 law and justice among all his people. Joab son of Zeruiah was in command of the army; Jehoshaphat son of Ahilud

16 was secretary of state; Zadok and Abiathar son of Ahimelech, son of Ahitub,[d] were priests; Shavsha was adjutant-

17 general; Benaiah son of Jehoiada commanded the Kerethite and Pelethite guards. The eldest sons of David were in attendance on the king.

---

* The sequence of events as pictured by the Chronicler is now worth setting out briefly, as it helps to explain the at first sight random order in which he has drawn upon material from 2 Samuel. David is chosen as king on the death of Saul (ch. 10), and all Israel rallies to him (chs. 11 and 12 – the lists of names were regarded by the Chronicler as being just as revealing as a piece of narrative would have been); then his first concern is the religious one, of establishing the Ark of God in his new capital at Jerusalem, and this is described in

[a] he brought with him: *so Pesh. and 2 Sam. 8: 10; Heb. om.*
[b] *So Pesh. and 2 Sam. 8: 10; Heb.* all vessels.
[c] *Verses 14–17: cp. 2 Sam. 8: 15–18; 20: 23–6; 1 Kgs. 4: 2–4.*
[d] and Abiathar...Ahitub: *prob. rdg., cp. 2 Sam. 8: 17; Heb.* son of Ahitub and Abimelech son of Abiathar.

chs. 13 and 15, with the necessary three months' break being occupied by David strengthening his position. The primary religious duties having been properly carried out (chs. 16 and 17), David is now sure of the divine support when he turns to the task of strengthening Israel against the attacks of external enemies, and this is the theme of the next three chapters. The material used is only part of that in 2 Samuel, and it is unwise to build any elaborate theories around the omissions, as has sometimes been done over, for example, the fact that the Chronicler does not introduce the story of David's adultery with Bathsheba. As we have seen already, the Chronicler assumes knowledge of the earlier sources. It is also worth bearing in mind that some at least of the enemies mentioned in the stories of David's wars will have been no more than names to his readers, living some 600 years after the events described; a picture of David, rather than precise historical information, is the Chronicler's aim.

1–7. This is based on 2 Sam. 8: 1–7. The omissions from the earlier source may be due to differences in textual transmission, or possibly to the obscurity of the original (the N.E.B. rendering of the 2 Samuel passage partly conceals some difficulties in interpretation).

8. *great quantity of bronze:* the booty is as recorded in 2 Samuel, though the city-names differ. Peculiar to the Chronicler is the link with the *Sea of bronze, the pillars, and the bronze vessels* in the temple. He is using the older text as a suitable opportunity for elaborating his theme of the extent of David's preparation for Solomon's temple-building.

9. *Tou:* in 2 Sam. 8 'Toi'. This is typical of many small differences in form, especially of names. It is misleading to speak of one as correct and the other as wrong; they represent different ways of spelling the same word, a matter on which the ancient world in general seems to have been less particular than some school-teachers today. But the form 'Hadoram' in verse 10 does seem more probable than 'Joram' of 2 Samuel – it is unlikely that the son of a *king of Hamath*, in the far north

of Palestine, would have a Yahwistic name like 'Joram'.

12–13. *Edom was defeated by Abishai:* variant traditions seem to have developed concerning this conflict. In 2 Sam. 8: 13 the victory is attributed to David himself, while the title of Ps. 60 (not in N.E.B.) ascribes it to 'Joab'.

13. *Thus the LORD gave victory to David wherever he went:* more basic than the differences in detail is the conviction, common to the author of Samuel and the Chronicler, that David's victory was brought about by the LORD, and reflected David's faithfulness to him. In his account of later wars, the Chronicler will stress to an even greater extent the direct nature of this divine intervention.

14–17. A brief note, following 2 Samuel, gives some information about David's administrative organization.

16. The text here has been altered (see the N.E.B. footnote) in the same way as the corresponding passage in 2 Sam. 8: 17. Historically this may well be right, but it then produces a discrepancy with the other genealogical note on Zadok (6: 8; and see the note there). *Shavsha:* in 2 Samuel he is given the more Israelite name 'Seraiah'. But it has been suggested that the Chronicler here, as sometimes elsewhere with proper names, has preserved a more original form, and that this official may have been of Egyptian origin. This might suggest that lists of this kind reflect the beginnings of a 'civil service' borrowed from Egyptian models. However this may be, it is scarcely likely that any recollection of this would be alive in the Chronicler's day, and David's officials are presented in the terms with which his own readers would be familiar.

17. *The eldest sons of David were in attendance on the king:* here there seems to be no serious doubt that the Chronicler has modified a text which was unacceptable to him. 2 Sam. 8: 18 has 'David's sons were priests', and the rigid distinction between the royal and priestly lines which the Chronicler maintains meant that such an identification was impossible, and so he substitutes this very generalized statement. *

THE AMMONITE AND OTHER WARS

Some time afterwards Nahash king of the Ammonites **19** 1[a]
died and was succeeded by his son. David said, 'I must 2
keep up the same loyal friendship with Hanun son of
Nahash as his father showed me', and he sent a mission to
condole with him on the death of his father. But when
David's envoys entered the country of the Ammonites to
condole with Hanun, the Ammonite princes said to 3
Hanun, 'Do you suppose David means to do honour to
your father when he sends you his condolences? These
men of his are spies whom he has sent to find out how to
overthrow the country.' So Hanun took David's ser- 4
vants, and he shaved them, cut off half their garments up
to the hips, and dismissed them. When David heard how 5
they had been treated, he sent to meet them, for they were
deeply humiliated, and ordered them to wait in Jericho
and not to return until their beards had grown again. The 6
Ammonites knew that they had brought themselves into
bad odour with David, so Hanun and the Ammonites
sent a thousand talents of silver to hire chariots and horsemen from Aram-naharaim,[b] Maacah, and Aram-zobah.[c]
They hired thirty-two thousand chariots and the king of 7
Maacah and his people, who came and encamped before
Medeba, while the Ammonites came from their cities and
mustered for battle. When David heard of it, he sent out 8
Joab and all the fighting men. The Ammonites came and 9
took up their position at the entrance to the city, while
the allied kings took up theirs in the open country. When 10

[a] *Verses 1–19: cp.* 2 Sam. 10: 1–19.　[b] *That is* Aram of Two Rivers.
[c] Maacah, and Aram-zobah: *prob. rdg.; Heb.* Aram-maacah, and Zobah.

Joab saw that he was threatened both front and rear, he
detailed some picked Israelite troops and drew them up
11 facing the Aramaeans. The rest of his forces he put under
his brother Abishai, who took up a position facing the
12 Ammonites. 'If the Aramaeans prove too strong for me,'
he said, 'you must come to my relief; and if the Ammonites prove too strong for you, I will relieve you.
13 Courage! Let us fight bravely for our people and for the
14 cities*a* of our God. And the LORD's will be done.' But
when Joab and his men came to close quarters with the
15 Aramaeans, they put them to flight; and when the
Ammonites saw them in flight, they too fled before his
brother Abishai and entered the city. Then Joab came to
16 Jerusalem. The Aramaeans saw that they had been
worsted by Israel, and they sent messengers to summon
other Aramaeans from the Great Bend of the Euphrates
17 under Shophach, commander of Hadadezer's army. Their
movement was reported to David, who immediately
mustered all the forces of Israel, crossed the Jordan and
advanced against them and took up battle positions. The
Aramaeans likewise took up positions facing David and
18 engaged him,*b* but were put to flight by Israel. David
slew seven thousand Aramaeans in chariots and forty
thousand infantry, killing Shophach the commander of
19 the army. When Hadadezer's men saw that they had been
worsted by Israel, they sued for peace and submitted to
David. The Aramaeans were never again willing to give
support to the Ammonites.

[a] *Or* altars.
[b] The Aramaeans...him: *so Sept.; Heb.* When David had taken up
position facing the Aramaeans, they engaged him.

At the turn of the year, when kings take the field, Joab **20** 1[a]
led the army out and ravaged the Ammonite country. He
came to Rabbah and laid siege to it, while David remained
in Jerusalem; he reduced the city and razed it to the
ground. David took the crown from the head of Milcom 2
and found that it weighed a talent of gold and was set
with a precious stone, and this he placed on his own head.
He also removed a great quantity of booty from the city;
he took its inhabitants and set them to work with saws 3
and other iron tools, sharp and toothed.[b] David did this
to all the cities of the Ammonites; then he and all his
people returned to Jerusalem.

Some time later war with the Philistines broke out in 4[c]
Gezer; it was then that Sibbechai of Hushah killed Sippai,
a descendant of the Rephaim, and the Philistines were
reduced to submission. In another war with the Philis- 5
tines, Elhanan son of Jair killed Lahmi brother of Goliath
of Gath, whose spear had a shaft like a weaver's beam. In 6
yet another war in Gath, there appeared a giant with six
fingers on each hand and six toes on each foot, twenty-
four in all; he too was descended from the Rephaim, and, 7
when he defied Israel, Jonathan son of David's brother
Shimea killed him. These giants were the descendants of 8
the Rephaim in Gath, and they all fell at the hands of
David and his men.

* The accounts of the wars recorded in these two chapters
are brought together by the Chronicler from different parts
of 2 Samuel, and the fighting against the Ammonites forms

[a] *Verses 1–3: cp. 2 Sam. 12: 26–31.*   [b] toothed: *so one MS., cp. 2
Sam. 12: 31; others* saws.   [c] *Verses 4–7: cp. 2 Sam. 21: 18–22.*

part of that section of the earlier work often called the 'succession narrative' (cp. p. 10). There it is introduced to give a context to David's marriage to Bathsheba; to the Chronicler it represented simply one illustration of the success which the LORD granted to his faithful servant. As already noted, it is not necessary to suppose that the Bathsheba episode is deliberately hushed up, for it would have been well enough known to the Chronicler's audience; it is rather the case that a deliberate stress is here laid upon the divine guidance of David. The details of ch. 19 follow 2 Sam. 10 closely in the account of the war against the Ammonites of the Transjordan.

4. *hips:* presumably a sense of delicacy led to the substitution of this more general term for the 'buttocks' of 2 Sam. 10: 4.

6–7. There are considerable differences in detail here from the account in 2 Samuel, the overall effect of which is to increase very greatly the forces ranged against David.

20: 1. This verse skilfully joins together 2 Sam. 11: 1 and 12: 26, passing over the intervening section which describes the adultery with Bathsheba and the murder of Uriah. The Chronicler also revises the earlier story so that Joab rather than David is responsible for capturing Rabbah, the capital of the Ammonites (the modern Amman, capital of Jordan).

2. *took the crown from the head of Milcom:* the change in the conqueror of the city leads to some inconsequence in this verse – David appears unexpectedly at Rabbah, and then either indicates the worthlessness of pagan deities (if the N.E.B. Milcom is correct), or perhaps ended the Ammonite king's independence, if 'took off the crown of their king' of the other English versions is to be followed.

4–8. The last section dealing with David's wars has its source in a different part of 2 Samuel (21: 18–22, one of the chapters added after the succession narrative in 2 Samuel).

4. *the Philistines were reduced to submission:* a state of finality is here implied which is hardly borne out by what we know of the later history of the Philistines.

5. *Elhanan son of Jair killed Lahmi brother of Goliath:* this appears to be a clear example of harmonization by the Chronicler. In the books of Samuel, the killing of Goliath is attributed to David in the well-known story of 1 Sam. 17, and to 'Elhanan' in 2 Sam. 21: 19, which is parallel to our passage. Various solutions of the discrepancy in Samuel have been proposed (see the commentary on 1 Sam. 17: 5 in this series); but by the Chronicler's time a difficulty was recognized, which he resolved by making Lahmi a proper name instead of part of the place name 'Bethlehem' and making this Lahmi to be Goliath's brother. Both this and the beginning of the next chapter provide good examples of the way in which part of the Chronicler's purpose appears to have been to comment on and smooth out irregularities in the earlier sacred writings which both he and his readers loved and revered. *

THE CENSUS AND ITS CONSEQUENCES

Now Satan, setting himself against Israel, incited David **21** 1[a] to count the people. So he instructed Joab and his public 2 officers to go out and number Israel, from Beersheba to Dan, and to report the number to him. Joab answered, 3 'Even if the LORD should increase his people a hundred-fold, would not your majesty still be king and all the people your slaves? Why should your majesty want to do this? It will only bring guilt on Israel.' But Joab was 4 overruled by the king; he set out and went up and down the whole country. He then came to Jerusalem and 5 reported to David the numbers recorded: those capable of bearing arms were one million one hundred thousand in Israel, and four hundred and seventy thousand in Judah.

[a] *Verses 1-27: cp. 2 Sam. 24: 1-25.*

6 Levi and Benjamin were not counted by Joab, so deep was his repugnance against the king's order.

7 God was displeased with all this and proceeded to 8 punish Israel. David said to God, 'I have done a very wicked thing: I pray thee remove thy servant's guilt, for 9 I have been very foolish.' And the LORD said to Gad, 10 David's seer, 'Go and tell David, "This is the word of the LORD: I have three things to offer you; choose one of 11 them and I will bring it upon you."' So Gad came to David and said to him, 'This is the word of the LORD: 12 "Make your choice: three years of famine, three months of harrying by your foes and close pursuit by the sword of your enemy, or three days of the LORD's own sword, bringing pestilence throughout the country, and the LORD's angel working destruction in all the territory of Israel." Consider now what answer I am to take back to 13 him who sent me.' Thereupon David said to Gad, 'I am in a desperate plight; let me fall into the hands of the LORD, for his mercy is very great; and let me not fall into 14 the hands of man.' So the LORD sent a pestilence through-15 out Israel, and seventy thousand men of Israel died. And God sent an angel to Jerusalem to destroy it; but, as he was destroying it, the LORD saw and repented of the evil, and said to the destroying angel at the moment when he was standing beside the threshing-floor of Ornan the Jebusite, 'Enough! Stay your hand.'

16 When David looked up and saw the angel of the LORD standing between earth and heaven, with his sword drawn in his hand and stretched out over Jerusalem, he and the elders, clothed in sackcloth, fell prostrate to the ground; 17 and David said to God, 'It was I who gave the order to

count the people. It was I who sinned, I, the shepherd,[a] who did wrong. But these poor sheep, what have they done? O LORD my God, let thy hand fall upon me and upon my family, but check this plague on the people.'[b]

✻ Another story from 2 Samuel is used, and here more than elsewhere in the Chronicler's writings, open criticism of David is expressed. But two aspects of the story make it of particular value for the overall purpose of the Chronicler: the prominence it gives to David's repentance (verses 8, 17); and the way in which it leads into the story of the preparation of the land for the future temple. This chapter may therefore be regarded as a transition, rounding off the account of David's success against his enemies, and passing on to the final and crowning achievement of his reign – the preparation of the temple and its organization.

1. *Satan*: again we have a very clear example of the way in which the Chronicler felt able to modify a part of the text of his source which presented unacceptable modes of speaking about Israel's past. In 2 Sam. 24: 1 we find 'the LORD...incited David...and gave him orders that Israel and Judah should be counted'. The Chronicler was aware of the obvious theological difficulties presented by such a statement and modified it. To do so, he introduces the character of Satan. Originally a common noun meaning 'adversary', a picture emerged of 'the Satan' as one of the members of the heavenly court (Job 1: 6; Zech. 3: 1), and this in turn led by the time of the Chronicler to a picture of a personal enemy whose purpose was to thwart God's doings. There is here no fully-fledged dualism of the kind characteristic of Persian thought and of some later Jewish writings; but we see one attempt at a solution of the problem of evident evil in the world.

3. The Chronicler here reproduces the distrust for the whole

[a] I, the shepherd: *prob. rdg.; Heb.* doing wrong.
[b] check...people: *prob. rdg.; Heb.* among thy people, not for a plague.

idea of a census, expressed in 2 Sam. 24: 3, and widespread in the ancient world, though the reasons for this are still not known. Ironically, the material he has used in earlier chapters, if it has any historical value at all, must have originated in something akin to a census. Joab's words are changed from those in 2 Samuel; the exact sense is not clear (and the translation offered by the N.E.B. is not the only possibility), but in general Joab appears to be stressing the loyalty of the people without the need of a census. The stress is clearly on the wrongness of the proposal: *It will only bring guilt on Israel*.

5. The numbers are different from those in 2 Samuel; but there is not the great exaggeration which the Chronicler sometimes employs. It seems likely that a variant tradition from that known to us is here used – numbers are peculiarly liable to such change.

6. *Levi and Benjamin were not counted:* the omission of Levi is easy to explain since they received no territorial allotment (6: 54–81); that of Benjamin is less easily understood, though it may be due to a desire to stress the loyalty of that tribe to the true centre of worship.

7. *God was displeased:* this is the corollary of the change already noted in verse 1. In 2 Samuel God had incited the census, and the realization of its wrongness had come from David; here God has not yet been mentioned, and so his displeasure (in an unspecified form) can properly be introduced at this point.

9. *Gad, David's seer:* in 2 Sam. 24: 11 he is also called 'the prophet'. By the time the Chronicler wrote the roles of 'prophet' and *seer* were probably regarded as distinct, and so the change is made for clarity. In any case Gad appears to have been a royal official, of a type often found in Old Testament accounts of the monarchical period.

13. Both here and in 2 Samuel the story is unclear at this point. Apparently David's words are to be understood (and were presumably understood by the Chronicler) as meaning

that he himself could not choose, but that he would accept whatever fate God decided upon.

15. *Ornan:* in 2 Samuel 'Araunah'. This difference may simply be due to variant forms of tradition, but the development in the remainder of the chapter which stresses the significance of this *threshing-floor* as the actual temple-site is much more probably a development due to the Chronicler himself.

16. *standing between earth and heaven:* the picture here is akin to that in later Old Testament books, of the angel as a divine messenger sent by God to carry out his commands upon earth. *he and the elders, clothed in sackcloth, fell prostrate to the ground:* all these details are additional to the source in 2 Samuel and have the effect of turning the occasion into the form of a regular service of penitence. It is likely that some of the individual laments in the Psalms should similarly be understood as being spoken by the king on behalf of the people. ✶

THE PURCHASE OF THE THRESHING-FLOOR

The angel of the LORD, speaking through the lips of 18 Gad, commanded David to go to the threshing-floor of Ornan the Jebusite and to set up there an altar to the LORD. David went up as Gad had bidden him in the 19 LORD's name. Ornan's four sons who were with him hid 20 themselves, but he was busy threshing his wheat when he turned and saw the angel. As David approached, Ornan 21 looked up and, seeing the king, came out from the threshing-floor and prostrated himself before him. David 22 said to Ornan, 'Let me have the site of the threshing-floor that I may build on it an altar to the LORD; sell it me at the full price, that the plague which has attacked my

23 people may be stopped.' Ornan answered David, 'Take
it and let your majesty do as he thinks fit; see, here are
the oxen for whole-offerings, the threshing-sledges for
the fuel, and the wheat for the grain-offering; I give you
24 everything.' But King David said to Ornan, 'No, I will
pay the full price; I will not present to the LORD what is
yours, or offer a whole-offering which has cost me
25 nothing.' So David gave Ornan six hundred shekels of
26 gold for the site, and built an altar to the LORD there; on
this he offered whole-offerings and shared-offerings, and
called upon the LORD, who answered him with fire falling
27 from heaven on the altar of whole-offering. Then, at the
LORD's command, the angel sheathed his sword.

28   It was when David saw that the LORD had answered
him at the threshing-floor of Ornan the Jebusite that he
29 offered sacrifice there. The tabernacle of the LORD and the
altar of whole-offering which Moses had made in the
30 wilderness were then at the hill-shrine in Gibeon; but
David had been unable to go there and seek God's
guidance, so shocked and shaken was he at the sight of the
22 angel's sword. Then David said, 'This is to be the house
of the LORD God, and this is to be an altar of whole-
offering for Israel.'

* The first part of this section is still based on the earlier
story in 2 Sam. 24, but it is given a new significance by the
fact that it is now clearly stated to be located at the site of the
projected temple. It is possible that such an identification was
already implicit in the story as told in 2 Samuel, but it is not
there made explicit, whereas for the Chronicler this is the
climax of the whole story, and the details of the plague that
has preceded are given much less prominence – indeed they

might almost be said to serve as no more than an occasion for this divine disclosure.

18. *The angel of the LORD, speaking through the lips of Gad:* the N.E.B. translation here is somewhat free, and the sense may be no more than that Gad received an intimation from God what he should say. Nevertheless, the phrase certainly emphasizes the solemnity of the command.

20. *Ornan's four sons:* no mention of them is made either in 2 Samuel or subsequently in this story; it may well be that the Chronicler's source differed somewhat from the version of the story known to us, and that the four sons originally had a more prominent part in the dénouement.

22–4. The details of the purchase of the *threshing-floor* put considerable emphasis on the fact that it was bought at *the full price*, so that David is not pictured as being dependent on any other human agency. In a similar way Abraham paid 'the full price' for a burial-place for himself and his family from the inhabitants of the land (Gen. 23: 9).

25. *six hundred shekels of gold:* the shekel was originally a measure of weight rather than of value. Modern equivalents of so vast a sum would be meaningless, but it is in marked contrast to the 'fifty shekels of silver' for 'the threshing-floor and the oxen' of 2 Sam. 24: 24. Such a sum no doubt seemed to the Chronicler grossly inadequate as 'the full price' of the temple site with which he and his readers were familiar.

26. *who answered him with fire falling from heaven:* the phrase has no equivalent in the 2 Samuel account, and an allusion is probably intended to the story of Elijah on Mount Carmel, whose prayer was shown to be efficacious in the same way (1 Kings 18: 37f.).

21: 28 – 22: 1. The account based on 2 Samuel (or parallel to it) ends with verse 27, but the Chronicler adds an extremely important epilogue to that story, stressing the identity of the threshing-floor with the temple, and indicating that the days when Gibeon would house the sacred objects believed to have been handed down from the wilderness period were now to end. The note in verse 30, *David had been unable to go there*, serves both to explain David's failure to take action so as to avert the disaster which had just taken place, and also gives an indication of the inadequacy of Gibeon as the true sanctuary.

22: 1. This verse is rightly printed with what precedes, for it serves as a climax to it. David stresses that here the *house of the LORD God* will be built, alluding back to the theme of ch. 17: that the one *altar of whole-offering* would be there, thus fulfilling the requirements of the Pentateuch; and that it would serve for all Israel, with the implicit point that all who deserted that altar were faithless to their God. ✳

The temple and its organization

2 DAVID NOW GAVE ORDERS to assemble the aliens resident in Israel, and he set them as masons to dress hewn stones and to build the house of God. He laid in a 3 great store of iron to make nails and clamps for the doors, 4 more bronze than could be weighed and cedar-wood without limit; the men of Sidon and Tyre brought David 5 an ample supply of cedar. David said, 'My son Solomon is a boy of tender years, and the house that is to be built to the LORD must be exceedingly magnificent, renowned and celebrated in every land; therefore I must make preparations for it myself.' So David made abundant preparation before his death.

6 He sent for Solomon his son and charged him to build 7 a house for the LORD the God of Israel. 'Solomon, my son,' he said, 'I had intended to build a house in honour

of the name of the LORD my God; but the LORD forbade 8
me and said, "You have shed much blood in my sight
and waged great wars; for this reason you shall not build
a house in honour of my name. But you shall have a son 9[a]
who shall be a man of peace; I will give him peace from
all his enemies on every side; his name shall be Solomon,
'Man of Peace', and I will grant peace[b] and quiet to Israel
in his days. He shall build a house in honour of my name; 10
he shall be my son and I will be a father to him, and I will
establish the throne of his sovereignty over Israel for
ever." Now, Solomon my son, the LORD be with you! 11
May you prosper and build the house of the LORD your
God, as he promised you should. But may the LORD grant 12
you wisdom and discretion, so that when he gives you
authority in Israel you may keep the law of the LORD
your God. You will prosper only if you are careful to 13
observe the decrees and ordinances which the LORD
enjoined upon Moses for Israel; be strong and resolute,
neither faint-hearted nor dismayed.

'In spite of all my troubles, I have here ready for the 14
house of the LORD a hundred thousand talents of gold and
a million talents of silver, with great quantities of bronze
and iron, more than can be weighed; timber and stone,
too, I have got ready; and you may add to them. Besides, 15
you have a large force of workmen, masons, sculptors,
and carpenters, and countless men skilled in work of
every kind, in gold and silver, bronze and iron. So now 16
to work, and the LORD be with you!'

David ordered all the officers of Israel to help Solomon 17
his son: 'Is not the LORD your God with you? Will he 18

[a] *Verse 9: cp. 1 Kgs. 5: 4.*   [b] *Heb.* shalom.

not give you peace on every side? For he has given the inhabitants of the land into my power, and they will be
19 subject to the LORD and his people. Devote yourselves, therefore, heart and soul, to seeking guidance of the LORD your God, and set about building his sanctuary, so that the Ark of the Covenant of the LORD and God's holy vessels may be brought into a house built in honour of his name.'

✳ The bringing of the Ark to Jerusalem has already provided one high-point for David's reign; now we have the second – the preparation of the temple, the description of which occupies the remainder of I Chronicles, together with some stress on the preparation of Solomon for his role as the actual builder of the temple. Both of these themes – the preparation of the house of the LORD, and the preparation of David's house in the person of Solomon, are found in this chapter.

2. *aliens resident in Israel:* the use of aliens for so important a task is in line with the positive attitude toward them shown by Deuteronomy, and provides another warning against too narrowly nationalistic an interpretation of the Chronicler. The tensions reported in Ezra concern especially those who might not be willing to recognize the uniqueness of Jerusalem.

5. *So David made abundant preparation:* here is found the basic theme of attributing as much as possible of the work in connection with the temple to David's foresight.

8. It has so far been assumed that it was known that Solomon rather than David would be the actual temple-builder, without any reason for this being offered. This is now spelt out more fully, in terms of the wars fought by David, and specifically the fact that he had *shed much blood.* The theme is an old one, being found already in I Kings 5: 3, but there the point is that David has had no opportunity for temple-building because of his continual wars. Here the association of the

temple with 'peace' is emphasized, appropriately in view of the fact that the Chronicler's audience were no longer part of a nation-state waging its wars with neighbouring countries, but part of a large empire, for whom the temple was the focus of unity.

9-10. The terms of the promise are those found in 2 Sam. 7 (cp. especially verse 14) and already used by the Chronicler in ch. 17.

9. *peace and quiet:* we may note here, not only that a deliberate play on the words for *peace* (Hebrew *shalom*) and *Solomon* (Hebrew *Shelomo*) is being introduced, but also that the idea of peace means more than the mere absence of war – what is implied is the whole idea of the community's being blessed by God and its consequent prosperity.

11-13. The command to Solomon is deliberately reminiscent of the farewell commands of Moses to Joshua in Deut. 31: 5-8. The Chronicler, by alluding to this in phrases that would be familiar to his readers, is able to show that Solomon is successor to David in a way analogous to that in which Joshua had succeeded Moses.

14. *a hundred thousand talents of gold:* these and the other greatly exaggerated figures which follow are not to be taken literally; they are intended to convey to the readers some idea of the immense amount of preparation which had gone into the building of the temple.

16-19. Solomon is given words of encouragement which will be further elaborated upon later (ch. 28); meanwhile David's final concern is to reiterate the basic fact that all this activity is only made possible by the providence of God. *

THE LEVITES IN THE TEMPLE SERVICE

David was now an old man, weighed down with years, **23** and he appointed Solomon his son king over Israel. He 2 gathered together all the officers of Israel, the priests, and

3 the Levites. The Levites were enrolled from the age of thirty upwards, their males being thirty-eight thousand 4 in all. Of these, twenty-four thousand were to be responsible for the maintenance and service of the house of the LORD, six thousand to act as officers and magistrates, 5 four thousand to be door-keepers, and four thousand to praise the LORD on the musical instruments which David[a] 6 had made for the service of praise. David organized them in divisions, called after Gershon, Kohath, and Merari, the sons of Levi.

7,8   The sons of Gershon: Laadan and Shimei. The sons of 9 Laadan: Jehiel the chief, Zetham and Joel, three.[b] These were the heads of the families grouped under Laadan. 10 The sons of Shimei: Jahath, Ziza,[c] Jeush and Beriah, four. 11 Jahath was the chief and Ziza the second, but Jeush and Beriah, having few children, were reckoned for duty as a single family.

12   The sons of Kohath: Amram, Izhar, Hebron and 13 Uzziel, four. The sons of Amram: Aaron and Moses. Aaron was set apart, he and his sons in perpetuity, to dedicate the most holy gifts,[d] to burn sacrifices before the LORD, to serve him, and to give the blessing in his name 14 for ever, but the sons of Moses, the man of God, were to 15 keep the name of Levite. The sons of Moses: Gershom 16 and Eliezer. The sons of Gershom: Shubael[e] the chief. 17 The sons of Eliezer: Rehabiah the chief. Eliezer had no 18 other sons, but Rehabiah had very many. The sons of

[a] *So Sept.; Heb.* I.   [b] *Prob. rdg.; Heb. adds* The sons of Shimei: Shelomith, Haziel and Haran, three.   [c] *So Sept.; Heb.* Zina.   [d] to dedicate...gifts: *or* to be hallowed as most holy.   [e] *So Sept.; Heb.* Shebuel.

Izhar: Shelomoth[a] the chief. The sons of Hebron: Jeriah 19
the chief, Amariah the second, Jahaziel the third and
Jekameam the fourth. The sons of Uzziel: Micah the 20
chief and Isshiah the second.

The sons of Merari: Mahli and Mushi. The sons of 21
Mahli: Eleazar and Kish. When Eleazar died, he left 22
daughters but no sons, and their cousins, the sons of Kish,
married them. The sons of Mushi: Mahli, Eder and 23
Jeremoth, three.

Such were the Levites, grouped by families in the 24
father's line whose heads were entered in the detailed list;
they performed duties in the service of the house of the
LORD, from the age of twenty upwards. For David said, 25
'The LORD the God of Israel has given his people peace
and has made his abode in Jerusalem for ever. The Levites 26
will no longer have to carry the Tabernacle or any of the
vessels for its service.' By these last words of David the 27
Levites were enrolled from the age of twenty upwards.
Their duty was to help the sons of Aaron in the service of 28
the house of the LORD: they were responsible for the care
of the courts and the rooms, for the cleansing of all holy
things, and the general service of the house of God; for 29
the rows of the Bread of the Presence, the flour for the
grain-offerings, unleavened wafers, cakes baked on the
griddle, and pastry, and for the weights and measures.
They were to be on duty continually before the LORD, 30
every morning and evening, giving thanks and praise to
him, and at every offering of whole-offerings to the LORD, 31
on sabbaths, new moons and at the appointed seasons,
according to their prescribed number. The Levites were 32

[a] *So one MS.; others* Shelomith.

to have charge of the Tent of the Presence and of the sanctuary, but the sons of Aaron their kinsmen were charged with the service of worship in the house of the LORD.

✻ It seems surprising that at this point the description of the preparation of the temple should be interrupted by further lists of names. It may indeed be the case that the material here and in the four following chapters was introduced into the total work at a relatively later stage and so interrupted the connection between chs. 22 and 28. Nevertheless, it is also true that this would not have been regarded as an interruption by the original readers in the way that we should so consider it, and the final editor of the book clearly felt it appropriate at this point to set out in detail the names of those who were engaged in the temple-service. Once again the exact provenance of the lists remains unknown, though we may suspect that in many cases the families listed here were those prominent in the Jerusalem community of the Chronicler's own day. There is in a number of cases a relation with the material already presented in the opening chapters, but not a word-for-word identity. In any case, we need to remember that for the Chronicler the preparation of the right people to minister in the sanctuary is at least as important as the preparation of the right materials for its building.

1. *David was now an old man...and he appointed Solomon his son king:* this is probably a brief allusion to the story in 1 Kings 1 and 2, which describe the appointment of Solomon at much greater length. The somewhat pathetic details of that story are not relevant to the Chronicler's purpose, and are not spelt out here; by contrast to the earlier work, only *Solomon* among David's sons is the object of attention.

2. *the priests, and the Levites:* it is noteworthy that the religious leaders are joined with *the officers of Israel* in the

recognition of the new king, whose authority must depend on the proper carrying out of religious requirements.

3. *the age of thirty:* later in this chapter the age is 'twenty' (verses 24 and 27), while in Numbers references are found to enrolment at thirty and at twenty-five years (Num. 4: 3; 8: 24). Custom in this matter may well have varied at different times. *thirty-eight thousand:* the statement presents an interesting contrast with the refusal to number the Levites in 21: 6.

4–5. This fourfold division of functions gives a clear picture of the role of the Levites, probably in the Chronicler's own time. It cannot be precisely correlated with the threefold 'divisions' of verse 6.

7–11. Comparison with ch. 6 shows that this version of the Gershonite line has enough similarity to be recognizably the same material, but with differences which are far more than mere variations of copying: we may note as examples the varying names *Gershon*/Gershom; the first son 'Libni' (6: 17), *Laadan* here; the listing of *Jahath* as a son of Libni (6: 20) or of *Shimei* here.

12–13. The traditions of the *sons of Kohath* correspond more closely with the names in other lists. *Aaron was set apart:* a brief résumé is given, based on various strands in the Pentateuch, to stress the role of the priestly line of Aaron and its significance.

14. *Moses:* earlier, Moses had simply been listed without comment as a name in a genealogy (6: 3), and in general no prominence is given to him by the Chronicler, for whom the great climax of his people's history came with David rather than with the exodus from Egypt. But it does not necessarily follow that the Chronicler had no place for Moses, as various allusions throughout the work indicate, and here he is given the title, reminiscent of Deut. 33: 1, *man of God*.

21–3. The information concerning *The sons of Merari* is regularly less than that for the other Levite families; here again there is some correspondence with, and some difference from, the information given in ch. 6.

27. *from the age of twenty upwards:* this verse reads like an attempt to account for the difference between the traditions within this chapter (verses 3 and 24) concerning the age of service for the Levites.

28–34. A valuable insight is here provided into the religious duties of the Levites; stress is laid upon the fact that their role was subsidiary (*to help the sons of Aaron*), but also on the importance and sacredness of the tasks involved, which are first set out in general terms and then with more specific detail.

29. *the rows of the Bread of the Presence:* this is the 'shew-bread' of the older English versions. The two rows of bread, left in the temple from one sabbath to the next, may originally have been connected with ideas of providing food for the deity, but had certainly lost all such connotations in historical times in Israel. The correct preparation and care of this Bread was an important part of the duties of the Levites (cp. also 9: 32).

32. According to 2 Chron. 1 the *Tent of the Presence* was at this time at Gibeon, but this section appears to come from a different source which shows no knowledge of that tradition. *

THE PRIESTS

24 The divisions of the sons of Aaron: his sons were
2 Nadab and Abihu, Eleazar and Ithamar. Nadab and Abihu died before their father, leaving no sons; therefore
3 Eleazar and Ithamar held the office of priest. David, acting with Zadok of the sons of Eleazar and with Ahimelech of the sons of Ithamar, organized them in divisions for the discharge of the duties of their office.
4 The male heads of families proved to be more numerous in the line of Eleazar than in that of Ithamar, so that sixteen heads of families were grouped under the line of
5 Eleazar and eight under that of Ithamar. He organized

them by drawing lots among them, for there were sacred officers[a] and officers of God in the line of Eleazar and in that of Ithamar. Shemaiah the clerk, a Levite, son of 6 Nethaneel, wrote down the names in the presence of the king, the officers, Zadok the priest, and Ahimelech son of Abiathar, and of the heads of the priestly and levitical families, one priestly family being taken from the line of Eleazar and one[b] from that of Ithamar. The first lot fell to 7 Jehoiarib, the second to Jedaiah, the third to Harim, the 8 fourth to Seorim, the fifth to Malchiah, the sixth to 9 Mijamin, the seventh to Hakkoz, the eighth to Abiah, the 10, 11 ninth to Jeshua, the tenth to Shecaniah, the eleventh to 12 Eliashib, the twelfth to Jakim, the thirteenth to Huppah, 13 the fourteenth to Jeshebeab,[c] the fifteenth to Bilgah, the 14 sixteenth to Immer, the seventeenth to Hezir, the 15 eighteenth to Aphses, the nineteenth to Pethahiah, the 16 twentieth to Jehezekel, the twenty-first to Jachin, the 17 twenty-second to Gamul, the twenty-third to Delaiah, 18 and the twenty-fourth to Maaziah. This was their order 19 of duty for the discharge of their service when they entered the house of the LORD, according to the rule prescribed for them by their ancestor Aaron, who had received his instructions from the LORD the God of Israel.

Of the remaining Levites: of the sons of Amram: 20 Shubael. Of the sons of Shubael: Jehdeiah. Of Rehabiah: 21 Isshiah, the chief of Rehabiah's sons. Of the line of Izhar: 22 Shelomoth. Of the sons of Shelomoth: Jahath. The sons 23 of Hebron:[d] Jeriah the chief,[e] Amariah the second,

[a] sacred officers: *or* officers of the sanctuary.   [b] one: *so some MSS.; others* taken.   [c] *One form of Sept. has* Ishbaal.   [d] Hebron: *so one MS.; others om.*   [e] the chief: *so Luc. Sept.; Heb. om.*

24 Jahaziel the third and Jekameam the fourth. The sons of
25 Uzziel: Micah. Of the sons of Micah: Shamir; Micah's
26 brother: Isshiah. Of the sons of Isshiah: Zechariah. The
sons of Merari: Mahli and Mushi and also[a] Jaaziah his son.
27 The sons of Merari: of Jaaziah: Beno, Shoham, Zaccur
28, 29 and Ibri. Of Mahli: Eleazar, who had no sons; of Kish:
30 the sons of Kish: Jerahmeel; and the sons of Mushi:
Mahli, Eder and Jerimoth. These were the Levites by
31 families. These also, side by side with their kinsmen the
sons of Aaron, cast lots in the presence of King David,
Zadok, Ahimelech, and the heads of the priestly and
levitical families, the senior and junior houses casting lots
side by side.

✶ Attention now focuses more precisely on the Aaronite
priests, with an explanation of the origin of the arrangements
for priestly duties.

1–4. *Eleazar and Ithamar:* during the last centuries before
Christ, great disputes arose within Judaism concerning priestly
genealogies. The Samaritans, for example, at their sanctuary
on Mount Gerizim, laid great stress on the importance of a
priestly line descended from Eleazar, as they claimed theirs
was; and condemned the Jerusalemite priesthood for its
inadequate claims based on descent from Ithamar. Here both
sons of Aaron are allowed a share in the priesthood, though
the prominence given to Eleazar in verse 4 is already significant; the fact that such families were *more numerous* is likely
to represent claims to genealogical superiority rather than
simply statements about numbers. No previous indication
has been given that Ahimelech was considered as a descendant
of Ithamar (cp. 18: 16, which does not link Ahimelech with
the lines of priests descended from Aaron).

[a] and also: *prob. rdg.; Heb.* the sons of.

7–19. There are indications from later Jewish writings and from the New Testament that this system of divisions of the priesthood was in effect in the last days of the temple. Thus John the Baptist's father was 'of the division of the priesthood called after Abijah' (Luke 1: 5), a division which is probably to be identified with the eighth division, that of Abiah here. Similarly Mattathias, father of the Maccabees, was 'of the Joarib family' (1 Macc. 2: 1), presumably the first division of Jehoiarib here. We do not know when the custom of such divisions grew up, but it was probably in the period after the exile, and it reflects the successful claim made by many to a priestly inheritance. The exercise of priesthood was thus a matter of inheritance, and was not a full-time occupation – those whose division was not on duty might follow a variety of other occupations.

20–31. The *remaining Levites* here listed appear to form a supplementary group, whose relation to other lists is not clear. Most of the family names have already been mentioned in ch. 23. The reference to casting *lots* in verse 31 may account for its inclusion at this point, after the casting of lots for the order of priestly divisions, but it is probable that the final compilers of the book were anxious to include all the information of this type that was available to them, and it was not always easy to build up a smoothly organized picture. ✳

THE MUSICIANS

David and his chief officers assigned special duties to **25** the sons of Asaph, of Heman, and of Jeduthun, leaders in inspired prophecy to the accompaniment of harps, lutes, and cymbals; the number of the men who performed this work in the temple was as follows. Of the sons of Asaph: 2 Zaccur, Joseph, Nethaniah and Asarelah; these were under Asaph, a leader in inspired prophecy under the

3 king. Of the sons of Jeduthun: Gedaliah, Izri,[a] Isaiah,
Shimei,[b] Hashabiah, Mattithiah, these six under their
father Jeduthun, a leader in inspired prophecy to the
accompaniment of the harp, giving thanks and praise to
4 the LORD. Of the sons of Heman: Bukkiah, Mattaniah,
Uzziel, Shubael,[c] Jerimoth, Hananiah, Hanani, Eliathah,
Giddalti, Romamti-ezer, Joshbekashah, Mallothi, Hothir,
5 and Mahazioth;[d] all these were sons of Heman the king's
seer, given to him through the promises of God for his
greater glory. God had given Heman fourteen sons and
6 three daughters, and they all served under their father for
the singing in the house of the LORD; they took part in
the service of the house of God, with cymbals, lutes, and
harps, while Asaph, Jeduthun, and Heman were under
7 the king. Reckoned with their kinsmen, trained singers of
the LORD, they brought the total number of skilled
8 musicians up to two hundred and eighty-eight. They cast
lots for their duties, young and old, master-singer and
apprentice side by side.

9   The first lot fell[e] to Joseph: he and his brothers and his
sons, twelve.[f] The second to Gedaliah: he and his bro-
10 thers and his sons, twelve. The third to Zaccur: his sons
11 and his brothers, twelve. The fourth to Izri: his sons and
12 his brothers, twelve. The fifth to Nethaniah: his sons and
13 his brothers, twelve. The sixth to Bukkiah: his sons and

[a] *Prob. rdg., cp. verse 11; Heb.* Zeri.   [b] *So one MS.; others om.*
[c] *So Sept., cp. verse 20; Heb.* Shebuel.   [d] Hananiah...Mahazioth:
*these nine proper names were probably originally the words of a prayer,
which may have had its place immediately after verse 3:* Be gracious to me,
O LORD, be gracious to me; my God art thou; I will magnify and exalt
thee, my helper. Lingering in hardship, I faint. Grant me vision after
vision.   [e] *Prob. rdg.; Heb. cdds* to Asaph.   [f] he...twelve: *prob.
rdg.; Heb. om.*

his brothers, twelve. The seventh to Asarelah:[a] his sons 14
and his brothers, twelve. The eighth to Isaiah: his sons and 15
his brothers, twelve. The ninth to Mattaniah: his sons 16
and his brothers, twelve. The tenth to Shimei: his sons and 17
his brothers, twelve. The eleventh to Azareel: his sons 18
and his brothers, twelve. The twelfth to Hashabiah: his 19
sons and his brothers, twelve. The thirteenth to Shubael: 20
his sons and his brothers, twelve. The fourteenth to 21
Mattithiah: his sons and his brothers, twelve. The 22
fifteenth to Jeremoth: his sons and his brothers, twelve.
The sixteenth to Hananiah: his sons and his brothers, 23
twelve. The seventeenth to Joshbekashah: his sons and his 24
brothers, twelve. The eighteenth to Hanani: his sons and 25
his brothers, twelve. The nineteenth to Mallothi: his sons 26
and his brothers, twelve. The twentieth to Eliathah: his 27
sons and his brothers, twelve. The twenty-first to Hothir: 28
his sons and his brothers, twelve. The twenty-second to 29
Giddalti: his sons and his brothers, twelve. The twenty- 30
third to Mahazioth: his sons and his brothers, twelve. The 31
twenty-fourth to Romamti-ezer: his sons and his brothers, twelve.

* We have already observed, in connection with the bringing
in of the Ark to Jerusalem, how important a part the musicians
played in the Chronicler's picture of true worship; and here
the names of the principal musicians are given, with once
again a notice of a twenty-four-fold division of the ranks.

1. *Asaph,...Heman, and...Jeduthun:* these are the musical
groups listed in 6: 31–48, with the substitution of Jeduthun
(already noted at 6: 44) for the 'Ethan' of the other lists.
leaders in inspired prophecy: the N.E.B. translation implies

[a] *So one form of Sept., cp. verse 2; Heb.* Yesarelah.

that the prophesying was accompanied by the musical instruments, but the Hebrew text could equally mean that the playing of the instruments was itself regarded as prophecy. Little is known of the place of prophets in the Chronicler's own day (to which this verse probably relates), but it may be that the temple prophets of earlier times had their successors in these groups of musicians.

4. *Hananiah . . . Mahazioth:* many commentators have recognized the strange character of this list of names, and have interpreted it as a psalm-like fragment along the lines suggested by the N.E.B. footnote. Perhaps the Chronicler treated the words as proper names so as to be able, with some slight modifications, to list his twenty-four courses, which are set out in verses 9–31, as a parallel to the corresponding lists of priestly courses. It is also possible, since the nine names here involved are not mingled with the others, and form the last nine courses, that the names of the courses had already arisen. The Chronicler – not knowing their origin – treated them as proper names.

5. *Heman the king's seer:* whereas the other two leaders are described in prophetic terms, Heman is spoken of as the royal seer. It is doubtful whether there was any significant difference between the two in ancient times, and if there was it has now been quite lost. In any case their role was expressed in terms of musical duties.

8. *master-singer and apprentice:* the N.E.B. translation is here somewhat fanciful – the words used simply mean 'teacher' and 'the one taught'. ＊

THE DOORKEEPERS AND OTHER LEVITES

26 The divisions of the door-keepers: Korahites: Meshele-
2 miah son of Kore, son of Ebiasaph.[a] Sons of Meshelemiah:
Zechariah the eldest, Jediael the second, Zebediah the

[a] son of Ebiasaph: *prob. rdg.*; *Heb.* from the sons of Asaph.

third, Jathniel the fourth, Elam the fifth, Jehohanan the 3
sixth, Elioenai the seventh. Sons of Obed-edom: She- 4
maiah the eldest, Jehozabad the second, Joah the third,
Sacar the fourth, Nethaneel the fifth, Ammiel the sixth, 5
Issachar the seventh, Peulthai the eighth (for God had
blessed him). Shemaiah, his son, was the father of sons 6
who had authority in their family, for they were men of
great ability. Sons of Shemaiah: Othni, Rephael, Obed, 7
Elzabad and[a] his brothers Elihu and Semachiah, men of
ability. All these belonged to the family of Obed-edom; 8
they, their sons and brothers, were men of ability, fit for
service in the temple; total: sixty-two. Sons and brothers 9
of Meshelemiah, all men of ability, eighteen. Sons of 10
Hosah, a Merarite: Shimri the chief (he was not the
eldest, but his father had made him chief), Hilkiah the 11
second, Tebaliah the third, Zechariah the fourth. Total of
Hosah's sons and brothers: thirteen.

The male heads of families constituted the divisions of 12
the door-keepers; their duty was to serve in the house of
the LORD side by side with their kinsmen. Young and old, 13
family by family, they cast lots for the gates. The lot for 14
the east gate fell to Shelemiah; then lots were cast for his
son Zechariah, a prudent counsellor, and he was allotted
the north gate. To Obed-edom was allotted the south 15
gate, and the gatehouse to his sons. Hosah[b] was allotted 16
the west gate, together with the Shallecheth gate on the
ascending causeway. Guard corresponded to guard. Six 17
Levites were on duty daily on the east side, four on the
north and four on the south, and two at each gatehouse;

[a] and: *so some MSS.; others om.*
[b] Hosah: *prob. rdg.; Heb.* Shuppim and Hosah.

18 at the western colonnade there were four at the causeway
19 and two at the colonnade itself. These were the divisions
of the door-keepers, Korahites and Merarites.

20 Fellow-Levites[a] were in charge of the stores of the
21 house of God and of the stores of sacred gifts. Of the
children of Laadan, descendants of the Gershonite line
through Laadan, heads of families in the group of Laadan
22 the Gershonite, Jehiel and[b] his brothers Zetham and Joel
23 were in charge of the stores of the house of the LORD. Of
the families of Amram, Izhar, Hebron and Uzziel,
24 Shubael[c] son of Gershom, son of Moses, was overseer of
25 the stores. The line of Eliezer his brother:[d] his son
Rehabiah, his son Isaiah, his son Joram, his son Zichri, and
26 his son Shelomoth. This Shelomoth and his kinsmen were
in charge of all the stores of the sacred gifts dedicated by
David the king, the heads of families, the officers over
units of a thousand and a hundred, and other officers of the
27 army. They had dedicated some of the spoils taken in the
28 wars for the upkeep of the house of the LORD. Everything
which Samuel the seer, Saul son of Kish, Abner son of
Ner, and Joab son of Zeruiah had dedicated, in short every
sacred gift, was under the charge of Shelomoth and his
29 kinsmen. Of the family of Izhar, Kenaniah and his sons
acted as clerks and magistrates in the secular affairs of
30 Israel. Of the family of Hebron, Hashabiah and his kinsmen, men of ability to the number of seventeen hundred,
had the oversight of Israel west of the Jordan, both in the
31 work of the LORD and in the service of the king. Also of

[a] Fellow-Levites: *so Sept.; Heb.* Levites, Ahijah. [b] Jehiel and: *prob.
rdg.; Heb.* Jehieli. The sons of Jehieli... [c] *So Vulg.; Heb.* Shebuel.
[d] The line...brother: *so Sept.; Heb. obscure.*

the family of Hebron, Jeriah was the chief. (In the fortieth year of David's reign search was made in the family histories of the Hebronites, and men of great ability were found among them at Jazer in Gilead.) His kinsmen, all 32 men of ability, two thousand seven hundred of them, heads of families, were charged by King David with the oversight of the Reubenites, the Gadites, and the half tribe of Manasseh, in religious and civil affairs alike.

<hr />

✻ The duties described in the first part of this chapter were probably more responsible than the conventional English translation 'door-keeper' might imply. Not only would financial responsibilities be involved, but it also became an important concern in Judaism to ensure that no-one should penetrate further into the temple than his standing within the community permitted.

1. *Korahites:* a link is here provided with the earlier reference to this group in 9: 19 (see the comment on 9: 19–20).

12–19. The traditions concerning the door-keepers in these verses seem to originate from a different source from that of the preceding verses, though several of the names mentioned are the same.

16. *Shallecheth gate on the ascending causeway:* as is often the case, topographical details which make good sense to those familiar with the area can be very confusing if the area is unknown. This is the only reference to this part of the temple precincts, and its whereabouts is unknown. The ancient versions in which the Hebrew is translated into other languages were already puzzled by this note.

18. *colonnade:* the meaning of this word is uncertain. The older English versions took it to be a proper name, Parbar, and various suggestions as to its meaning have been made – courtyard, pavilion, or, as here, colonnade.

20–8. A separate list, this time of 'the Gershonite line',

gives details of those who were responsible for the stores and
the offerings. The names in these lists are basically similar to
those in 23: 7–19.

28. *Everything which Samuel the seer, Saul son of Kish, Abner
son of Ner, and Joab son of Zeruiah had dedicated:* there are a
number of noteworthy features about this phrase. The first
is the joining together of the names – all of them well known,
though not elsewhere closely connected with one another
(save that Joab had killed Abner in blood revenge, 2 Sam.
3: 27). The second is that none of the first three, and probably
not Joab, could have lived to see the building of the Jerusalem
temple. The third is the sympathetic note, of which we have
already seen some evidence in the case of the Chronicler's
treatment of Saul's family. Samuel is here described as *the
seer*, as in 1 Sam. 9; there is no trace of the tradition which
gave him priestly status as in 1 Chron. 6: 28.

29–32. Some indication is given in these verses of the role
that the priestly families played in the whole of Israel's life
in the Chronicler's time. The N.E.B. phrase 'secular affairs'
(verse 29) may be a somewhat free translation, but conveys
the sense well enough.

31. *In the fortieth year:* the origin of this apparently historical
note is unknown. It is contrary to the Chronicler's usual
practice which does not concern itself with the developing
chronology of the reign. It may be related to a tradition
available to the author concerning the Transjordanian tribes
mentioned in verse 32. This area was not in Judah's control
in the Chronicler's own day. ✳

THE ORGANIZATION OF THE KINGDOM

27 The number of the Israelites – that is to say, of the heads
of families, the officers over units of a thousand and a
hundred, and the clerks who had their share in the king's
service in the various divisions which took monthly turns

of duty throughout the year – was twenty-four thousand in each division.

First, Jashobeam son of Zabdiel commanded the divi- 2 sion for the first month with twenty-four thousand in his division; a member of the house of Perez, he was chief 3 officer of the temple staff for the first month. Eleazar son 4 of[a] Dodai the Ahohite[b] commanded the division for the second month with twenty-four thousand in his division. Third, Benaiah son of Jehoiada the chief priest, comman- 5 der of the army, was the officer for the third month with twenty-four thousand in his division (he was the Benaiah 6 who was one of the thirty warriors and was a chief among the thirty); but his son Ammizabad commanded[c] his division. Fourth, Asahel, the brother of Joab, was the 7 officer commanding for the fourth month with twenty-four thousand in his division; and his successor was Zebediah his son. Fifth, Shamhuth the Zerahite[d] was the 8 officer commanding for the fifth month with twenty-four thousand in his division. Sixth, Ira son of Ikkesh, a man 9 of Tekoa, was the officer commanding for the sixth month with twenty-four thousand in his division. Seventh, 10 Helez an Ephraimite, from a place unknown, was the officer commanding for the seventh month with twenty-four thousand in his division. Eighth, Sibbecai the Husha- 11 thite, of the family of Zerah, was the officer commanding for the eighth month with twenty-four thousand in his division. Ninth, Abiezer, from Anathoth in Benjamin, 12 was the officer commanding for the ninth month with

[a] Eleazar son of: *prob. rdg., cp. 11: 12; Heb. om.*   [b] *So Sept.; Heb.* adds and his division and Mikloth the prince.   [c] commanded: *so Sept.; Heb. om.*   [d] the Zerahite: *prob. rdg.; Heb.* the Izrah.

13 twenty-four thousand in his division. Tenth, Maharai the Netophathite, of the family of Zerah, was the officer commanding for the tenth month with twenty-four
14 thousand in his division. Eleventh, Benaiah the Pirathonite, from Ephraim, was the officer commanding for the eleventh month with twenty-four thousand in his
15 division. Twelfth, Heldai the Netophathite, of the family of Othniel, was the officer commanding for the twelfth month with twenty-four thousand in his division.

16 The following were the principal officers in charge of the tribes of Israel: of Reuben, Eliezer son of Zichri; of
17 Simeon, Shephatiah son of Maacah; of Levi, Hashabiah
18 son of Kemuel; of Aaron, Zadok; of Judah, Elihu a
19 kinsman of David; of Issachar, Omri son of Michael; of Zebulun, Ishmaiah son of Obadiah; of Naphtali, Jeri-
20 moth son of Azriel; of Ephraim, Hoshea son of Azaziah;
21 of the half tribe of Manasseh, Joel son of Pedaiah; of the half of Manasseh in Gilead, Iddo son of Zechariah; of
22 Benjamin, Jaasiel son of Abner; of Dan, Azareel son of Jeroham. These were the officers in charge of the tribes of Israel.

23 David took no census of those under twenty years of age, for the LORD had promised to make the Israelites as
24 many as the stars in the heavens. Joab son of Zeruiah did begin to take a census but he did not finish it; this brought harm upon Israel, and the census was not entered in the chronicle of King David's reign.

25 Azmoth son of Adiel was in charge of the king's stores; Jonathan son of Uzziah was in charge of the stores in the country, in the cities, in the villages and in the fortresses.
26 Ezri son of Kelub had oversight of the workers on the

land; Shimei of Ramah was in charge of the vine- 27
dressers, while Zabdi of Shephem had charge of the produce of the vineyards for the wine-cellars. Baal-hanan 28
the Gederite supervised the wild olives and the sycomore-
figs in the Shephelah; Joash was in charge of the oil-
stores. Shitrai of Sharon was in charge of the herds grazing 29
in Sharon, Shaphat son of Adlai of the herds in the vales.
Obil the Ishmaelite was in charge of the camels, Jehdeiah 30
the Meronothite of the asses. Jaziz the Hagerite was in 31
charge of the flocks. All these were the officers in charge
of King David's possessions. David's favourite nephew 32
Jonathan, a counsellor, a discreet and learned man, and
Jehiel the Hachmonite, were tutors to the king's sons.
Ahithophel was a king's counsellor; Hushai the Archite 33
was the King's Friend. Ahithophel was succeeded by 34
Jehoiada son of Benaiah, and Abiathar. Joab was commander of the army.

* The more obviously religious lists, of those associated with
the temple, are now followed by details of the organization
of the kingdom in general. Once again it is likely that we
should see here the kind of structure in which the country
was organized in the Chronicler's own day. It has been
suggested that some of these lists attributing Davidic origin
to various offices have as their purpose the reform of the
system of the Chronicler's own time, but if this is so such
details of internal politics are no longer clear to us.

2–15. All the names of those listed here have already been
mentioned among the lists of warriors in ch. 11, as is implied
in some of the allusions here. In one case, that of Eleazar
(verse 4), the N.E.B. has supplied the name on this basis,
though it is lacking in the Hebrew text, and it is surprising
that a comparable modification has not been made at verse 15,

where *Heldai* is found instead of the variant form 'Heled' of 11: 30.

16. *principal officers in charge of the tribes of Israel:* the 'all Israel' theme is here once again brought out. It is impossible to tell how many different tribal groups were in fact represented in the Israel of the Chronicler's day, but the claim was certainly made that his community was the repository of all the tribal traditions. A curiosity of this list is that the twelve-fold structure is different from that found anywhere else in the Old Testament – Levi is included, and both halves of Manasseh, and this leads to the exclusion of Asher and Gad. The names found here do not appear ·elsewhere as a list, though they are all familiar in themselves.

23. *David took no census:* it appears as if this may be a variant tradition to that found in ch. 21. This verse may be an attempt at harmonization, by the way it limits those involved in David's census; while the following verse shifts the responsibility for the census from David to Joab. Both ch. 21 and this brief section indicate how the census represented a theological problem for David's reputation.

25–34. A further list of officers is provided. In the first section there are few links with other traditions that have been preserved to us, and we are left to speculate whether the Chronicler here had access to ancient lists, or was basing his information on the state of affairs in his own day. By contrast the names in verses 33–4 are familiar from the stories in 2 Samuel.

32. *David's favourite nephew Jonathan:* otherwise unknown. Further, the relationship is not clear, the older English versions taking Jonathan as David's uncle. It may be that an allusion is being made to the son of Saul, who was also a favourite of David (1 Sam. 18: 2). ✳

FINAL PREPARATIONS FOR THE TEMPLE

David assembled at Jerusalem all the officers of Israel, the **28** officers over the tribes, over the divisions engaged in the king's service, over the units of a thousand and a hundred, and those in charge of all the property and the cattle of the king and of his sons, as well as the eunuchs, the heroes and all the men of ability. Then King David rose 2 to his feet and said, 'Hear me, kinsmen and people. I had in mind to build a house as a resting-place for the Ark of the Covenant of the LORD which might serve as a footstool for the feet of our God, and I made preparations to build it. But God said to me, "You shall not build a 3 house in honour of my name, for you have been a fighting man and you have shed blood." Nevertheless, the LORD 4 the God of Israel chose me out of all my father's family to be king over Israel in perpetuity; for it was Judah that he chose as ruling tribe, and, out of the house of Judah, my father's family; and among my father's sons it was I whom he was pleased to make king over all Israel. And 5 out of all my sons – for the LORD gave me many sons – he chose Solomon to sit upon the throne of the LORD's sovereignty over Israel; and he said to me, "It is Solomon 6 your son who shall build my house and my courts, for I have chosen him to be a son to me and I will be a father to him. I will establish his sovereignty in perpetuity, if 7 only he steadfastly obeys my commandments and my laws as they are now obeyed." Now therefore, in the 8 presence of all Israel, the assembly of the LORD, and within the hearing of our God, I bid you all study carefully the commandments of the LORD your God, that you

may possess this good land and hand it down as an in-
9 heritance for all time to your children after you. And you,
Solomon my son, acknowledge your father's God and
serve him with whole heart and willing mind, for the
LORD searches all hearts and discerns every invention of
men's thoughts. If you search for him, he will let you
find him, but if you forsake him, he will cast you off for
10 ever. Remember, then, that the LORD has chosen you to
build a house for a sanctuary: be steadfast and do it.'
11   David gave Solomon his son the plan of the porch of
the temple[a] and its buildings, strong-rooms, roof-
chambers and inner courts, and the shrine of expiation;[b]
12 also the plans of all he had in mind for the courts of the
house of the LORD and for all the rooms around it, for the
stores of God's house and for the stores of the sacred gifts,
13 for the divisions of the priests and the Levites, for all the
work connected with the service of the house of the LORD
14 and for all the vessels used in its service. He prescribed the
weight of gold for all the gold vessels[c] used in the
various services, and the weight of silver[d] for all the silver
15 vessels used in the various services; and the weight of gold
for the gold lamp-stands and their lamps; and the weight
of silver for the silver lamp-stands, the weight required
for each lamp-stand and its lamps according to the use of
16 each; and the weight of gold for each of the tables for the
rows of the Bread of the Presence, and of silver for the
17 silver tables. He prescribed also the weight of pure gold
for the forks, tossing-bowls and cups, the weight of gold

[a] of the temple: *prob. rdg.; Heb. om.*   [b] the shrine...expiation: *or*
the place for the Ark with its cover.   [c] for...vessels: *prob. rdg.;*
Heb. for gold.   [d] of silver: *prob. rdg.; Heb. om.*

for each of the golden dishes and of silver[a] for each of the
silver dishes; the weight also of refined gold for the altar 18
of incense, and of gold for the model of the chariot, that
is the cherubim with their wings outspread to screen the
Ark of the Covenant of the LORD. 'All this was drafted 19
by the LORD's own hand,' said David; 'my part was to
consider the detailed working out of the plan.'

Then David said to Solomon his son, 'Be steadfast and 20
resolute and do it; be neither faint-hearted nor dismayed,
for the LORD God, my God, will be with you; he will
neither fail you nor forsake you, until you have finished
all the work needed for the service of the house of the
LORD. Here are the divisions of the priests and the Levites, 21
ready for all the service of the house of God. In all the
work you will have the help of every willing craftsman
for any task; and the officers and all the people will be
entirely at your command.'

✶ It appears likely that chs. 23–7 have been inserted, perhaps
from another source, into the main narrative, which is concerned with the preparation of the people and of Solomon for
the building of the temple as the final climax of David's reign.
In these last two chapters of the book, therefore, the themes
developed as far as ch. 22 are taken up again.

1. *all the officers of Israel...all the men of ability:* the 'all
Israel' theme is found once again, this time with the particular
emphasis that the final dispositions of David were shared by
all the people, who thus shared both in the privilege and the
responsibilities of true worship.

2. *a house as a resting-place for the Ark:* it seems likely that
originally the Ark and the temple represented rather sharply
contrasted ways of envisaging the presence of God with his
people. The Chronicler, however, stresses the links, and

[a] of silver: *prob. rdg.; Heb. om.*

thereby the continuity of Israel's tradition from the wilderness period onwards.

3. *you have been a fighting man and you have shed blood:* that David had in fact not been the builder of the temple was inescapable, and yet it posed something of a problem for the Chronicler, as we have already noted in considering ch. 22. The solution offered to this difficulty differs markedly from that found in 2 Sam. 7: 5f. The earlier work preserved a tradition of God not requiring a temple at all; for the Chronicler, it was impossible to envisage true worship other than in the temple, and so a different type of explanation is put forward.

5. *out of all my sons:* the choice of Solomon is here seen as divinely inspired, with none of the intrigues and warfare described in 2 Samuel.

6f. The promises expressed in general terms in 2 Sam. 7: 13f. are here made specific to Solomon.

11–19. Although Solomon is the temple builder, once again it is stressed that all the preparations had been made by David, and, indeed, had been *drafted by the LORD's own hand* (verse 19). The details here set out were probably those familiar to the Chronicler and his readers from their own time.

20f. The speech here appears to be a variant of the commissioning of Solomon already described in ch. 22. ✻

THE DEATH OF DAVID AND THE ACCESSION
OF SOLOMON

29 King David then said to the whole assembly, 'My son Solomon is the one chosen by God, Solomon alone, a boy of tender years; and this is a great work, for it is a
2 palace not for man but for the LORD God. Now to the best of my strength I have made ready for the house of my God gold for the gold work, silver for the silver,

bronze for the bronze, iron for the iron, and wood for the woodwork, together with cornelian and other gems for setting, stones for mosaic work, precious stones of every sort, and marble in plenty. Further, because I delight in the house of my God, I give my own private store of gold and silver for the house of my God – over and above all the store which I have collected for the sanctuary – namely three thousand talents of gold, gold from Ophir, and seven thousand talents of fine silver for overlaying the walls of the buildings, for providing gold for the gold work, silver for the silver, and for any work to be done by skilled craftsmen. Now who is willing to give with open hand to the LORD today?'

Then the heads of families, the officers administering the tribes of Israel, the officers over units of a thousand and a hundred, and the officers in charge of the king's service, responded willingly and gave for the work of the house of God five thousand talents of gold, ten thousand darics, ten thousand talents of silver, eighteen thousand talents of bronze, and a hundred thousand talents of iron. Further, those who possessed precious stones gave them to the treasury of the house of the LORD, into the charge of Jehiel the Gershonite. The people rejoiced at this willing response, because in the loyalty of their hearts they had given willingly to the LORD; King David also was full of joy, and he blessed the LORD in the presence of all the assembly and said, 'Blessed art thou, LORD God of our father Israel, from of old and for ever. Thine, O LORD, is the greatness, the power, the glory, the splendour, and the majesty; for everything in heaven and on earth is thine;[a]

[a] is thine: *prob. rdg.; Heb. om.*

thine, O Lord, is the sovereignty, and thou art

12 exalted over all as head. Wealth and honour come from thee; thou rulest over all; might and power are of thy disposing; thine it is to give power and strength to all.

13 And now, we give thee thanks, our God, and praise thy glorious name.

14 'But what am I, and what is my people, that we should be able to give willingly like this? For everything comes from thee, and it is only of thy gifts that we give to thee.

15 We are aliens before thee and settlers, as were all our fathers; our days on earth are like a shadow, we have no

16 abiding place. O Lord our God, from thee comes all this wealth that we have laid up to build a house in honour

17 of thy holy name, and everything is thine. I know, O my God, that thou dost test the heart and that plain honesty pleases thee; with an honest heart I have given all these gifts willingly, and have rejoiced now to see thy people

18 here present give willingly to thee. O Lord God of Abraham, Isaac and Israel our fathers, maintain this purpose for ever in thy people's thoughts and direct their

19 hearts toward thyself. Grant that Solomon my son may loyally keep thy commandments, thy solemn charge, and thy statutes, that he may fulfil them all and build the palace for which I have prepared.'

20 Then, turning to the whole assembly, David said, 'Now bless the Lord your God.' So all the assembly blessed the Lord the God of their fathers, bowing low and prostrating themselves before the Lord and the king.

21 The next day they sacrificed to the Lord and offered whole-offerings to him, a thousand oxen, a thousand rams, a thousand lambs, with the prescribed drink-

offerings, and abundant sacrifices for all Israel. So they 22
ate and drank before the LORD that day with great
rejoicing. They then appointed Solomon, David's son,
king a second time and anointed him as the LORD's prince,
and Zadok as priest. So Solomon sat on the LORD's throne 23
as king in place of his father David, and he prospered and
all Israel obeyed him. All the officers and the warriors, as 24
well as all the sons of King David, swore fealty to King
Solomon. The LORD made Solomon stand very high in 25
the eyes of all Israel, and bestowed upon him sovereignty
such as no king in Israel had had before him.

David son of Jesse had ruled over the whole of Israel, 26
and the length of his reign over Israel was forty years; he 27
ruled for seven years in Hebron, and for thirty-three in
Jerusalem. He died in ripe old age, full of years, wealth, 28
and honour; and Solomon his son ruled in his place. The 29
events of King David's reign from first to last are recorded in the books of Samuel the seer, of Nathan the
prophet, and of Gad the seer, with a full account of his 30
reign, his prowess, and of the times through which he and
Israel and all the kingdoms of the world had passed.

✳ The death of David and his succession by Solomon are
described in the context of the completion of preparations for
the temple. David's task of preparation is accomplished, and
his death is presented, after his final prayer of blessing, as
the appropriate end to his life in God's service.
  1. *a boy of tender years*: this theme – found also at 1 Kings
3: 7 – is intended to emphasize his dependence on his God.
The absence of the usual accession-formula for kings in
Solomon's case means that no tradition of his actual age has
survived.

6. David's own generosity is matched by that of the whole community, which is pictured as totally committed to the task in hand.

7. *darics:* this mention of coined money appears to be an anachronism. The *daric* was a Persian gold coin – the name may be connected with that of the Persian king Darius – and coined money was not used in David's time. There is little point in attempting to calculate the modern equivalents of the enormous sums here envisaged; the point is precisely that they are beyond calculation, a way of stressing the magnificence of the temple and the generosity of the people's response.

8. *Jehiel:* has previously only been mentioned in lists (23: 8; 26: 21).

10–19. David's prayer in these verses has often been used in Christian worship; such prayers, expressed in the form of a blessing, have many parallels in Jewish usage. Several individual phrases can be paralleled elsewhere in the Old Testament, but it is unlikely that these should be regarded as specific 'sources'; the Chronicler is here using the language of prayer with which he and his readers will have been familiar and which was made appropriate for the occasion being described by the addition of verse 19 with its reference to Solomon.

20. *bless the LORD your God:* just as God's blessing might be invoked, so often in the Old Testament we find to 'bless God' as itself a form of prayer and adoration. *bowing low and prostrating themselves:* though the usual posture for prayer seems to have been standing, reference to prostration is not infrequent when an impression of a specially intense prayer is to be conveyed.

21. As with the monetary gifts, so here an impression is created of overwhelming generosity in response to the divine initiative.

22–5. In 1 Kings, Solomon's accession is described in an atmosphere of intrigue, with plots and counter-plots. Here the contrast is marked: *all Israel obeyed* (verse 23), with no suggestion of any rival candidates for the throne; *all...swore fealty* (verse 24). Despite the difference in presentation, a number of phrases are taken from the 1 Kings account, and it appears as if the allusions are deliberate – the same scene is being described, though with a very different emphasis.

25. *sovereignty such as no king in Israel had had before him:* a curious expression, in view of the fact that only Saul and David had preceded Solomon. It is probably an allusion to the promise made by God to Solomon in the dream at Gibeon (2 Chron. 1: 12).

28. *in ripe old age:* a comparison is probably being made with Abraham, of whom the same expression is used (Gen. 25: 8 – N.E.B. 'good old age').

29. *Samuel*, *Nathan* and *Gad* are all well-known figures from David's reign, but nothing more is known of the sources here listed. It seems improbable that any literary sources relating to this period were available to the Chronicler – if there were, they have left few traces in his work – and it seems more likely that this reference is simply to the material within our books of Samuel and Kings.

30. *all the kingdoms of the world:* possibly the N.E.B. translation here gives a misleading impression. It is likely that the reference is to the countries surrounding Israel, rather than to any more extended area. ✵

THE SECOND BOOK OF THE
CHRONICLES

THE CHARACTERISTICS OF 2 CHRONICLES

We have seen already that 1 and 2 Chronicles should not be regarded as separate works; they are two parts of one presentation of God's dealings with his people. The point of division is nevertheless an appropriate one. In 1 Chronicles the stage has been set by the genealogies, and the divine promises made in and through David, seen as the ideal ruler preparing the ideal institution for the ideal community, have been set out. In the next section of the work, the story is taken forward nearly four centuries, to the time when Judah ceased to exist as an independent nation. That fact is in itself sufficient indication that an important element in the story will be human sinfulness, a failure to make an adequate response to the divine graciousness.

For the modern reader, however, the difficulty in coming to a sympathetic understanding of 2 Chronicles is likely to arise largely from its relationship with the books of Kings. The difficulty will be caused both by its similarity to, and by its differences from, the earlier work. Many sections are so close to Kings that it is difficult to know why the material needs to be reproduced at all; others differ from Kings in such a way as to raise grave doubts as to their historical credibility. In the light of what has been said already on pp. 4–7 about the Chronicler as historian, perhaps this latter point need not be further dwelt upon here; but the sections which closely follow 1 and 2 Kings must be considered more fully. To some extent such a reproduction of earlier material was necessary in order to produce a coherent story, and often there is no need to look further for a reason; but there are also many parts of the work where such a necessity is not apparent, or where the following of the earlier material is not exact in detail. Here, we need to remember the importance of the Chronicler's role as an interpreter of earlier traditions. Very frequently we shall discover that he is using earlier material, not simply as a source to be reproduced slavishly, but in order to put his own distinctive interpretation on it, in the light of his own circumstances and those of the community for whom he was writing. Such an interpretative process has already been observable in 1 Chronicles; in 2 Chronicles it becomes a major element in the presentation.

The Chronicler thus provides us with important evidence concerning the way in which a group of writings came to be accepted as sacred. We cannot with certainty state what those writings were, nor the precise form in which the Chronicler found them; but it is clear that he accepted, and expected his audience to recognize, a substantial part of the Law and the Prophets (i.e. the first two parts of the Hebrew Bible) as authoritative texts. But that authority did not yet mean fixity; and so the passages quoted or alluded to might often be modified in detail or placed in some new context. Of all of this we shall see examples in the course of 2 Chronicles.

Reasons of space will prevent us from commenting fully on those passages which have already been dealt with in the commentaries on 1 or 2 Kings, and most attention must be given to those sections which are peculiar to this book; nevertheless, it is hoped that sufficient information will be given to provide the broad outline of the historical development, so that the present volume need not necessarily be supplemented by others.

✻   ✻   ✻   ✻   ✻   ✻   ✻   ✻   ✻   ✻   ✻   ✻   ✻

The reign of Solomon and dedication of the temple

1 KING SOLOMON, David's son, strengthened his hold on the kingdom, for the LORD his God was with him and made him very great.

2   Solomon spoke to all Israel, to the officers over units of a thousand and of a hundred, the judges and all the leading

3 men of Israel, the heads of families; and he, together with all the assembled people, went to the hill-shrine at Gibeon; for the Tent of God's Presence, which Moses the LORD's servant had made in the wilderness, was there.

4 (But David had brought up the Ark of God from Kiriath-jearim to the place which he had prepared for it,

5 for he had pitched a tent for it in Jerusalem.) The altar of bronze also, which Bezalel son of Uri, son of Hur, had made, was there[a] in front of the Tabernacle of the LORD;

6 and Solomon and the assembly resorted to it.[b] There Solomon went up to the altar of bronze before the LORD in the Tent of the Presence and offered on it a thousand

7[c] whole-offerings. That night God appeared to Solomon

8 and said, 'What shall I give you? Tell me.' Solomon answered, 'Thou didst show great and constant love to David my father and thou hast made me king in his

9 place. Now, O LORD God, let thy word to David my father be confirmed, for thou hast made me king over a

[a] was there: *so many MSS.; others* he placed   [b] resorted to it: *or* worshipped him.   [c] *Verses 7–12: cp. 1 Kgs. 3: 5–14.*

people as numerous as the dust on the earth. Give me now 10
wisdom and knowledge, that I may lead this people; for
who is fit to govern this great people of thine?' God 11
answered Solomon, 'Because this is what you desire,
because you have not asked for wealth or possessions or
honour[a] or the lives of your enemies or even long life for
yourself, but have asked for wisdom and knowledge to
govern my people over whom I have made you king,
wisdom and knowledge are given to you; I shall also give 12
you wealth and possessions and honour[a] such as no king
has had before you and none shall have after you.' Then 13
Solomon returned from the hill-shrine at Gibeon, from
before the Tent of the Presence, to Jerusalem and ruled
over Israel.

Solomon got together many chariots and horses; he 14[b]
had fourteen hundred chariots and twelve thousand
horses, and he stabled some in the chariot-towns and kept
others at hand in Jerusalem. The king made silver and 15
gold as common in Jerusalem as stones, and cedar as
plentiful as sycomore-fig in the Shephelah. Horses were 16
imported from Egypt and Coa for Solomon; the royal
merchants obtained them from Coa by purchase. Chariots 17
were imported from Egypt for six hundred silver shekels
each, and horses for a hundred and fifty; in the same way
the merchants obtained them for export from all the
kings of the Hittites and the kings of Aram.

☆ The main part of this chapter, from verse 7 onwards, is
based on material already found in 1 Kings, but the opening
verses give it an entirely fresh context. In particular, as we

[a] Or riches.   [b] Verses 14–17: cp. 9: 25–8; 1 Kgs. 10: 26–9.

shall see, these verses give a new significance to the place of
Gibeon, as against the central sanctuary of Jerusalem, in terms
which both emphasize the propriety of Solomon's visit –for
the 'Tent of God's Presence' (verse 3) was there – and also
indicate that Gibeon's importance is soon to pass, for the
Tent will soon be brought to Jerusalem (ch. 5). We do not
know enough of the condition of Gibeon in the Chronicler's
own day to be certain whether this reference had a contemporary point, or whether the Chronicler was simply reshaping
the ancient traditions in such a way as to ensure that Gibeon's
importance was not exaggerated.

3. *he, together with all the assembled people:* the occasion is
presented as an official pilgrimage. *the Tent of God's Presence...
was there:* this is a reference back to 1 Chron. 16, which
described how the 'Tabernacle' had been left at Gibeon.
Modern scholars commonly differentiate between the *Tent
of the Presence* and the 'Tabernacle', as representing different
ancient traditions; but such a distinction is unknown to the
Chronicler, who again stresses the continuity with Israel's
beginnings.

4. This may be a later note making clear the difference
between the *Ark* and the 'Tent of the Presence'.

7. *That night God appeared to Solomon:* in 1 Kings, it is
specified that the context was a dream, but the Chronicler
never mentions dreams. There are passages in Jeremiah which
suggest that they may have fallen into disrepute as a means of
divine disclosure (cp. Jer. 23: 25–32).

8–13. The remainder of the section is clearly based on
1 Kings 3, though the correspondence here is much less close
than in many parts of the Chronicler's work. The tradition
of Solomon as the greatest of wise men was a strong one
throughout the Old Testament period, and is very prominent
in the Chronicler's treatment of his reign.

14–17. This section is found in virtually identical terms in
9: 25–8, and each is based on the accounts of Solomon's
administration in 1 Kings 10. A secondary insertion may be

suspected here, but it is not clear why a note of such peripheral importance should have been included twice.

16. *Egypt and Coa:* both these place-names are suspect, *Egypt* because a well-known area has probably been substituted for a little-known one with a similar name; *Coa* because its precise identification has never been possible, and it was for long not recognized as a place-name at all (cp. the Authorized Version 'linen yarn'). Both may originally have been in what is now South-east Turkey. It is likely that both these misunderstandings had already taken place by the time of the Chronicler. ✻

THE PREPARATIONS FOR THE TEMPLE

Solomon resolved to build a house in honour of the **2** 1[a] name of the LORD, and a royal palace for himself. He 2[b] engaged seventy thousand hauliers and eighty thousand quarrymen, and three thousand six hundred men to superintend them. Then Solomon sent this message to 3[c] Huram king of Tyre: 'You were so good as to send my father David cedar-wood to build his royal residence. Now I am about to build a house in honour of the name 4 of the LORD my God and to consecrate it to him, so that I may burn fragrant incense in it before him, and present the rows of the Bread of the Presence regularly, and whole-offerings morning and evening, on the sabbaths and the new moons and the appointed festivals of the LORD our God; for this is a duty laid upon Israel for ever. The house I am about to build will be a great house, 5 because our God is greater than all gods. But who is able 6 to build him a house when heaven itself, the highest

[a] *1: 18 in Heb.*   [b] *2: 1 in Heb.*   [c] *Verses 3–16: cp. 1 Kgs. 5: 2–11.*

heaven, cannot contain him? And who am I that I should
build him a house, except that I may burn sacrifices before
7 him? Send me then a skilled craftsman, a man able to
work in gold and silver, copper[a] and iron, and in purple,
crimson, and violet yarn, who is also an expert engraver
and will work with my skilled workmen in Judah and in
8 Jerusalem who were provided by David my father. Send
me also cedar, pine, and algum[b] timber from Lebanon,
for I know that your men are expert at felling the trees of
9 Lebanon; my men will work with yours to get an ample
supply of timber ready for me, for the house which I
10 shall build will be great and wonderful. I will supply pro-
visons[c] for your servants, the woodmen who fell the
trees: twenty thousand kor of wheat and twenty thousand
kor of barley, with twenty thousand bath of wine and
twenty thousand bath of oil.'

11   Huram king of Tyre sent this answer by letter to
Solomon: 'It is because of the love which the LORD has
for his people that he has made you king over them.' The
12 letter went on to say, 'Blessed is the LORD the God of
Israel, maker of heaven and earth, who has given to King
David a wise son, endowed with intelligence and understanding, to build a house for the LORD and a royal
13 palace for himself. I now send you a skilful and experi-
14 enced craftsman, master Huram. He is the son of a Danite
woman, his father a Tyrian; he is an experienced worker
in gold and silver, copper[a] and iron, stone and wood, as
well as in purple, violet, and crimson yarn, and in fine
linen; he is also a trained engraver who will be able to

[a] *Or* bronze.   [b] almug *in 1 Kgs. 10: 11.*   [c] provisions: *so Vulg.
cp. 1 Kgs. 5: 11; Heb.* plagues.

work with your own skilled craftsmen and those of my
lord David your father, to any design submitted to him.
Now then, let my lord send his servants the wheat and 15
the barley, the oil and the wine, which he promised; we 16
will fell all the timber in Lebanon that you need and float
it as rafts to the roadstead at Joppa, and you will convey
it from there up to Jerusalem.'

Solomon took a census of all the aliens resident in 17
Israel, similar to the census which David his father had
taken; these were found to be a hundred and fifty-three
thousand six hundred. He made seventy thousand of them 18
hauliers and eighty thousand quarrymen, and three
thousand six hundred superintendents to make the people
work.

* With Solomon established as king, the work with which
he was above all else associated could now begin – the building
of the temple. Though in this and the succeeding chapters,
there is much that is dependent on the material in 1 Kings,
there is also material without parallel elsewhere. In view of
the obvious importance of the subject to the Chronicler, it
may well be that much of this additional material represents
his own interpretation of the temple-building.

2. These figures are found also in 1 Kings, but there the
reference to Adoniram (1 Kings 5: 14) suggests a link with
forced-labour gangs, for Adoniram was in charge of this side
of Solomon's economy. Here, nothing which might imply
forced labour is mentioned.

3. *Huram:* the name is regularly found in this form in the
Chronicler as against the 'Hiram' of Kings. Solomon's
message to him is greatly elaborated by comparison with the
corresponding passage in 1 Kings 5 in terms of the theological
significance of the temple, many of the phrases being found

elsewhere in Kings; the details of the price to be paid also show some variation.

7. The *craftsman* here requested is very similar in his skills to Bezalel who had been responsible for preparing the Tabernacle (Exod. 35: 30–6), and who had been referred to in the previous chapter (1: 5); this link between Tabernacle and temple is characteristic of the Chronicler's concern for continuity.

8. *algum:* the variation between this form and 'almug' of 1 Kings is probably due to the fact that the identity of this wood was as unknown to the editors as it is to us today.

10. The details of these measures are to be found in the Appendix to the N.E.B. (see below, p. 311).

13. *master Huram:* a good deal of confusion has been caused by the description of the *craftsman* sent from Tyre. The text here has been understood as naming him 'Huramabi' (so the Revised Standard Version), or as meaning 'of Huram my father'. A modern suggestion followed by the N.E.B. is that the suffix 'abi', literally 'my father', here means, 'my master', i.e. my chief craftsman. As with the royal name, 1 Kings has 'Hiram'.

14. *son of a Danite woman:* this link may be stressed so as to avoid the implication of a major role in the building of the temple being played by one of foreign descent. The parallel text in 1 Kings mentions 'the son of a widow of the tribe of Naphtali', and no reason for the change can be given unless it is to stress the comparison with Bezalel, whose helpers in Exod. 35 were from Dan. The account of his skill in 1 Kings 7 has been greatly expanded by the Chronicler.

16. *float it as rafts to the roadstead at Joppa:* this technique is alluded to again in Ezra 3: 7, but is not attested by any non-biblical source. The Israelites were not a seafaring people, and there are few references to ports on the Mediterranean coast, though Joppa is mentioned also in the story of Jonah.

17. *all the aliens resident:* again the point is made that no native Israelite was engaged in the forced-labour corvée. *

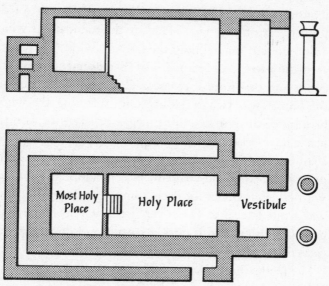

Most Holy Place

Holy Place

Vestibule

1. The Jerusalem temple. The Chronicler's description of the temple, its ministers and furnishings, was probably based on the second temple, built about 520 B.C., with which he and his readers were familiar. Of its construction we know nothing in detail, but it is likely that its general structure was similar to that of Solomon's temple, the probable plan and elevation of which are shown here.

THE TEMPLE BUILT

Then Solomon began to build the house of the LORD **3** in Jerusalem on Mount Moriah, where the LORD had appeared to his father David, on the site which David had prepared[a] on the threshing-floor of Ornan the

[a] on...prepared: *so Sept.; Heb.* which he had prepared on David's site.

2 ^{a} Jebusite. He began to build in the second month^b of the
3 fourth year of his reign. These are the foundations which
Solomon laid for building the house of God: the length,
according to the old standard of measurement, was sixty
4 cubits and the breadth twenty. The vestibule in front of
the house^c was twenty cubits long, spanning the whole
breadth of the house, and its height was twenty;^{d} on the
5 inside he overlaid it with pure gold. He panelled the large
chamber with pine, covered it with fine gold and carved
6 on it palm-trees and chain-work. He adorned the house
with precious stones for decoration, and the gold he used
7 was from Parvaim. He covered the whole house with
gold, its rafters and frames, its walls and doors; and he
carved cherubim on the walls.

8   He made the Most Holy Place twenty cubits long,
corresponding to the breadth of the house, and twenty
cubits broad. He covered it all with six hundred talents
9 of fine gold, and the weight of the nails was fifty shekels
of gold. He also covered the upper chambers with gold.
10 ^{e} In the Most Holy Place he carved two images^f of
11 cherubim and overlaid them with gold. The total span of
the wings of the cherubim was twenty cubits. A wing of
the one cherub extended five cubits to reach the wall of
the house, while its other wing reached out five cubits to
12 meet a wing of the other cherub. Similarly, a wing of the
second cherub extended five cubits to reach the other
wall of the house, while its other wing met a wing of the
13 first cherub. The wings of these cherubim extended

[a] *Verses 2–4: cp. 1 Kgs. 6: 1–3.*   [b] *So some MSS.; others add* on the
second.   [c] house: *prob. rdg.; Heb.* length.   [d] *So Sept.; Heb.* a
hundred and twenty.   [e] *Verses 10–13: cp. 1 Kgs. 6: 23–8.*   [f] *Mng.
of Heb. word uncertain.*

twenty cubits; they stood with their feet on the ground, facing the outer chamber. He made the Veil of violet, 14 purple, and crimson yarn, and fine linen, and embroidered cherubim on it.

In front of the house he erected two pillars eighteen[a] 15[b] cubits high, with an architrave five cubits high on top of each. He made chain-work like a necklace[c] and set it 16 round the tops of the pillars, and he carved a hundred pomegranates and set them in the chain-work. He erected 17 the two pillars in front of the temple, one on the right and one on the left; the one on the right he named Jachin[d] and the one on the left Boaz.[e]

✻ The Chronicler here has drastically shortened the account of the building of the temple found in 1 Kings. Possibly some of the architectural description was incomprehensible to him, as it has continued to puzzle commentators ever since, but it is more likely that here he is content to comment on a well-known source, picking out for special emphasis those features of the earlier description which he regarded as needing special comment.

1. *on Mount Moriah*: this identification is of special importance and interest, for it is the first illustration known to us of the tradition (still widely accepted in Islam and Judaism) that the Solomonic temple was built upon the spot where Abraham had been about to sacrifice Isaac. We need not suppose this identification to be an invention of the Chronicler, for he may have received it in the traditions he inherited, but once again the theme of continuity between the ancient promises and the cultic practice of the contemporary community is

[a] So Pesh., cp. 1 Kgs. 7: 15; Heb. thirty-five.   [b] Verses 15–17: cp. 1 Kgs. 7: 15–21.   [c] necklace: prob. rdg.; Heb. obscure.   [d] Or Jachun, meaning It shall stand.   [e] Or Booz, meaning In strength.

brought out. The remainder of the verse provides a link back to David's preparations described in 1 Chron. 21.

2. *the fourth year of his reign:* both David and Solomon are given conventional forty year reigns, so accurate dating is scarcely possible, but the approximate period is the mid-tenth century. The deuteronomic editor of 1 Kings saw in this date an opportunity for an elaborate chronology linking these events with the exodus from Egypt (1 Kings 6: 1); but the exodus is less prominent in the Chronicler's reckoning, and is not here mentioned.

3. *foundations:* the word is unexpected and emendations have often been suggested. A similar phrase is found in Ezra 3: 11, and the reference may not be to foundations in the modern sense, but more generally to the inauguration of the building. *the length, according to the old standard of measurement, was sixty cubits:* a cubit was 'the measure from the elbow to the knuckles of the closed fist' (see p. 311). The length of the temple would therefore have been about 100 ft (30 metres) – which may seem remarkably small to us. *the old standard* here probably is an allusion to the fact that it was known that a change in custom had taken place between the time of building of the temple and the time when the Chronicler was writing.

6. *gold...from Parvaim:* if this is a district it is unknown, but the suggestion has been made that it refers to a particular quality of gold. There is no corresponding passage in Kings, and the reference to gold ornamentation is much greater throughout the Chronicler's account.

10–17. The cherubim – half human, half winged creatures – and the free-standing pillars (with their strange names, translated in the N.E.B. footnotes) were originally features common to the Phoenician temples with which Solomon's temple may be compared. By the Chronicler's time, however, such alien antecedents were no longer recognized, and the description of them is simply reproduced in its main features from 1 Kings 6 and 7, with, once again, emphasis on the gold ornamentation.

16. *like a necklace:* many commentators have made the
same emendation as the N.E.B. to arrive at this meaning
here, but it must remain a matter of speculation. *

THE FURNISHINGS OF THE TEMPLE

He then made an altar of bronze, twenty cubits long, **4**
twenty cubits broad, and ten cubits high. He also made 2ª
the Sea of cast metal; it was round in shape, the diameter
from rim to rim being ten cubits; it stood five cubits high,
and it took a line thirty cubits long to go round it. Under 3
the Sea, on every side, completely surrounding the thirty[b]
cubits of its circumference, were what looked like
gourds,[c] two rows of them, cast in one piece with the
Sea itself. It was mounted on twelve oxen, three facing 4
north, three west, three south, and three east, their hind
quarters turned inwards; the Sea rested on top of them.
Its thickness was a hand-breadth; its rim was made like 5
that of a cup, shaped like the calyx of a lily; when full it
held three thousand bath. He also made ten basins for 6
washing, setting five on the left side and five on the right;
in these they rinsed everything used for the whole-
offering. The Sea was made for the priests to wash in.

He made ten golden lamp-stands in the prescribed man- 7
ner and set them in the temple, five on the right side and
five on the left. He also made ten tables and placed them 8
in the temple, five on the right and five on the left; and
he made a hundred golden tossing-bowls. He made the 9
court of the priests and the great precinct and the doors

[a] *Verses 2–5: cp. 1 Kgs. 7: 23–6.*   [b] *Prob. rdg.; Heb.* ten.
[c] *Prob. rdg., cp. 1 Kgs. 7: 24; Heb.* oxen.

157

10 for it, and overlaid the doors of both with copper; he put the Sea at the right side, at the south-east corner of the temple.

11[a] Huram made the pots, the shovels, and the tossing-bowls. So he finished the work which he had undertaken
12 for King Solomon on the house of God. The two pillars; the two bowl-shaped capitals[b] on the tops of the pillars; the two ornamental networks to cover the two bowl-
13 shaped capitals on the tops of the pillars; the four hundred pomegranates for the two networks, two rows of pomegranates for each network, to cover the two bowl-
14 shaped capitals on the two[c] pillars; the ten[d] trolleys and
15 the ten[d] basins on the trolleys; the one Sea and the twelve
16 oxen which supported it; the pots, the shovels, and the tossing-bowls[e] – all these[f] objects master Huram made of bronze, burnished work for King Solomon for the house
17 of the LORD. In the Plain of the Jordan the king cast them,
18 in the foundry between Succoth and Zeredah. Solomon made great quantities of all these objects; the weight of the copper[g] used was beyond reckoning.

19 Solomon made also all the furnishings for the house of God: the golden altar, the tables upon which was set the
20 Bread of the Presence, the lamp-stands of red gold whose lamps burned before the inner shrine in the prescribed
21 manner, the flowers and lamps and tongs of solid[h] gold,
22 the snuffers, tossing-bowls, saucers, and firepans of red

[a] 4: 11 – 5: 1: cp. 1 Kgs. 7: 40–51.   [b] bowl-shaped capitals: *prob. rdg.*, cp. 1 Kgs. 7: 41; *Heb.* the bowls and the capitals.   [c] two: *prob. rdg.*, cp. 1 Kgs. 7: 42; *Heb.* surface of the.   [d] the ten: *prob. rdg.*, cp. 1 Kgs. 7: 43; *Heb.* he made the...   [e] tossing-bowls: *prob. rdg.*, cp. 1 Kgs. 7: 45; *Heb.* forks.   [f] *Prob. rdg.*, cp. 1 Kgs. 7: 45; *Heb.* their.   [g] *Or* bronze.   [h] *Mng. of Heb. word uncertain.*

gold, and, at the entrance to the house, the inner doors leading to the Most Holy Place and those leading to the sanctuary, of gold.

When all the work which Solomon did for the house **5** of the LORD was completed, he brought in the sacred treasures of his father David, the silver, the gold, and the vessels, and deposited them in the storehouses of the house of God.

✻ The description of the furnishings of the temple broadly follows the account in 1 Kings 7, again with a good deal of abbreviation of the more obscure details.

1. *an altar of bronze:* altars of this type have been discovered in other ancient near-eastern shrines, so that this may be an ancient element in the description, even though it is not mentioned in the 1 Kings account. Its dimensions indicate that it must have occupied the full width of the temple.

6. *The Sea was made for the priests to wash in:* though the description of the Sea is for the most part based on 1 Kings (as the N.E.B. footnote indicates), this final note is an addition, and seems to stress the utilitarian nature of the Sea. This very large vessel may originally have symbolized in some way the great waters of the primaeval deep, believed to be a hostile power overcome by God (cp., e.g., Isa. 51: 9f.).

7–9. This section has no parallel in Kings; instead it alludes to the instruction given to Aaron in Exod. 25 and 27, in connection with the furnishings of the Tabernacle. The unity of the different traditions is thereby emphasized.

4: 11 – 5: 1. Here, by contrast, the text follows very closely that of 1 Kings, as the N.E.B. footnote indicates. The footnotes also show that in a number of cases where the meaning is doubtful, the translation has been brought even closer to that of Kings than it is in the Hebrew. ✻

THE DEDICATION OF THE TEMPLE

2[a] Then Solomon summoned the elders of Israel, and all the
heads of the tribes who were chiefs of families in Israel, to
assemble in Jerusalem, in order to bring up the Ark of the
Covenant of the LORD from the City of David, which is
3 called Zion. All the men of Israel assembled in the king's
4 presence at the pilgrim-feast in the seventh month. When
the elders of Israel had all come, the Levites took the Ark
5 and carried it up with the Tent of the Presence and all the
sacred furnishings of the Tent: it was the priests and[b] the
6 Levites together who carried them up. King Solomon
and the whole congregation of Israel, assembled with him
before the Ark, sacrificed sheep and oxen in numbers past
7 counting or reckoning. Then the priests brought in the
Ark of the Covenant of the LORD to its place, the inner
shrine of the house, the Most Holy Place, beneath the
8 wings of the cherubim. The cherubim spread their wings
over the place of the Ark, and formed a covering above
9 the Ark and its poles. The poles projected, and their ends
could be seen from the Holy Place[c] immediately in front
of the inner shrine, but from nowhere else outside; they
10 are[d] there to this day. There was nothing inside the Ark
but the two tablets which Moses had put there at Horeb,
the tablets of the covenant[e] which the LORD made with
the Israelites when they left Egypt.

11   Now when the priests came out of the Holy Place (for
all the priests who were present had hallowed themselves

[a] *Verses 2–10: cp. 1 Kgs. 8: 1–9.*   [b] and: *so some MSS.; others om.*
[c] Holy Place: *so Sept.; Heb.* Ark.   [d] *So many MSS.; others it is.*
[e] the tablets of the covenant: *prob. rdg., cp. 1 Kgs. 8: 9; Heb. om.*

without keeping to their divisions), all the levitical 12
singers, Asaph, Heman, and Jeduthun, their sons and
their kinsmen, clothed in fine linen, stood with cymbals,
lutes, and harps, to the east of the altar, together with a
hundred and twenty priests who blew trumpets. Now the 13
trumpeters and the singers joined in unison to sound forth
praise and thanksgiving to the LORD, and the song was
raised with trumpets, cymbals, and musical instruments,
in praise of the LORD, because 'that*a* is good, for his love
endures for ever'; and the house was filled with the cloud
of the glory*b* of the LORD. The priests could not con- 14
tinue to minister because of the cloud, for the glory of the
LORD filled the house of God. Then Solomon said: **6** 1*c*

O LORD who hast chosen to dwell in thick darkness,
  here have I built thee a lofty house,   2
    a habitation for thee to occupy for ever.

And as they stood waiting, the king turned round and 3
blessed all the assembly of Israel in these words: 'Blessed 4
be the LORD the God of Israel who spoke directly to my
father David and has himself fulfilled his promise. For he
said, "From the day when I brought my people out of 5
Egypt, I chose no city out of all the tribes of Israel where
I should build a house for my Name to be there, nor did
I choose any man to be prince over my people Israel. But 6
I chose Jerusalem for my Name to be there, and I chose
David to be over my people Israel." My father David 7
had in mind to build a house in honour of the name of
the LORD the God of Israel, but the LORD said to him, 8

[a] *Or* he.   [b] glory: *so Sept.; Heb.* house.   [c] *Verses 1–39: cp. 1 Kgs.
8: 12–50.*

"You purposed to build a house in honour of my name;
9 and your purpose was good. Nevertheless, you shall not
build it; but the son who is to be born to you, he shall
10 build the house in honour of my name." The LORD has
now fulfilled his promise: I have succeeded my father
David and taken his place on the throne of Israel, as the
LORD promised; and I have built the house in honour of
11 the name of the LORD the God of Israel. I have installed
there the Ark containing the covenant of the LORD which
he made with Israel.'

✶ What follows is a section in which the Chronicler to a
large extent follows the Kings text, but his own additions and
the way he handles parts of the earlier text enable us to see his
own distinctive theological emphases. It is widely held that
the account in 1 Kings 8 owes its present form and emphasis
to a deuteronomic editor; here we may see the Chronicler
both accepting that tradition and also remoulding it for his
own purpose.

3. *the pilgrim-feast* here mentioned is the Autumn festival,
Tabernacles.

4. *the Levites:* in the earlier presentation, priests and
Levites were regarded as synonymous terms. For the Chronicler there were important differences in function and status,
and so *Levites* is substituted for the earlier 'priests' here. In
view of this, it may be doubted whether the correction introduced by the N.E.B. at verse 5 necessarily gives the correct
impression.

9. *they are there to this day:* this could, of course, be regarded
as no more than an unintelligent piece of copying, overlooking
the fact of the temple's destruction by the Babylonians.
Much more likely, it is a deliberate assertion of continuity
between Solomon's temple and the temple of the Chronicler's

day. The phrase *to this day* often seems to imply a sense of perpetuity.

11–13. These verses have no equivalent in Kings; they represent the Chronicler's own presentation, which should probably be understood in terms of the religious ceremonial with which his audience would have been familiar. The duties of 'priests', 'levitical singers', and 'trumpeters' are carried out in accordance with what had been prepared by David in 1 Chronicles, while the refrain was that used at the end of the ceremony of installing the Ark (1 Chron. 16: 34). This section is skilfully worked into the Kings account, which is picked up again with the reference to the 'cloud'.

13. *the cloud of the glory of the LORD:* the minor emendation followed by the N.E.B. here is a probable one, and provides a link with a different way of expressing the divine presence. Whereas in Kings, and the deuteronomic writings generally, this is expressed by God making his 'name' dwell among men, Ezekiel refers to 'the glory of the LORD' to express the same idea. Similarly the *cloud* is a frequent way of expressing the divine presence in the Old Testament (cp. Ezek. 10: 4). Here, as elsewhere, the Chronicler shows himself the heir to more than one tradition.

6: 5. *nor did I choose any man to be prince:* another addition to the Kings text, stressing that David was the first to be chosen.

11. *the covenant of the LORD which he made with Israel:* a curious feature of the work of the Chronicler is the lack of emphasis on the events of the exodus and wandering in the wilderness, so that here, for example, the allusion to the exodus found in the Kings text is omitted. It would be misleading to say that the Chronicler denies all significance to these events; but he certainly wishes to keep the revelation through David in the forefront of his picture. ✻

SOLOMON'S PRAYER

12 Then Solomon, standing in front of the altar of the
LORD, in the presence of the whole assembly of Israel,
13 spread out his hands. He had made a bronze[a] platform,
five cubits long, five cubits broad, and three cubits high,
and had placed it in the centre of the precinct. He mounted it and knelt down in the presence of the assembly,
14 and, spreading out his hands towards heaven, he said, 'O
LORD God of Israel, there is no god like thee in heaven or
on earth, keeping covenant with thy servants and showing them constant love while they continue faithful to
15 thee in heart and soul. Thou hast kept thy promise to thy
servant David my father; by thy deeds this day thou hast
16 fulfilled what thou didst say to him in words. Now,
therefore, O LORD God of Israel, keep this promise of
thine to thy servant David my father: "You shall never
want for a man appointed by me to sit on the throne of
Israel, if only your sons look to their ways and conform
17 to my law, as you have done in my sight." And now, O
LORD God of Israel, let the word which thou didst speak
to thy servant David be confirmed.
18   'But can God indeed dwell with man on the earth?
Heaven itself, the highest heaven, cannot contain thee;
19 how much less this house that I have built! Yet attend to
the prayer and the supplication of thy servant, O LORD
my God; listen to the cry and the prayer which thy ser-
20 vant utters before thee, that thine eyes may ever be upon
this house day and night, this place of which thou didst

[a] Or copper.

say, "It shall receive my Name"; so mayest thou hear
thy servant when he prays towards this place. Hear thou 21
the supplications of thy servant and of thy people Israel
when they pray towards this place. Hear from heaven
thy dwelling and, when thou hearest, forgive.

'When a man wrongs his neighbour and he is adjured 22
to take an oath, and the adjuration is made before thy
altar in this house, then do thou hear from heaven and 23
act: be thou thy servants' judge, requiting the guilty man
and bringing his deeds upon his own head, acquitting the
innocent and rewarding him as his innocence may
deserve.

'When thy people Israel are defeated by an enemy 24
because they have sinned against thee, and they turn back
to thee, confessing thy name and making their prayer and
supplication before thee in this house, do thou hear from 25
heaven; forgive the sin of thy people Israel and restore
them to the land which thou gavest to them and to their
forefathers.

'When the heavens are shut up and there is no rain, 26
because thy servant*a* and thy people Israel have sinned
against thee, and when they pray towards this place, confessing thy name and forsaking their sin when they feel
thy punishment, do thou hear in*b* heaven and forgive 27
their sin; so mayest thou teach them the good way which
they should follow, and grant rain to thy land which
thou hast given to thy people as their own possession.

'If there is famine in the land, or pestilence, or black 28
blight or red, or locusts new-sloughed or fully grown, or

[a] *So Pesh.; Heb.* servants.
[b] *Or, with Sept.,* from.

165

if their enemies besiege them in any[a] of their cities, or if
29 plague or sickness befall them, then hear the prayer or
supplication of every man among thy people Israel, as
each one, prompted by his own suffering and misery,
30 spreads out his hands towards this house; hear it from
heaven thy dwelling and forgive. And, as thou knowest a
man's heart, reward him according to his deeds, for thou
31 alone knowest the hearts of all men; and so they will fear
and obey thee all their lives in the land thou gavest to our
forefathers.

32 'The foreigner too, the man who does not belong to
thy people Israel, but has come from a distant land because of thy great fame and thy strong hand and arm
outstretched, when he comes and prays towards this
33 house, hear from heaven thy dwelling and respond to the
call which the foreigner makes to thee, so that like thy
people Israel all peoples of the earth may know thy fame
and fear thee, and learn that this house which I have built
bears thy name.

34 'When thy people go to war with their enemies,
wherever thou dost send them, and they pray to thee,
turning towards this city which thou hast chosen and
towards this house which I have built in honour of thy
35 name, do thou from heaven hear their prayer and
supplication, and grant them justice.

36 'Should they sin against thee (and what man is free
from sin?) and shouldst thou in thy anger give them over
to an enemy, who carries them captive to a land far or
37 near; if in the land of their captivity they learn their
lesson and turn back and make supplication to thee in

[a] in any: *prob. rdg.*; *Heb.* in the land.

that land and say, "We have sinned and acted perversely and wickedly", if they turn back to thee with heart and 38 soul in the land of their captivity to which they have been taken, and pray, turning towards their land which thou gavest to their forefathers and towards this city which thou didst choose and this house which I have built in honour of thy name; then from heaven thy dwelling do 39 thou hear their prayer and supplications and grant them justice. Forgive thy people their sins against thee. Now, 40 O my God, let thine eyes be open and thy ears attentive to the prayer made in this place. Arise now, O LORD God, 41 and come to thy place of rest, thou and the Ark of thy might. Let thy priests, O LORD God, be clothed with salvation and thy saints rejoice in prosperity. O LORD 42 God, reject not thy anointed prince;*a* remember thy servant David's loyal service.'*b*

---

* In this section the Chronicler is content to draw upon the earlier material almost verbatim. In two ways in particular it is likely to have expressed what he wanted to emphasize to his own readers: the picture of a God whom heaven and earth could not contain and who yet condescended to let his name dwell in this temple; and the picture of the community in exile, who might still be restored to divine favour through prayer and repentance. It is likely that the prayer in I Kings 8 did not reach its present form until the leaders of the people were exiled to Babylon, and this viewpoint would tie in well with the Chronicler's own emphasis on the exile of all the faithful community. The theology of the whole prayer deserves careful study; it is possible here only to comment on

[a] *So many MSS.; others* princes.
[b] thy servant...service: *or* thy constant love for David thy servant.

those sections which appear to embody a distinctive contribution by the Chronicler.

13. This verse is an addition to the earlier text, probably
representing the liturgical custom of the Chronicler's own
day and associating it with Solomonic practice.

16. *conform to my law:* an addition characteristic of the period
after the exile, when the law (*torah*) was increasingly becoming
the guiding principle of Israel's life. We need not suppose
any formal canonization had taken place to recognize here
the beginnings of the idea of a body of sacred scripture.

32–3. The fact that the Chronicler includes this section of
the prayer from 1 Kings is notable in view of the charge
sometimes laid against him of a narrow nationalistic attitude.
The specific measures taken by Ezra and Nehemiah against
foreign marriages should not be seen as a contradiction of this.

40–2. Instead of a reference to the deliverance from Egypt,
which closes the Kings version of the prayer, the Chronicler
has substituted a hymnic section based on Ps. 132: 8–10, a
psalm associated with the bringing of the Ark into Jerusalem. ✶

SOLOMON'S PRAYER ACCEPTED

7 When Solomon had finished this prayer, fire came down
from heaven and consumed the whole-offering and the
sacrifices, while the glory of the LORD filled the house.
2 The priests were unable to enter the house of the LORD
3 because the glory of the LORD had filled it. All the Israelites
were watching as the fire came down with the glory of
the LORD on the house, and where they stood on the
paved court they bowed low to the ground and worshipped and gave thanks to the LORD, because 'that[a] is
good, for his love endures for ever.'

[a] *Or* he.

Then the king and all the people offered sacrifice before 4
the LORD. King Solomon offered a sacrifice of twenty- 5
two thousand oxen and a hundred and twenty thousand
sheep; in this way the king and all the people dedicated
the house of God. The priests stood at their appointed 6
posts; so too the Levites with their musical instruments
for the LORD's service, which King David had made for
giving thanks to the LORD – 'for his love endures for
ever' – whenever he rendered praise with their help;
opposite them, the priests sounded their trumpets; and
all the Israelites were standing there.

Then Solomon consecrated the centre of the court 7*a*
which lay in front*b* of the house of the LORD; there he
offered the whole-offerings and the fat portions of the
shared-offerings, because the bronze altar which he had
made could not take the whole-offering, the grain-
offering, and the fat portions. So Solomon and all Israel 8
with him, a very great assembly from Lebo-hamath to
the Torrent of Egypt, celebrated the pilgrim-feast at that
time for seven days. On the eighth day they held a closing 9
ceremony; for they had celebrated the dedication of the
altar for seven days; the pilgrim-feast lasted seven days.
On the twenty-third day of the seventh month he sent 10
the people to their homes, happy and glad at heart for all
the prosperity granted by the LORD to David and Solomon and to his people Israel.

When Solomon had finished the house of the LORD and 11
the royal palace and had successfully carried out all that
he had planned for the house of the LORD and the palace,
the LORD appeared to him by night and said, 'I have 12

[a] *Verses 7–22: cp. 1 Kgs. 8: 64 – 9: 9.*   [b] *Or to the east.*

heard your prayer and I have chosen this place to be my
13 place of sacrifice. When I shut up the heavens and there is
no rain, or command the locusts to consume the land, or
14 send a pestilence against my people, if my people whom
I have named my own submit and pray to me and seek
me and turn back from their evil ways, I will hear from
15 heaven and forgive their sins and heal their land. Now my
eyes will be open and my ears attentive to the prayers
16 which are made in this place. I have chosen and consecrated this house, that my Name may be there for all time
17 and my eyes and my heart be fixed on it for ever. And if
you, on your part, live in my sight as your father David
lived, doing all I command you, and observing my
18 statutes and my judgements, then I will establish your
royal throne, as I promised by a covenant granted to your
father David when I said, "You shall never want for a
19 man to rule over Israel." But if you turn away and forsake my statutes and my commandments which I have
set before you, and if you go and serve other gods and
20 prostrate yourselves before them, then I will uproot you*a*
from my land which I gave you,*a* I will reject this house
which I have consecrated in honour of my name, and
make it a byword and an object-lesson among all peoples.
21 And this house will become a ruin;*b* every passer-by will
be appalled at the sight of it, and they will ask, "Why
22 has the LORD so treated this land and this house?" The
answer will be, "Because they forsook the LORD the God
of their fathers, who brought them out of Egypt, and
clung to other gods, prostrating themselves before them

[a] *So Sept.; Heb.* them.
[b] will become a ruin: *so Pesh.; Heb.* which was high.

and serving them; that is why the LORD has brought this great evil on them.'"

* Though much of the material here is found in Kings it is differently ordered, and it appears that the Chronicler's purpose is to emphasize the direct divine response to prayer when rightly and faithfully offered. This is brought out both by the dramatic picture in the first verse and by the divine promises in the last part of the chapter.

1. The divine response is immediate; God's acceptance of prayer is set out in words reminiscent both of 1 Chron. 21: 26 and of the response to Elijah's prayer in the contest on Mount Carmel (1 Kings 18: 38). Once again, as in 5: 13, reference is made to *the glory of the LORD*, as if it were a physical object which *filled the house*, indicating by its presence the divine favour.

3. '*that is good, for his love endures for ever*': a further link with 5: 13 is provided by the use by the assembly of this liturgical refrain, found frequently in the Psalms (cp. Ps. 136) and referred to once again in verse 6.

6. Emphasis is laid upon all the liturgical arrangements being carried out correctly in accordance with the provision laid down by David.

7–23. As the N.E.B. footnote indicates, the remainder of the chapter corresponds closely with 1 Kings. Where there are minor differences, it is not easy to determine whether they are deliberate changes by the Chronicler, or whether the text of Kings which he had before him differed somewhat from that available to us. This might well explain the minor variations in the dating (verses 8–9), as well as the expansion of the Kings text as known to us at verses 13–15. The omission of the Kings reference to Gibeon (verse 12; cp. 1 Kings 9: 2) is more likely to be deliberate; attention is now to be focused on Jerusalem.

21. *this house will become a ruin*: as the N.E.B. footnote

indicates, the translators have here followed the Syriac rather than the Hebrew text. It may be that both have retained parts of the correct original, and that we should translate: 'this house which is high will become a ruin'. By contrast with the Kings text the emphasis here is more markedly on the fate of the temple than on that of the people.

22. *who brought them out of Egypt:* it is noteworthy that not all references to the exodus have been omitted.   ✴

SOLOMON'S OTHER ACHIEVEMENTS

8 1[a] Solomon had taken twenty years to build the house of
2 the LORD and his own palace, and he rebuilt the cities which Huram had given him and settled Israelites in
3, 4 them. He went to Hamath-zobah and seized it, and rebuilt Tadmor in the wilderness and all the store-cities
5 which he had built in Hamath. He also built Upper Beth-horon and Lower Beth-horon as fortified cities with walls
6 and barred gates, and Baalath, as well as all his store-cities, and all the towns where he quartered his chariots and horses; and he carried out all his cherished plans for building in Jerusalem, in the Lebanon, and throughout
7 his whole dominion. All the survivors of the Hittites, Amorites, Perizzites, Hivites, and Jebusites, who did not
8 belong to Israel – that is their descendants who survived in the land, wherever the Israelites had been unable to exterminate them – were employed by Solomon on
9 forced labour, as they still are. He put none of the Israelites to forced labour for his public works; they were his fighting men, his captains and lieutenants,[b] and the com-

[a] *Verses 1–18: cp. 1 Kgs. 9: 10–28.* [b] his captains and lieutenants: so Sept.; Heb. the captains of his lieutenants.

manders of his chariots and of his cavalry. These were 10
King Solomon's officers, two hundred and fifty of them,
in charge of the foremen who superintended the people.

Solomon brought Pharaoh's daughter up from the 11
City of David to the house he had built for her, for he
said, 'No wife of mine shall live in the house of David
king of Israel, because this place which the Ark of the
LORD has entered is[a] holy.'

Then Solomon offered whole-offerings to the LORD on 12
the altar which he had built to the east of the vestibule,
according to what was required for each day, making 13
offerings according to the law of Moses for the sabbaths,
the new moons, and the three annual appointed feasts –
the pilgrim-feasts of Unleavened Bread, of Weeks, and
of Tabernacles.[b] Following the practice of his father 14
David, he drew up the roster of service for the priests and
that for the Levites for leading the praise and for waiting
upon the priests, as each day required, and that for the
door-keepers at each gate; for such was the instruction
which David the man of God had given. The instructions 15
which David had given concerning the priests and the
Levites and concerning the treasuries were not forgotten.

By this time all Solomon's work was achieved, from 16
the foundation of the house of the LORD to its completion;
the house of the LORD was perfect. Then Solomon went 17
to Ezion-geber and to Eloth on the coast of Edom, and 18
Huram sent ships under the command of his own officers
and manned by crews of experienced seamen; and these,
in company with Solomon's servants, went to Ophir and

[a] this place which...is: *prob. rdg.; Heb.* those which...are.
[b] *Or* Booths.

brought back four hundred and fifty talents of gold, which they delivered to King Solomon.

* A modern historian, describing the reign of Solomon, would probably give only a small place to the temple-building, and would lay greater emphasis on the other public buildings which were larger and no doubt more impressive. Such an assessment is quite foreign to the point of view of the biblical writers, and in both Kings and Chronicles the description of the temple and its dedication are the main matters of concern. Now a summary account of the rest of Solomon's achievement is given. For the most part 1 Kings 9 is followed, as the footnote indicates, but there are a number of minor points of difference.

2. *he rebuilt the cities which Huram had given him:* in the days before critical study of the Bible began, great ingenuity was exercised over this verse, for the Kings text is specific that Solomon had ceded the cities, not received them. Instead of elaborating theories about otherwise unknown events, it is much more realistic to recognize that the Chronicler simply could not believe that Solomon would have had to part with any land, however worthless (cp. 1 Kings 9: 13 and the N.E.B. footnote there), and so he pictured the transaction as taking place in the other direction.

3. *He went to Hamath-zobah and seized it:* nothing else is known of such a campaign on Solomon's part, which would have taken him far to the north. It is doubtful whether a genuine historical memory is preserved here, for – though Hamath and Zobah are each referred to separately in Samuel and Kings – there is no evidence to link them together earlier than the Persian period. Hamath is the ideal northern boundary of Israel (cp. 7: 8); the exact location of Zobah is unknown.

4. *Tadmor in the wilderness:* this is the great oasis city of Palmyra, a site of vital importance on the caravan route from

Mesopotamia to Palestine. But once again the Chronicler's imagination has been at work in the glorification of Solomon, for the original reference was to Tamar (1 Kings 9: 18), a much more modest spot in the Judaean wilderness.

10. *two hundred and fifty of them:* the difference from 1 Kings 9: 23, where the number is 'five hundred and fifty', is no doubt due to textual corruption, but we have no means of telling which figure is original and more likely to be correct.

11. *No wife of mine shall live in the house of David king of Israel:* this ungallant-sounding remark is attributed to Solomon by the Chronicler, who has added it to the Kings text. No reference has been made to the Kings account of Solomon's marriage with the Pharaoh's daughter. But this fact is taken for granted, and suitable religious sentiments attributed to Solomon which help to modify any offence his action might have caused. *this place:* the N.E.B. has modified the Hebrew text here (see footnote) – this may be correct, or the original reference may be to all places associated with the procession of the Ark.

12–15. Once again the theme of Solomon's faithfulness to the plans laid down by David in accordance with the Mosaic Law is stressed.

16. *the house of the LORD was perfect:* the idea here being expressed is not simply that the work was now complete – implicit also is the notion of its fittingness and acceptability.

17. *Solomon went to Ezion-geber:* such a detail is historically improbable and is not supported by 1 Kings. The intention is probably to stress how Solomon himself takes the initiative and is not dependent upon Huram. ✶

SOLOMON'S WEALTH

The queen of Sheba heard of Solomon's fame and came **9** 1[a] to test him with hard questions. She arrived in Jerusalem with a very large retinue, camels laden with spices, gold

[a] *Verses 1–24: cp. 1 Kgs. 10: 1–25.*

in abundance, and precious stones. When she came to
Solomon, she told him everything she had in her mind,
2 and Solomon answered all her questions; not one of them
3 was too abstruse for him to answer. When the queen of
Sheba saw the wisdom of Solomon, the house which he
4 had built, the food on his table, the courtiers sitting round
him, his attendants and his cup-bearers in their livery
standing behind, and the stairs by which he went up to*a*
the house of the LORD, there was no more spirit left in her.
5 Then she said to the king, 'The report which I heard in
my own country about you*b* and your wisdom was true,
6 but I did not believe what they told me until I came and
saw for myself. Indeed, I was not told half of the greatness of your wisdom; you surpass the report which I had
7 of you. Happy are your wives,*c* happy these courtiers of
yours who wait on you every day and hear your wisdom!
8 Blessed be the LORD your God who has delighted in you
and has set you on his throne as his king; because in his
love your God has elected Israel to make it endure for
ever, he has made you king over it to maintain law and
9 justice.' Then she gave the king a hundred and twenty
talents of gold, spices in great abundance, and precious
stones. There had never been any spices to equal those
which the queen of Sheba gave to King Solomon.

10   Besides all this, the servants of Huram and of Solomon,
who had brought gold from Ophir, brought also cargoes
11 of algum wood and precious stones. The king used the
wood to make stands*d* for the house of the LORD and for

[a] stairs...up to: *or, with Sept.*, whole-offerings which he used to
offer in...   [b] *Lit.* your affairs.   [c] *So Luc. Sept.; Heb.* men.
[d] *Mng. of Heb. word uncertain.*

the royal palace, as well as harps and lutes for the singers.
The like of them had never before been seen in the land of
Judah.

King Solomon gave the queen of Sheba all she desired, 12
whatever she asked, besides his gifts in return for*a* what
she had brought him. Then she departed and returned
with her retinue to her own land.

Now the weight of gold which Solomon received 13
yearly was six hundred and sixty-six talents, in addition 14
to the tolls*b* levied on merchants and on traders who imported goods; all the kings of Arabia and the regional
governors also*c* brought gold and silver to the king.

King Solomon made two hundred shields of beaten 15
gold, and six hundred shekels of gold went to the making
of each one; he also made three hundred bucklers of 16
beaten gold, and three hundred shekels of gold went to
the making of each buckler. The king put these into the
House of the Forest of Lebanon.

The king also made a great throne of ivory and over- 17
laid it with pure gold. Six steps and a footstool for the 18
throne were all encased in gold. There were arms on each
side of the seat, with a lion standing beside each of them,
and twelve lions stood on the six steps, one at either end 19
of each step. Nothing like it had ever been made for any
monarch. All Solomon's drinking vessels were of gold, 20
and all the plate in the House of the Forest of Lebanon
was of red gold; silver was reckoned of no value in the
days of Solomon. The king had a fleet of ships plying to 21
Tarshish with Huram's men; once every three years this

[a] his gifts...for: *prob. rdg.; Heb. om.*   [b] *So Pesh.; Heb.* men.
[c] all...also: *or* and on all the kings of Arabia and the regional
governors who...

fleet of merchantmen[a] came home, bringing gold and silver, ivory, apes, and monkeys.

22, 23 Thus King Solomon outdid all the kings of the earth in wealth and wisdom, and all the kings of the earth courted him, to hear the wisdom which God had put in his heart.

24 Each brought his gift with him, vessels of silver and gold, garments, perfumes and spices, horses and mules, so much year by year.

25[b] Solomon had standing for four thousand horses and chariots, and twelve thousand cavalry horses, and he stabled some in the chariot-towns and kept others at hand

26 in Jerusalem. He ruled over all the kings from the Euphrates to the land of the Philistines and the border of

27 Egypt. He made silver as common in Jerusalem as stones, and cedar as plentiful as sycomore-fig in the Shephelah.

28 Horses were imported from Egypt and from all countries for Solomon.

29[c] The rest of the acts of Solomon's reign, from first to last, are recorded in the history of Nathan the prophet, in the prophecy of Ahijah of Shiloh, and in the visions of

30 Iddo the seer concerning Jeroboam son of Nebat. Solomon ruled in Jerusalem over the whole of Israel for forty

31 years. Then he rested with his forefathers and was buried in the city of David his father, and he was succeeded by his son Rehoboam.

* The account continues to follow that in 1 Kings in broad outline, though now with a major and significant omission. Whereas the Kings account, after a highly favourable des-

[a] *Lit.* ships of Tarshish.   [b] *Verses 25–8: cp. 1: 14–17; 1 Kgs. 10: 26–9.*   [c] *Verses 29–31: cp. 1 Kgs. 11: 41–3.*

cription of Solomon and his achievements, turns in its last chapter (11) to a condemnation of his many foreign wives and concubines and his involvement with foreign religious practice, the Chronicler passes over this in silence. The Kings account prepares its readers for the division of the kingdom by recounting prophetic signs which were already given in Solomon's reign; the Chronicler introduces the break as a bolt from the blue, and no sign of impending disaster clouds the picture of Solomon, second only to David in the divine favour.

1–12. The story of the queen of Sheba follows that in Kings, with only minor differences.

7. The N.E.B. emendation of the Hebrew text is a very minor one (see footnote), but may not be correct; it would scarcely be acceptable for the Chronicler to hear Solomon's (foreign) wives praised.

18. *Six steps and a footstool for the throne were all encased in gold:* for the most part the account of Solomon's wealth follows Kings very closely, but a detail here is omitted ('at the back of the throne there was the head of a calf', 1 Kings 10: 19), probably because it was felt to transgress the second commandment.

21. *ships plying to Tarshish:* this may be a 'learned' correction by the Chronicler. The Kings text had 'ships of Tarshish' as does the later part of this verse (cp. N.E.B. footnote, and 1 Kings 10: 22), but by the Chronicler's time Tarshish was known of as a place in the far distance to which ships might sail (Jonah 1: 3). The Chronicler therefore imagines that Solomon's fleet was in the Mediterranean, rather than in the Red Sea.

25–8. These verses have already appeared in very similar form in 1: 14–17 (see N.E.B. footnote), and thus provide further evidence of a continuing editorial process within the circle which we call 'the Chronicler'.

26. *from the Euphrates to the land of the Philistines and the border of Egypt:* the Old Testament contains numerous

statements of what the borders of Israel were, or were thought ideally to be. This is one of the most extensive visions, and is paralleled in 1 Kings 4: 21.

29. *The rest of the acts:* as the N.E.B. footnote shows, the Chronicler passes directly from 1 Kings 10 to 1 Kings 11: 41. This means that the whole of the condemnation of Solomon is omitted. It is probably too simple to say that he wished to hide that aspect, which must have been familiar to his readers; rather, he wished to focus attention especially on the positive aspect of Solomon's reign and in particular the temple-building. *the history of Nathan the prophet:* this has already been mentioned in 1 Chron. 29: 29. It seems unlikely that any of the three works mentioned here are genuine ancient records to which the Chronicler had access, especially in view of his heavy dependence on Kings for his account of Solomon's reign. The references to Nathan and Ahijah are probably allusions to the material in Kings; Iddo is unknown, though there are further references to him in 12: 15 and 13: 22. *

The kings of Judah from Rehoboam to Ahaz

* The remainder of 2 Chronicles, save for the last three verses, deals with the period covered by 1 Kings 12 – 2 Kings 25, and, as with the account of Solomon's reign, is for the most part dependent on the earlier work as its source. But there are important differences to be borne in mind: the Chronicler's attention is focused on the southern kingdom, so the Kings material dealing with the north is omitted; on the other hand, the Chronicler introduces a number of stories which have no corresponding material in Kings. In the past

these stories have been judged in accordance with scholars' estimates of their historical reliability (which have generally been disparaging), but, as has already been suggested, it is more helpful to consider them primarily as contributions to the Chronicler's own theological presentation. This point should also be borne in mind in a number of places in which the Chronicler makes significant changes in the Kings material. ✻

THE ACCESSION OF REHOBOAM

REHOBOAM WENT TO SHECHEM, for all Israel had 10 1[a] gone there to make him king. When Jeroboam son 2 of Nebat heard of it in Egypt, where he had taken refuge to escape Solomon, he returned from Egypt. They now 3 recalled him, and he and all Israel came to Rehoboam and said, 'Your father laid a cruel yoke upon us; but if you 4 will now lighten the cruel slavery he imposed on us and the heavy yoke he laid on us, we will serve you.' 'Give 5 me three days,' he said, 'and come back again.' So the people went away. King Rehoboam then consulted the 6 elders who had been in attendance on his father Solomon while he lived: 'What answer do you advise me to give to this people?' And they said, 'If you show yourself 7 well-disposed to this people and gratify them by speaking kindly to them, they will be your servants ever after.' But he rejected the advice which the elders gave him. 8 He next consulted those who had grown up with him, the young men in attendance, and asked them, 'What 9 answer do you advise me to give to this people's request that I should lighten the yoke which my father laid on

[a] *Verses 1–19: cp. 1 Kgs. 12: 1–19.*

181

10 them?' The young men replied, 'Give this answer to the
people who say that your father made their yoke heavy
and ask you to lighten it; tell them: "My little finger is
11 thicker than my father's loins. My father laid a heavy
yoke on you; I will make it heavier. My father used the
12 whip on you; but I will use the lash."' Jeroboam and the
people all came back to Rehoboam on the third day, as
13 the king had ordered. And the king gave them a harsh
answer. He rejected the advice which the elders had given
14 him and spoke to the people as the young men had
advised: 'My father made[a] your yoke heavy; I will make
it heavier. My father used the whip on you; but I will
15 use the lash.' So the king would not listen to the people;
for the LORD had given this turn to the affair, in order
that the word he had spoken by Ahijah of Shiloh to
Jeroboam son of Nebat might be fulfilled.

16   When all Israel saw[b] that the king would not listen to
them, they answered:

> What share have we in David?
> We have no lot in the son of Jesse.
> Away to your homes, O Israel;
> now see to your own house, David.

17 So all Israel went to their homes, and Rehoboam ruled
over those Israelites who lived in the cities of Judah.
18   Then King Rehoboam sent out Hadoram, the commander of the forced levies, but the Israelites stoned him
to death; whereupon King Rehoboam mounted his
19 chariot in haste and fled to Jerusalem. From that day to
this, Israel has been in rebellion against the house of David.

[a] My father made: *so some MSS.; others* I will make.   [b] saw: *prob.
rdg., cp. 1 Kgs. 12: 16; Heb. om.*

* This section is reproduced from 1 Kings 12: 1–19 almost without change, but the overall impression given is very different. The stress in 1 Kings 11 on the falling-away of Solomon led naturally to the expectation of trouble following his death; here no mention has been made of Solomon's misdeeds, and so Rehoboam is envisaged as following him in the natural order of events, and the division of the kingdom becomes a rebellion against God's chosen one. Only in verse 15 is there any indication that this action is agreeable to the divine plan, and even that allusion might be taken as implying a divine plan for the rejection of the northerners.

1. *Shechem:* this ancient site in the central hill-country was in later times the home of the Samaritans, but neither here nor elsewhere in Chronicles is there any indication of hostility towards it or its inhabitants. *all Israel:* here the Chronicler's use of this expression appears to us somewhat confusing. It was frequently used in Kings, and referred to the inhabitants of the northern kingdom, and in this chapter the Chronicler, following his source, has the same usage (see, in addition to this verse, verses 3 and 16). Elsewhere, however, the Chronicler uses it in a more restricted sense of the true people of God, i.e. those who remained loyal to the Davidic king in Jerusalem (so 12: 1 and elsewhere). The meaning in any given case can only be determined by the context.

2. *Jeroboam:* in 1 Kings he has already been introduced in the story of Solomon's reign; in Chronicles the only allusion so far has been the note in 2 Chron. 9: 29, so no mention is made of the rebellion which had led to his flight into Egypt. This appears to be part of the Chronicler's view that all was well in the time of Solomon.

3. In 1 Kings 12: 3 the suppliants are described as a *qahal* (N.E.B.: 'the assembly of Israel'). In the Chronicler's usage, however, the word *qahal* has become a religious term to describe the true followers of God, and is unacceptable in this context; he therefore omits it.

7. *If you show yourself well-disposed:* again perhaps a

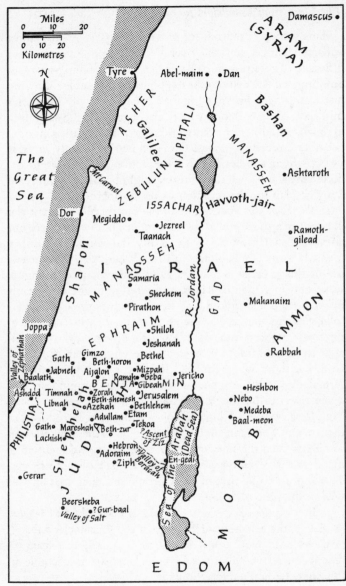

2. Map of the divided kingdoms.

184

deliberate modification of 'If today you are willing to serve' (1 Kings 12: 7).

15. *the word he had spoken by Ahijah of Shiloh:* here, as often in Chronicles, the wording of the source is followed, even though the event referred to is not included. Here the reference is to 1 Kings 11: 31–9, where Jeroboam is promised the rule over ten of the twelve tribes.

16–19. This section follows its source in Kings very closely and reaches its climax in the statement that the action of the northern tribes was 'rebellion against the house of David' (verse 19). The description of Jeroboam's establishment as king, in 1 Kings 12: 20, is omitted, and from this point the Chronicler refers to northern rulers only if the context of affairs in the south demands it.

16. This poetic fragment is found in 2 Sam. 20: 1, as well as in the source of its quotation here (1 Kings 12: 16). Its preservation by the Chronicler is remarkable, in view of the extreme reverence which he shows for David and his house; his view is closer to that expressed in 1 Chron. 12: 18, when Amasai's oath had emphasized continuing loyalty. The present passage enables us to see something of the great diversity which lay behind the façade of unity under David and Solomon as presented by both Kings and Chronicles.

18. *Hadoram:* this official's name is found in varying forms– Adoniram (1 Kings 4: 6), Adoram (1 Kings 12: 18, the source of this passage). He has not previously been mentioned by the Chronicler, since his idealized picture of Israel under Solomon left no room for *forced levies.* ✳

REHOBOAM ESTABLISHED AS KING

When Rehoboam reached Jerusalem, he assembled the **11** [a] tribes of Judah and Benjamin, a hundred and eighty thousand chosen warriors, to fight against Israel and

[a] *Verses 1–4: cp. 1 Kgs. 12: 21–4.*

2 recover his kingdom. But the word of the LORD came to
3 Shemaiah the man of God: 'Say to Rehoboam son of
Solomon, king of Judah, and to all the Israelites in Judah
4 and Benjamin, "This is the word of the LORD: You shall
not go up to make war on your kinsmen. Return to your
homes, for this is my will."' So they listened to the word
of the LORD and abandoned their campaign against Jeroboam.

5 Rehoboam resided in Jerusalem and built up the de-
6 fences of certain cities in Judah. The cities in Judah and
Benjamin which he fortified were Bethlehem, Etam,
7, 8 Tekoa, Beth-zur, Soco, Adullam, Gath, Mareshah, Ziph,
9, 10 Adoraim, Lachish, Azekah, Zorah, Aijalon, and Hebron.
11 He strengthened the fortifications of these fortified cities,
and put governors in them, as well as supplies of food,
21 oil, and wine. Also he stored shields and spears in every
one of the cities, and strengthened their fortifications.
Thus he retained possession of Judah and Benjamin.

* The establishment of Rehoboam's kingdom is first described, with an explanation of the continuing division, which
is seen as God's will as revealed to a man of God. His defensive
measures are then described in a section which is not paralleled
in Kings.

1. *a hundred and eighty thousand chosen warriors:* just as the
accounts of the cultic arrangements under David and Solomon
often contained impossibly large numbers, so the size of the
armies in the various battles fought during the time of the
divided monarchy will show the same phenomenon. Little
purpose is served by seeking detailed explanations – they are
meant simply to create an impression of great size. Such a
device was not first used by the Chronicler – in this case, it
was already in his source (1 Kings 12: 21).

2. *Shemaiah* is one of the few prophets from the southern kingdom who is mentioned in the historical accounts. Like Moses, Elijah and other great prophetic figures, he is described as a *man of God*, a term used to denote anyone whose words and actions showed him to be in specially close touch with the divine.

6–10. The cities listed are all identifiable with a fair degree of confidence (see p. 184). The Chronicler had access to a source other than Kings, but we have no means of telling whether the fortifications here described really date to the time of Rehoboam or should be ascribed to a later ruler.   ✳

REHOBOAM'S RELIGIOUS STANDING

Now the priests and the Levites throughout the whole 13 of Israel resorted to Rehoboam from all their territories; for the Levites had left all their common land and their 14 own patrimony and had gone to Judah and Jerusalem, because Jeroboam and his successors rejected their services as priests of the LORD, and he appointed his own priests 15 for the hill-shrines, for the demons,[a] and for the calves which he had made. Those, from all the tribes of Israel, 16 who were resolved to seek the LORD the God of Israel followed the Levites to Jerusalem to sacrifice to the LORD the God of their fathers. So they strengthened the king- 17 dom of Judah and for three years made Rehoboam son of Solomon secure, because he[b] followed the example of David and Solomon during that time.

Rehoboam married Mahalath, whose father was Jeri- 18 moth son of David and whose mother was Abihail daughter of Eliab son of Jesse. His sons by her were: 19

[a] *Or* satyrs.   [b] *So Sept.; Heb.* they.

20 Jeush, Shemariah and Zaham. Next he married Maacah granddaughter*a* of Absalom, who bore him Abijah, Attai,
21 Ziza and Shelomith. Of all his wives and concubines, Rehoboam loved Maacah most; he had in all eighteen wives and sixty concubines and became the father of
22 twenty-eight sons and sixty daughters. He appointed Abijah son of Maacah chief among his brothers, making him crown prince and planning*b* to make him his succes-
23 sor on the throne. He showed discretion in detailing his sons to take charge of all the fortified cities throughout the whole territory of Judah and Benjamin; he also made generous provision for them and procured them*c* wives.

✶ The previous section saw the kingdom established on a solid political and military foundation; now all true religious leaders gather to Rehoboam. The account of his reign is given in a way which is very characteristic of the Chronicler's treatment of kings of Judah. During part of his reign Rehoboam is pictured as carrying out God's will and prospering as a result; the next chapter will show how his falling-away led to the withdrawal of divine favour. The reigns of several kings are described either in this form (e.g. Josiah in ch. 35) or by picturing a period of wickedness followed by repentance (e.g. Manasseh in ch. 33). Such an appraisal is clearly to be described as theological rather than historical.

13. *the priests and the Levites throughout the whole of Israel:* the faithfulness of these groups is axiomatic for the Chronicler, and he therefore elaborates the note at 1 Kings 12: 31, which speaks of Jeroboam appointing non-Levitical priests, to show how all true priests and Levites rallied round the true sanctuary in Jerusalem.

[a] *Lit.* daughter.   [b] planning: *so Vulg.; Heb. om.*   [c] procured them: *prob. rdg.; Heb.* asked for a multitude of...

15. *for the demons, and for the calves which he had made:* exactly what form of worship is implied by *demons* is not known: the word comes from a root meaning 'hairy ones' and the N.E.B. footnote 'satyrs' may suggest goat-formed deities. There may be a reference to Lev. 17: 7, where the same word is used, and Jeroboam is pictured as contravening the law. *the calves* provide a more specific reference to the setting up of such images by Jeroboam at Bethel and Dan (1 Kings 12: 28-33), an action regarded as idolatrous by the editors of Kings, a judgement which the Chronicler takes for granted.

16. *to seek the LORD:* the implication clearly is that Jeroboam had altogether forsaken true worship, though historically such a judgement seems questionable. On the Chronicler's presuppositions no true worship was possible outside Jerusalem – hence the contrast with the man-made objects of worship of the north.

17. *three years:* the reference is apparently to the period before the falling-away described in 12: 1 took place, and therefore the Hebrew text, which refers to the behaviour of the whole people rather than to Rehoboam alone, may be correct (cp. the N.E.B. footnote).

18-23. These details of Rehoboam's family are not found in 1 Kings, save for the reference to Maacah, and it is possible that here the Chronicler had access to ancient and reliable information.

20. *granddaughter of Absalom:* on the assumption that the Absalom here mentioned is the son of David, the N.E.B. has *granddaughter* in place of the original 'daughter' (see footnote), for 2 Sam. 14: 27 implies that Absalom's only daughter was Tamar, who would no doubt have been past child-bearing age by this time. But the details of Absalom's family are in any case confused (cp. 2 Sam. 18: 18), and the identity of Maacah remains uncertain (cp. also 13: 2).

22. *Abijah:* in 1 Kings he is called 'Abijam', but here as in a few other cases it is possible that the Chronicler has

preserved a more accurate form, which means 'Yah(weh) is my father'.

23. The first half of this verse shows Rehoboam carrying on his father Solomon's policy; the meaning of the last phrase is not clear. The Hebrew reads: 'he asked for a multitude of wives' (cp. the N.E.B. footnote), and many suggestions have been made as to how this text might be understood or emended to make sense – e.g. that the 'asking' refers to resorting to the foreign gods whom his wives worshipped; on the whole the N.E.B. rendering, though speculative, is as likely as any. *

REHOBOAM FALLS AWAY AND IS PUNISHED

12 When the kingdom of Rehoboam was on a firm foot-
ing and he became strong, he forsook the law of the LORD,
2 he and all Israel with him. In the fifth year of Rehoboam's
reign, because of this disloyalty to the LORD, Shishak king
3 of Egypt attacked Jerusalem with twelve hundred chariots
and sixty thousand horsemen, and brought with him
from Egypt an innumerable following of Libyans,
4 Sukkites, and Cushites.*[a]* He captured the fortified cities of
5 Judah and reached Jerusalem. Then Shemaiah the prophet
came to Rehoboam and the leading men of Judah, who
had assembled in Jerusalem before the advance of Shishak,
and said to them, 'This is the word of the LORD: You
have abandoned me; therefore I now abandon you to
6 Shishak.' The princes of Israel and the king submitted and
7 said, 'The LORD is just.' When the LORD saw that they
had submitted, there came from him this word to
Shemaiah: 'Because they have submitted I will not destroy them, I will let them barely escape; my wrath shall

[a] *Or* Nubians.

190

not be poured out on Jerusalem by means of Shishak, but 8
they shall become his servants; then they will know the
difference between serving me and serving the rulers of
other countries.' Shishak king of Egypt in his attack on 9ᵃ
Jerusalem removed the treasures of the house of the
LORD and of the royal palace. He seized everything, including the shields of gold that Solomon had made. King 10
Rehoboam replaced them with bronze shields and entrusted them to the officers of the escort who guarded the
entrance of the royal palace. Whenever the king entered 11
the house of the LORD, the escort entered, carrying the
shields; afterwards they returned them to the guard-
room. Because Rehoboam submitted, the LORD's wrath 12
was averted from him, and he was not utterly destroyed;
Judah enjoyed prosperity.

✻ The invasion of Palestine by Egyptian forces is seen by the
Chronicler as being caused by Rehoboam's failure to remain
loyal to God. Whereas in other similar instances retribution
followed, Rehoboam is pictured as repenting and therefore
being spared extreme punishment. As so often in the Chronicler, genuine historical reminiscence is shaped in such a way
as to bring out the theological point which the writer wishes
to convey.

1. *he became strong*: the word translated *strong* usually has a
meaning similar to that in English, but here, as in some other
(mostly late) Old Testament passages, it means 'stubborn' or
'obstinate'. The same expression is used in 2 Chronicles of
Uzziah (26: 16), and a closely similar one of Pharaoh in
Exodus (7: 13; N.E.B. 'Pharaoh . . . was obstinate'). Perhaps
the Chronicler's intention was to contrast the two situations;
earlier the LORD had been with the Israelites in Egypt, and the

[a] *Verses 9–11: cp. 1 Kgs. 14: 25–8.*

Egyptian king stubbornly resists; now the LORD gives power to the Egyptian king against the stubbornness of his own people's king. *all Israel:* this refers to the faithful community around Jerusalem loyal to the Davidic king. For the Chronicler Israel is a religious rather than a political entity (cp. on 10: 1 above).

2. *Shishak:* the account of this invasion is partly based on 1 Kings 14: 25-8, but another source of information is also incorporated. Shishak was the Pharaoh Shoshenq I, who ruled over Egypt about 935-914 B.C., and who was originally a Libyan chieftain who had seized the throne.

3. *Sukkites:* not mentioned elsewhere in the Old Testament, they appear from Egyptian texts to have been light-armed mercenaries, perhaps of foreign origin.

5-8. *Shemaiah*, already mentioned in 11: 2, appears here as the mediator of God's word, both as bringing punishment and as accepting repentance. The speeches appear to be free compositions by the Chronicler and incorporate characteristic motifs from his theology. The theme of verse 5 is found again at 15: 2; of verse 7a at 7: 14; and of 7b at 34: 25. *

THE DEATH OF REHOBOAM

13[a] Thus King Rehoboam increased his power in Jerusalem. He was forty-one years old when he came to the throne, and he reigned for seventeen years in Jerusalem, the city which the LORD had chosen out of all the tribes of Israel as the place to receive his Name. Rehoboam's 14 mother was a woman of Ammon called Naamah. He did what was wrong, he did not make a practice of seeking 15 guidance of the LORD. The events of Rehoboam's reign, from first to last, are recorded in the histories of She-

[a] *Verses 13-16: cp. 1 Kgs. 14: 29-31.*

maiah the prophet and Iddo the seer.[a] There was continual fighting between Rehoboam and Jeroboam. He 16
rested with his forefathers and was buried in the city of
David; and he was succeeded by his son Abijah.

* This section is partially taken from the concluding summary of Rehoboam's reign in 1 Kings 14, where the judgement
upon him is less favourable than that of the Chronicler.

13. The dates of Rehoboam's reign were approximately
930 to 914 B.C.; certainty in dating is not possible at this
period, and many scholars have supposed that Rehoboam did
not in fact reign as long as is stated here and at 1 Kings 14: 21.

15. *the histories of Shemaiah the prophet and Iddo the seer:*
the latter of these works has already been referred to (9: 29);
both of them seem likely to be a means of claiming authen-
ticity for the Chronicler's work rather than survivals of
ancient writings. The Hebrew text adds a phrase 'to be
enrolled by genealogy', which is banished to a footnote by
most modern translations including the N.E.B. It appears to
be an abbreviation of a longer phrase whose meaning is no
longer known, but is perhaps concerned with Levitical
lists. *

ABIJAH'S 'SERMON ON THE MOUNT'

In the eighteenth year of King Jeroboam's reign Abijah 13
became king of Judah. He reigned in Jerusalem for three 2
years; his mother was Maacah[b] daughter of Uriel of
Gibeah. There was fighting between Abijah and Jeroboam. Abijah drew up his army of four hundred thousand 3
picked troops in order of battle, while Jeroboam formed

[a] *Prob. rdg.; Heb. adds* to be enrolled by genealogy.
[b] *So Sept., cp. 1 Kgs. 15: 2; Heb.* Micaiah.

up against him with eight hundred thousand picked
4 troops. Abijah took up position on the slopes of Mount
Zemaraim in the hill-country of Ephraim and called out,
5 'Hear me, Jeroboam and all Israel: Ought you not to
know that the LORD the God of Israel gave the kingship
over Israel to David and his descendants in perpetuity by
6 a covenant of salt? Yet Jeroboam son of Nebat, the servant of Solomon son of David, rose in rebellion against
7 his lord, and certain worthless scoundrels gathered round
him, who stubbornly opposed Solomon's son Rehoboam
when he was young and inexperienced, and he was no
8 match for them. Now you propose to match yourselves
against the kingdom of the LORD as ruled by David's sons,
you and your mob of supporters and the golden calves
9 which Jeroboam has made to be your gods. Have you not
dismissed from office the Aaronites, priests of the LORD,
and the Levites, and followed the practice of other lands
in appointing priests? Now, if any man comes for consecration with an offering of a young bull and seven rams,
10 you accept him as a priest to a god that is no god. But as
for us, the LORD is our God and we have not forsaken
him; we have Aaronites as priests ministering to the LORD
11 with the Levites, duly discharging their office.[a] Morning
and evening, these burn whole-offerings and fragrant
incense to the LORD and offer the Bread of the Presence
arranged in rows on a table ritually clean; they also kindle
the lamps on the golden lamp-stand every evening. Thus
we do indeed keep the charge of the LORD our God,
12 whereas you have forsaken him. God is with us at our
head, and his priests stand there with trumpets to signal

[a] duly...office: *so Sept.; Heb.* in the work.

the battle-cry against you. Men of Israel, do not fight the
LORD the God of your fathers; you will have no success.'

* Save for the introductory chronological note with the
reference to wars with Jeroboam, this section has no parallel
in 1 Kings. It has been described as Abijah's 'sermon on the
mount', in which the legitimacy of Jerusalem and of its cult
and worship is maintained against all rival claims.

2. *Maacah daughter of Uriel of Gibeah:* the variant traditions
enshrined here (notice the N.E.B. footnote) may suggest that
the Chronicler had more than one source, giving different
versions of Abijah's parentage (cp. also 11: 20). The Chronicler's source already mentioned wars between Abijah and
Jeroboam (1 Kings 15: 7), and it is unlikely that any further
independent information is enshrined here.

4. *Zemaraim:* the site is unknown, though it may be the
same as a place of the same name mentioned in Josh. 18: 22.

4*a*-12. The speech put into Abijah's mouth is intended for
the Chronicler's own contemporaries – not least those living
in the north – to reflect upon. It stresses the legitimacy of the
Davidic line as against the merely usurped claims of Jeroboam
and those who succeeded him; the continuation in Jerusalem
alone of the correct cult carried out by the proper ministers
of sacrifice; and the confidence that God would be with those
who remained loyal to him. All these themes would be
appropriate at any time for a speech asserting the claims of
Jerusalem, but it was particularly in the last centuries B.C.
that claims concerning true priesthood were a matter of
dispute.

5. *covenant of salt:* a permanent covenant. There may be an
allusion to Num. 18: 19, to show that the covenant there made
with Israel in the wilderness was equally applicable to the
Davidic line.

6f. Jeroboam's revolt against Solomon (1 Kings 11: 26-40)
is not mentioned in Chronicles, since it forms part of the

criticism of Solomon found in Kings of which the Chronicler makes no mention. Here as elsewhere (e.g. 10: 15), the author assumes knowledge of his sources. The picture of Rehoboam as *young and inexperienced* scarcely accords with the note that he was forty-one years old at the time of his accession (12: 13).

9. *the Aaronites:* the theory that all true priests were descendants of Aaron was developed in Jerusalem in the period after the exile, and is not alluded to in earlier writings. *a young bull and seven rams:* this is an exaggeration of the requirements of Exod. 29: 1, but that is a late text, and different customs concerning the consecration of priests may have existed.

10. The maintenance of the correct ritual at Jerusalem is affirmed, with the consequent assurance of God's presence.

12. *do not fight the LORD:* in a remarkable climax, Abijah asserts that to fight against Jerusalem is to fight against God himself, in which inevitably they will *have no success.* This last theme is picked up by Gamaliel in Acts 5: 39. *

THE LORD FIGHTS FOR HIS PEOPLE

13 Jeroboam sent a detachment of his troops to go round and lay an ambush in the rear, so that his main body faced
14 Judah while the ambush lay behind them. The men of Judah turned to find that they were engaged front and rear. Then they cried to the LORD for help. The priests
15 sounded their trumpets, and the men of Judah raised a shout, and when they did so, God put Jeroboam and all
16 Israel to rout before Abijah and Judah. The Israelites fled before the men of Judah, and God delivered them into
17 their power. So Abijah and his men defeated them with very heavy losses, and five hundred thousand picked
18 Israelites fell in the battle. After this, the Israelites were

reduced to submission, and Judah prevailed because they relied on the LORD the God of their fathers. Abijah fol- 19 lowed up his victory over Jeroboam and captured from him the cities of Bethel, Jeshanah, and Ephron, with their villages. Jeroboam did not regain his power during the 20 days of Abijah; finally the LORD struck him down and he died.

* This passage admirably reflects the Chronicler's idea of warfare. No human design is needed, nor can strategy prevail against God; God himself defeats his enemy's plans without human intervention.

18. *the Israelites were reduced to submission:* this is a theological reflection arising from the battle which has just been described and has no known historical basis. What is fairly certain historically is that there was continuous fighting between the two kingdoms; 1 Kings 14: 30 and 15: 7, 16f. imply constant hostility, which may well have been fiercest in the border-areas represented by the towns listed in verse 19.

20. *struck him down:* the verb is the same as that translated 'put...to rout' in verse 15, and would normally imply that Jeroboam died a violent death. There is no other evidence of this, and the intention here may simply be to stress that his death was the result of divine displeasure. *

THE DEATH OF ABIJAH

But Abijah established his position; he married fourteen 21 wives and became the father of twenty-two sons and sixteen daughters. The other events of Abijah's reign, 22 both what he said and what he did, are recorded in the story of the prophet Iddo. Abijah rested with his fore- **14** 1[a]

[a] *13: 23 in Heb.*

fathers and was buried in the city of David; and he was succeeded on the throne by his son Asa. In his days the land was at peace for ten years.

✲ This brief note contrasts the blessings which Abijah received with the fate of Jeroboam. The Chronicler's verdict on Abijah is in marked contrast with that found in 1 Kings 15: 3.

22. *the story of the prophet Iddo:* this is presumably the same source as is referred to in 9: 29 and 12: 15. The Hebrew word here translated *story* is *midrash*, a word found in the Old Testament in only two places, here and 2 Chron. 24: 27. In post-biblical Judaism this became extremely important as a term for the interpretation of biblical texts, often in a way that may seem to us very far-fetched, or to collections of such interpretations. Whether the word had already acquired this meaning when the Chronicler wrote is uncertain – there is a sense in which the work of the Chronicler could itself be regarded as a *midrash* on earlier biblical texts. But it may mean no more than 'book', with the more developed meaning of the word coming later. (See also *The Making of the Old Testament* in this series, pp. 169–71.)

14: 1. The period of peace referred to may have been in Abijah's reign or in Asa's – both the Hebrew and the N.E.B. are ambiguous at this point. ✲

KING ASA

2[a] Asa did what was good and right in the eyes of the
3 LORD his God. He suppressed the foreign altars and the
hill-shrines, smashed the sacred pillars and hacked down
4 the sacred poles, and ordered Judah to seek guidance of

[a] 14: 1 in Heb.

the LORD the God of their fathers and to keep the law and the commandments. He also suppressed the hill-shrines 5 and the incense-altars in all the cities, and the kingdom was at peace under him. He built fortified cities in Judah, 6 for the land was at peace. He had no war to fight during those years, because the LORD had given him security. He 7 said to the men of Judah, 'Let us build these cities and fortify them, with walls round them, and towers and barred gates. The land still lies open before us. Because we have sought guidance of the LORD our God, he has sought us and given us security on every side.' So they built and prospered.

Asa had an army equipped with shields and spears; 8 three hundred thousand men came from Judah, and two hundred and eighty thousand from Benjamin, shield-bearers and archers; all were valiant warriors. Zerah the 9 Cushite came out against them with an army a million strong and three hundred chariots. When he reached Mareshah, Asa came out to meet him and they took up 10 position in the valley of Zephathah at Mareshah. Asa 11 called upon the LORD his God and said, 'There is none like thee, O LORD, to help men, whether strong or weak; help us, O LORD our God, for on thee we rely and in thy name we have come out against this horde. O LORD, thou art our God, how can man vie with thee?' So the LORD 12 gave Asa and Judah victory over the Cushites and they fled, and Asa and his men pursued them as far as Gerar. 13 The Cushites broke before the LORD and his army, and many of them fell mortally wounded; and Judah carried off great loads of spoil. They destroyed all the cities around 14 Gerar, for the LORD had struck the people with panic; and

they plundered the cities, finding rich spoil in them all.
15 They also killed the herdsmen and seized many sheep and
camels, and then they returned to Jerusalem.

∗ Asa's reign, dealt with quite briefly in 1 Kings 15, is treated
at much greater length by the Chronicler and the account
illustrates many of his basic theological concerns. At the outset
he is pictured in wholly favourable terms, as is illustrated by
the defeat of the Cushites (verse 12) – an episode otherwise
unknown, the historicity of which is suspect. Human military
preparations are useless and the only proper preparation is
prayer to God. If this is rightly offered, he will bring about
the defeat of Israel's enemies. Such an understanding of war
is a prominent theme in 2 Chronicles.

3. *suppressed...the hill-shrines:* this statement is in flat
contradiction of 1 Kings 15: 14, and if the Chronicler's work
is understood as historical in intention, a problem is raised –
either he is an incompetent historian, or some form of harmonization must be resorted to. But if we understand the
overall aim of the Chronicler here as being to give an appraisal
of Asa's reign, then this is simply an indication of his good
standing before God.

3-5. The religious reforms here envisaged appear to be what
the Chronicler regarded as appropriate for a faithful ruler
rather than a record derived from an ancient source.

8f. In these verses, as on several previous occasions, the
numbers are greatly exaggerated; their significance is in the
impression they create of the greatness of God's saving acts.

10. *Mareshah:* this was one of the cities in the south which
had been fortified by Rehoboam (11: 8); *Zephathah* is
nowhere else mentioned in the Old Testament, so the exact
site envisaged for the battle is unknown.

11f. The pattern here described is one several times found
in the work of the Chronicler; when hostile armies are met,
the proper course of action is prayer, which leads to the

direct intervention of God on behalf of his people and ends
with a decisive victory.

13. *Gerar:* this city in the Philistine country south-west of
Judah is known from the story of Abraham and Isaac and
Abimelech in Gen. 20 and 26, but otherwise it is only men-
tioned here. It would appear from the references here to
have been in the disputed border area between Israel and
Egypt. ✶

ASA'S RELIGIOUS REFORMATION

The spirit of God came upon Azariah son of Oded, and **15** 1, 2
he went out to meet Asa and said to him, 'Hear me, Asa
and all Judah and Benjamin. The LORD is with you when
you are with him; if you look for him, he will let himself
be found; if you forsake him, he will forsake you. For a 3
long time Israel was without the true God, without a
priest to interpret the law and without law.*a* But when, 4
in their distress, they turned to the LORD the God of
Israel and sought him, he let himself be found by them.
At those times there was no safety for people as they went 5
about their business; the inhabitants of every land had
their fill of trouble; there was ruin on every side, nation 6
at odds with nation, city with city, for God harassed them
with every kind of distress. But now you must be strong 7
and not let your courage fail; for your work will be
rewarded.' When Asa heard these words,*b* he resolutely 8
suppressed the loathsome idols in all Judah and Benjamin
and in the cities which he had captured in the hill-country
of Ephraim; and he repaired the altar of the LORD which
stood before the vestibule of the LORD's house.*c* Then he 9

[*a*] without law: *or* without the law.   [*b*] *Prob. rdg.; Heb. adds* and the
prophecy, Oded the prophet.   [*c*] house: *prob. rdg.; Heb. om.*

assembled all Judah and Benjamin and all who had come from Ephraim, Manasseh, and Simeon to reside among them; for great numbers had come over to him from Israel, when they saw that the LORD his God was with
10 him. So they assembled at Jerusalem in the third month
11 of the fifteenth year of Asa's reign, and that day they sacrificed to the LORD seven hundred oxen and seven thousand sheep from the spoil which they had brought.
12 And they entered into a covenant to seek guidance of the LORD the God of their fathers with all their heart and
13 soul; all who would not seek the LORD the God of Israel were to be put to death, young and old, men and women
14 alike. Then they bound themselves by an oath to the LORD, with loud shouts of acclamation while trumpets
15 and horns sounded; and all Judah rejoiced at the oath, because they had bound themselves with all their heart and had sought him earnestly, and he had let himself be found by them. So the LORD gave them security on every
16[a] side. King Asa also deprived Maacah his grandmother[b] of her rank as queen mother because she had an obscene object made for the worship of Asherah; Asa cut it down, ground it to powder and burnt it in the gorge of the
17 Kidron. Although the hill-shrines were allowed to remain
18 in Israel, Asa himself remained faithful all his life. He brought into the house of God all his father's votive offerings and his own, gold and silver and sacred vessels.
19 And there was no more war until the thirty-fifth year of Asa's reign.

[a] *Verses 16–18: cp. 1 Kgs. 15: 13–15.* [b] *Lit.* mother.

* The acceptable policy of Asa already outlined in 14: 3–5 is now described in greater detail, and shown to be the result of prophetic preaching. The greater part of this chapter is found only in Chronicles, but the last verses have a parallel in 1 Kings 15.

1. *The spirit of God:* the idea, found in many of the early parts of the Old Testament, of the *spirit* (perhaps better: 'breath') *of God* guiding the actions of holy men is revived from the time of Ezekiel onwards, and is characteristic of the Chronicler. It is not confined to prophets; the same expression is used of a Levite in 20: 14 and of a priest in 24: 20. *Azariah son of Oded:* the name Azariah is a common one in the Old Testament, but there seems to be no ground for identifying this one with any of the others mentioned. He appears to be considered as a prophet, like his father (cp. the N.E.B. footnote to verse 8).

3. The period of the Judges appears to be envisaged here, though the book of Judges does not express Israel's deprivation in these terms. But for the Chronicler to be *without a priest* and *without law* (*torah*: it may be that the reference here is to the completed Pentateuch) was to be *without the true God*.

5–6. The picture here appears to be a summary of the anarchic conditions described at the end of Judges: 'In those days there was no king in Israel and every man did what was right in his own eyes' (Judg. 21: 25). The only way to overcome such a state of affairs is to suppress all alien forms of worship.

8. It seems likely that there was some confusion in the Chronicler's sources as to the origin of this prophecy, which is attributed to Azariah in verse 1 and to Oded according to the Hebrew text (see the N.E.B. footnote) here. It may be that to describe Azariah as 'son of Oded' (verse 1) is itself a harmonization of these discrepant traditions. It is a common occurrence in the Old Testament for the same prophecy to be attributed to different prophets. *loathsome idols:* this is only one word in Hebrew, since all idols were loathsome! It is

not found elsewhere in Chronicles, but the same word is used in Daniel concerning the idol put in the temple by the heathen king, 'the abominable thing that causes desolation' (Dan. 11: 31).

9. *Ephraim, Manasseh, and Simeon:* the grouping is curious, since Ephraim and Manasseh represented the two most important northern tribes, whereas Simeon was in the far south and had long since been absorbed into Judah. The twelve-tribe grouping was a religious rather than a political entity. In any case the sequel makes it clear that what is stated as past fact is really intended as present appeal: that all allegedly dissident elements throughout Israel should rally to the true Israel now to be found in Jerusalem. Such an appeal is a dominant concern of the Chronicler.

17. *in Israel:* the remainder of verses 16–18 follows 1 Kings 15: 13–15, but these words are inserted to avoid the inconsistency that would otherwise be present between this statement and that in 14: 3, 5 and 15: 8. *Israel* here must be taken to mean the northern kingdom. ✳

ASA'S WAR WITH BAASHA

16 1[a] In the thirty-sixth year of the reign of Asa, Baasha king of Israel invaded Judah and fortified Ramah to cut off all
2 access to Asa king of Judah. So Asa brought out silver and gold from the treasuries of the house of the LORD and the royal palace, and sent this request to Ben-hadad king of
3 Aram, whose capital was Damascus: 'There is an alliance between us, as there was between our fathers. I now send you herewith silver and gold; break off your alliance with Baasha king of Israel, so that he may abandon his cam-
4 paign against me.' Ben-hadad listened willingly to King

[a] *Verses 1–6: cp. 1 Kgs. 15: 17–22.*

Asa and ordered the commanders of his armies to move against the cities of Israel, and they attacked Iyyon, Dan, Abel-mayim, and all the store-cities of Naphtali. When 5 Baasha heard of it, he ceased fortifying Ramah and stopped all work on it. Then King Asa took with him all the 6 men of Judah and they carried away the stones of Ramah and the timbers with which Baasha had fortified it; and he used them to fortify Geba and Mizpah.

At that time the seer Hanani came to Asa king of Judah 7 and said to him, 'Because you relied on the king of Aram and not on the LORD your God, the army of the king of Israel[a] has escaped. The Cushites and the Libyans, were 8 they not a great army with a vast number of chariots and horsemen? Yet, because you relied on the LORD, he delivered them into your power. The eyes of the LORD 9 range through the whole earth, to bring aid and comfort to those whose hearts are loyal to him. You have acted foolishly in this affair; you will have wars from now on.' Asa was angry with the seer and put him in the stocks; 10 for these words of his had made the king very indignant. At the same time he treated some of the people with great brutality.

✵ Events described in 1 Kings are now used to show how different a fate befell Asa when he trusted in human alliances rather than praying for divine aid. At first all seems well, but a seer is sent to show Asa the folly of his ways.

1. *In the thirty-sixth year:* the chronology here cannot be reconciled with that of 1 Kings 15: 33. It is not clear why the Chronicler should have spoken of the thirty-sixth year, since the corresponding section in 1 Kings refers to war between the

[a] Israel: *so Luc. Sept.; Heb.* Aram.

205

two kings 'all through their reigns' (15: 16). But it is worth remembering that the Chronicler did not give the dates of northern rulers, so that the difficulty only arises if we compare the two presentations. It was not the Chronicler's purpose to resolve chronological problems.

2. The account in Kings is modified; there all the gold and silver were sent to Ben-hadad; here only some gold and silver were brought out, and a message sent to the Aramaean king. The offence of Asa is thus less heinous, and the continuity of the temple treasury emphasized.

7. The Aramaean diversionary attack in the north seems to mean that Asa's tactics have been successful, and in Kings they are so represented, but the Chronicler adds a note of condemnation. *Hanani* is presumably the father of Jehu, mentioned at 19: 2 and in 1 Kings 16. In 1 Kings, Jehu's words are directed against Baasha; here it is Asa whose faithlessness is condemned. *king of Israel:* this correction may be acceptable, but it is possible to understand the 'Aram' of the Hebrew text as implying that faithfulness would have brought Asa victory over all opposition.

10. The turning-away of Asa from the right path is now total, as is evidenced by his treatment of Hanani. The picture here may be influenced by the account of Jeremiah being similarly treated (Jer. 20: 2). *

SUMMARY OF ASA'S REIGN

11[a] The events of Asa's reign, from first to last, are recor-
12 ded in the annals of the kings of Judah and Israel. In the thirty-ninth year of his reign Asa became gravely affected with gangrene in his feet; he did not seek guidance of the
13 LORD but resorted to physicians. He rested with his fore-
14 fathers, in the forty-first year of his reign, and was buried in the tomb which he had bought[b] for himself in the city

[a] *Verses 11–14: cp. 1 Kgs. 15: 23, 24.*   [b] *Or* dug.

of David, being laid on a bier*a* which had been heaped with all kinds of spices skilfully compounded; and they kindled a great fire in his honour.

* This closing summary is largely based on 1 Kings, but the Chronicler stresses the continued falling away of Asa.

11. *are recorded in the annals of the kings of Judah and Israel:* whereas in the books of Kings a consistent pattern is followed in the summary accounts at the end of a king's reign, no such pattern is found in 2 Chronicles. The reference here might be to our books of Kings; but may also be regarded simply as a literary embellishment by the author.

12. *gangrene:* in a number of passages the Chronicler notes that both the onset of disease and the reaction to it are indicative of a king's standing before God (cp. 21: 18; 26: 21; 32: 24). The nature of the disease cannot be identified; it is possible that *feet* here, as elsewhere in the Old Testament, is a euphemism for the sexual organs. *physicians:* literally, healers. The objection is not to resorting to doctors as such – though in a pre-scientific age this may have been associated with suspicion of magical practices – but to Asa's failure to turn to God. In this he is contrasted with Hezekiah (32: 24–6).

14. Little is known of burial practice in the Old Testament world, and so the meaning of the rites alluded to here cannot be determined. It is possible, however, that in some quarters at least such customs suggest belief in a life beyond the grave. *

KING JEHOSHAPHAT

Asa was succeeded by his son Jehoshaphat, who deter- **17** mined to resist Israel by force. He posted troops in all the **2** fortified cities of Judah and stationed officers*b* throughout

[*a*] *Or* in a niche. [*b*] *Or* garrisons.

Judah and in the cities of Ephraim which his father Asa
3 had captured. The LORD was with Jehoshaphat, for he
followed the example his father*a* had set in his early years
4 and did not resort to the Baalim; he sought guidance of
the God of his father and obeyed his commandments and
5 did not follow the practices of Israel. So the LORD estab-
tished the kingdom under his rule, and all Judah brought
him gifts, and his wealth and fame*b* became very great.
6 He took pride in the service of the LORD; he also suppressed the hill-shrines and the sacred poles in Judah.

✻ The account of Asa's reign was in terms of a pattern of
loyalty and disobedience. Something similar can be discerned
in the account of his son and successor Jehoshaphat. In general,
however, he is regarded more favourably, as is appropriate
for one whose name means 'Yahweh judges'. (The significance
of such a name is brought out especially clearly in the account
in ch. 19.) This opening summary gives a sketch of what
should be the attributes of a faithful king.

1. The use of *Israel* here to denote the northern kingdom
may indicate that the Chronicler was following a source. But
it is also possible that no other way of describing that kingdom
was readily open to him.

3. *his father:* the N.E.B. may be right in making this refer
to Asa, but most Hebrew manuscripts indicate a comparison
with David (cp. the N.E.B. footnote), and this would certainly be appropriate for Jehoshaphat.

6. *suppressed the hill-shrines:* this statement is contradicted
in 20: 33, and so we have a similar problem to that of Asa's
reign (see on 14: 3 and 15: 17). The suggestion that different
sources lie behind the different statements is not much help,
for we can scarcely suppose that the author took over his
sources without any smoothing out of inconsistencies. It

[a] *So some MSS.; others add* David.   [b] *Or* riches.

seems more probable that the different statements were allowed to stand as indicative of that pattern of loyalty and disobedience which we have already noted. ✷

JEHOSHAPHAT'S SUCCESS

In the third year of his reign he sent his officers, Ben- 7 hayil, Obadiah, Zechariah, Nethaneel, and Micaiah, to teach in the cities of Judah, together with the Levites, 8 Shemaiah, Nethaniah, Zebadiah, Asahel, Shemiramoth, Jehonathan, Adonijah, Tobiah, and Tob-adonijah,[a] accompanied by the priests Elishama and Jehoram. They 9 taught in Judah, having with them the book of the law of the LORD; they went round the cities of Judah, teaching the people.

So the dread of the LORD fell upon all the rulers of the 10 lands surrounding Judah, and they did not make war on Jehoshaphat. Certain Philistines brought a gift, a great 11 quantity of silver, to Jehoshaphat; the Arabs too brought him seven thousand seven hundred rams and seven thousand seven hundred he-goats. Jehoshaphat became 12 ever more powerful and built fortresses and store-cities in Judah; and he had much work on hand in the cities of 13 Judah. He had regular, seasoned troops in Jerusalem, enrolled according to their clans in this way: of Judah, the 14 officers over units of a thousand: Adnah the commander, together with three hundred thousand seasoned troops; and next to him the commander Johanan, with two 15 hundred and eighty thousand; and next to him Amasiah 16 son of Zichri, who had volunteered for the service of the

[a] *Prob. rdg.; Heb. adds* the Levites.

17 LORD, with two hundred thousand seasoned troops; and of Benjamin: an experienced soldier Eliada, with two hundred thousand men armed with bows and shields; 18 next to him Jehozabad, with a hundred and eighty thou-19 sand fully-armed men. These were the men who served the king, apart from those whom the king had posted in the fortified cities throughout Judah.

* This section is without parallel in Kings – where Jeho-shaphat's reign is dealt with much more briefly – and the Chronicler has here drawn upon sources which we cannot now identify. His purpose was, however, clear: to show how in all aspects of the nation's life Jehoshaphat took care to carry out the principles of true Yahwism, and was duly rewarded for his zeal. So the teaching mission of verses 7–9 leads to 'the dread of the LORD' falling 'upon all the rulers of the lands surrounding Judah' (verse 10).

7f. There are fewer lists of names in this part than anywhere else in the Chronicler's work, but he introduces such lists wherever possible to indicate the unity and loyalty of the true community throughout its history. None of these names is known elsewhere; the list is notable chiefly as beginning with the lay members.

9. *the book of the law of the LORD:* such references always provoke speculation as to the identity of the 'book' in question, but it is doubtful whether an identification is now possible. More likely the reference is intended to stress the loyalty of the king and his servants to the demands of Yahweh.

11. *Arabs:* though tribesmen from different parts of Arabia are referred to in all parts of the Old Testament, the use of the word 'Arab' to describe them is confined to the writings of the Chronicler, which may suggest that he is using terms familiar from his own time to describe earlier events.

14–19. Like the lists of names, the numbers are to be regarded as symbolic of the divine favour rather than as accurate records. The figures listed here total well over one million men; it has been estimated that the total population of Judah cannot in fact have been as much as a quarter of that figure. ✳

JEHOSHAPHAT AND AHAB AT RAMOTH-GILEAD

When Jehoshaphat had become very wealthy and **18** famous,*a* he allied himself with Ahab by marriage. Some 2*b* years afterwards he went down to visit Ahab in Samaria, and Ahab slaughtered many sheep and oxen for him and his retinue, and incited him to attack Ramoth-gilead. What Ahab king of Israel said to Jehoshaphat king of 3 Judah was this: 'Will you join me in attacking Ramoth-gilead?' And he answered, 'What is mine is yours, myself and my people; I will join with you in the war.' Then 4 Jehoshaphat said to the king of Israel, 'First let us seek counsel from the LORD.' The king of Israel assembled the 5 prophets, some four hundred of them, and asked them, 'Shall I*c* attack Ramoth-gilead or shall I refrain?' 'Attack,' they answered; 'God will deliver it into your hands.' Jehoshaphat asked, 'Is there no other prophet of the LORD 6 here through whom we may seek guidance?' 'There is 7 one more', the king of Israel answered, 'through whom we may seek guidance of the LORD, but I hate the man, because he never prophesies any good for me; never anything but evil. His name is Micaiah son of Imla.' Jehoshaphat exclaimed, 'My lord king, let no such word pass your lips!' So the king of Israel called one of his 8

[a] Or rich. [b] Verses 2–34: cp. 1 Kgs. 22: 2–35.
[c] So Sept.; Heb. we (and similarly in verse 14).

eunuchs and told him to fetch Micaiah son of Imla with all speed.

9 The king of Israel and Jehoshaphat king of Judah were seated on their thrones, clothed in their royal robes and in shining armour, at the entrance to the gate of Samaria,

10 and all the prophets were prophesying before them. One of them, Zedekiah son of Kenaanah, made himself horns of iron and said, 'This is the word of the LORD: "With horns like these you shall gore the Aramaeans and make

11 an end of them."' In the same vein all the prophets prophesied, 'Attack Ramoth-gilead and win the day; the

12 LORD will deliver it into your hands.' The messenger sent to fetch Micaiah told him that the prophets had with one voice given the king a favourable answer. 'And mind

13 you agree with them', he added. 'As the LORD lives,' said Micaiah, 'I will say only what my God tells me to say.'

14 When Micaiah came into the king's presence, the king said to him, 'Micaiah, shall I attack Ramoth-gilead or shall I refrain?' 'Attack and win the day,' he said, 'and it

15 will fall into your hands.' 'How often must I adjure you', said the king, 'to tell me nothing but the truth in the

16 name of the LORD?' Then Micaiah said, 'I saw all Israel scattered on the mountains, like sheep without a shepherd; and I heard the LORD say, "They have no master; let

17 them go home in peace."' The king of Israel said to Jehoshaphat, 'Did I not tell you that he never prophesies

18 good for me, nothing but evil?' Micaiah went on, 'Listen now to the word of the LORD: I saw the LORD seated on his throne, with all the host of heaven in attendance on his

19 right and on his left. The LORD said, "Who will entice

Ahab to attack and fall on[a] Ramoth-gilead?" One said
one thing and one said another; then a spirit came for- 20
ward and stood before the LORD and said, "I will entice
him." "How?" said the LORD. "I will go out", he said, 21
"and be a lying spirit in the mouth of all his prophets."
"You shall entice him," said the LORD, "and you shall
succeed; go and do it." You see, then, how the LORD has 22
put a lying spirit in the mouth of all these prophets of
yours, because he has decreed disaster for you.' Then 23
Zedekiah son of Kenaanah came up to Micaiah and struck
him in the face: 'And how did the spirit of the LORD pass
from me to speak to you?' he said. Micaiah answered, 24
'That you will find out on the day when you run into an
inner room to hide yourself.' Then the king of Israel 25
ordered Micaiah to be arrested and committed to the
custody of Amon the governor of the city and Joash the
king's son.[b] 'Lock this fellow up', he said, 'and give him 26
prison diet of bread and water until I come home in
safety.' Micaiah retorted, 'If you do return in safety, the 27
LORD has not spoken by me.'[c]

So the king of Israel and Jehoshaphat king of Judah 28
marched on Ramoth-gilead, and the king of Israel said to
Jehoshaphat, 'I will disguise myself to go into battle, but 29
you shall wear your royal robes.' So he went into battle
in disguise. Now the king of Aram had commanded the 30
captains of his chariots not to engage all and sundry but
the king of Israel alone. When the captains saw Jehosha- 31
phat, they thought he was the king of Israel and wheeled to
attack him. But Jehoshaphat cried out, and the LORD came

[a] *Or* at.   [b] son: *or* deputy.   [c] *Prob. rdg.; Heb. adds* and he said,
'Listen, peoples, all together.'

213

32 to his help; and God drew them away from him. When the captains saw that he was not the king of Israel, they
33 broke off the attack on him. But one man drew his bow at random and hit the king of Israel where the breastplate joins the plates of the armour. So he said to his driver, 'Wheel round and take me out of the line; I am wounded.'
34 When the day's fighting reached its height, the king of Israel was facing the Aramaeans, propped up in his chariot; he remained so till evening, and at sunset he died.

19 As Jehoshaphat king of Judah returned in safety to his
2 home in Jerusalem, Jehu son of Hanani, the seer, went out to meet him and said, 'Do you take delight in helping the wicked and befriending the enemies of the LORD? The
3 LORD will make you suffer for this.*a* Yet there is some good in you, for you have swept away the sacred poles from the land and have made a practice of seeking guidance of God.'

☆ The Chronicler here takes over, with very few changes, a lengthy section from 1 Kings. No doubt his veneration for Jehoshaphat led him to incorporate all the available material dealing with that king, though in 1 Kings 22 this chapter is preserved within a body of material dealing with prophetic activity in the northern kingdom, and Jehoshaphat appears in a somewhat inglorious light as little more than a vassal. This impression is softened, though not entirely dispelled, by the Chronicler's modifications of the story.

1. *When Jehoshaphat had become very wealthy and famous:* there is nothing in 1 Kings corresponding to this introduction, which may be intended to modify the picture otherwise given of Jehoshaphat's subordinate status. *Ahab:* it is likely that the original form of this story told of an anonymous northern king, and that the episode was subsequently asso-

[a] The LORD...for this: *lit*. Wrath from the LORD will come upon you.

ciated with Ahab. Clearly this association, first found in
1 Kings 22: 20, was accepted by the time of the Chronicler,
who will have inherited the judgement of the compilers of
Kings concerning the wickedness of Ahab.

2. *Ramoth-gilead:* in Transjordan, the whole area was the
scene of continual fighting between Israel and the Aramaean
kingdom of Damascus. It is noteworthy that the Chronicler
omits 1 Kings 22: 3, 'You know that Ramoth-gilead belongs
to us', for it would scarcely have been acceptable to have
Jehoshaphat helping to legitimize the territory of an apostate
kingdom.

3. *I will join with you in the war:* not in 1 Kings. The
Chronicler may wish to imply that Jehoshaphat was blame-
worthy through becoming involved with the apostate
northern kingdom, but it is also possible that he simply
wishes to stress Jehoshaphat's independence. The same point
may be intended by the Hebrew text of verse 5 which has
'shall we attack?' (see the N.E.B. footnote).

7. *Imla:* the same name in Kings is always spelt 'Imlah'.
This is a good example in quite a trivial matter of the way in
which the text of Kings which the Chronicler had as his
source probably differed from the one known to us.

9. *all the prophets were prophesying:* the very vivid picture
in this section clearly implies that prophecy was seen as a
mixture of words and action, the message of encouragement
being accompanied by symbolic actions.

14–27. This section follows the corresponding text, 1 Kings
22: 15–28, very closely, and provides one of the most important descriptions in the Old Testament of the nature of genuine
prophecy. The prophet must be in the presence of the LORD,
must listen to his voice and receive his spirit; only then can
he be sure that the message he gives will be a true one. (For
further consideration of this section, see the commentary on
1 Kings.)

The Chronicler has made a few significant changes in his
source. In verse 14, even though Micaiah is there speaking

ironically, the Chronicler felt it necessary to change 'the LORD will deliver it into your hands' of 1 Kings 22: 15 to the more neutral 'it will fall into your hands' – the LORD would not work for an apostate king.

27. The words in the N.E.B. footnote are found both in Kings and Chronicles in the Hebrew text; they are the first prophetic words in the book of Micah (1: 2) and are an early example of a tendency, which later became more common, of linking people of the same name as having a similar role to perform. In this instance Micah and Micaiah (these are variant forms of the same name) lived at quite different periods of history.

31. *the LORD came to his help:* in the Kings version, the Aramaeans turn away from Jehoshaphat when they realize that he is not their target, but this is both slighting in its judgement upon Jehoshaphat, and gives insufficient prominence to divine intervention.

19: 1. *As Jehoshaphat...returned in safety:* in 1 Kings 22, the story, which is of northern origin, has no further interest in Jehoshaphat. Here, by contrast, the Chronicler can comment both on his safe return and on the condemnation which his action merits.

2. *Jehu son of Hanani, the seer:* this reference provides a link both with the condemnations of this same *Jehu* addressed to Baasha in 1 Kings 16: 1, and with his father *Hanani*'s condemnation of Asa in 2 Chron. 16: 7. The judgement that follows is a qualified one; to be taken more as a warning of what might happen than as any kind of outright rejection. *

JEHOSHAPHAT ENFORCES GOD'S LAWS

4 Jehoshaphat had his residence in Jerusalem, but he went out again among his people from Beersheba to the hill-country of Ephraim and brought them back to the LORD 5 the God of their fathers. He appointed judges throughout

the land, one in each of the fortified cities of Judah, and 6
said to them, 'Be careful what you do; you are there as
judges, to please not man but the LORD, who is with you
when you pass sentence. Let the dread of the LORD be 7
upon you, then; take care what you do, for the LORD our
God will not tolerate injustice, partiality, or bribery.'

In Jerusalem Jehoshaphat appointed some of the Levites 8
and priests and some heads of families by paternal descent
in Israel to administer the law of the LORD and to arbi-
trate in lawsuits among the inhabitants*a* of the city, and he 9
gave them these instructions: 'You must always act in the
fear of the LORD, faithfully and with singleness of mind.
In every suit which comes before you from your kins- 10
men, in whatever city they live, whether cases of blood-
shed or offences against the law or the commandments,
against statutes or regulations, you shall warn them to
commit no offence against the LORD; otherwise you and
your kinsmen will suffer for it.*b* If you act thus, you will be
free of all offence. Your authority in all matters which 11
concern the LORD is Amariah the chief priest, and in
those which concern the king it is Zebediah son of Ishmael, the prince of the house of Judah; the Levites are
your officers. Be strong and resolute, and may the LORD
be on the side of the good!'

✻ The elaboration of the account of Jehoshaphat continues,
with material that has no counterpart in Kings. This chapter
provides as clear an example as any of sharply diverging
scholarly judgements upon the historical reliability of the

[a] in...inhabitants: *prob. rdg., cp. Sept.; Heb. obscure.*
[b] *Lit.* otherwise wrath will come upon you and your kinsmen.

material peculiar to Chronicles. Some have taken this as a valuable source, describing a major change in Judah's judicial system and even arguing that the present form of the tenth commandment (Exod. 20: 17), with its reference to coveting rather than to seizure of possessions, originated from this time. Others have been much more sceptical, denying any historical basis to the story, and seeing it as a *midrash* (see note on 13 : 22) on Jehoshaphat's name, which means 'Yahweh judges'. In view of the lack of specific detail concerning the reform, and the absence of any other supporting evidence, this more cautious attitude may be nearer the mark.

4. *from Beersheba to the hill-country of Ephraim:* the extent of Judah's boundaries is greater here than in most other notices which mention them, possibly as an indication of the favour which Jehoshaphat enjoyed.

5. *judges throughout the land:* whether or not this incident is historical, we see here evidence of the continuing tension between the idea of justice as residing with the local elders and as being dependent on central control.

6–7. Jehoshaphat's commands to the judges are couched in language strongly reminiscent of – perhaps actually quoting – the book of Deuteronomy, and it is clearly the Chronicler's intention to portray him as carrying out all that had there been laid down.

8–11. What is here described is the setting-up of a court of appeal, to deal with cases beyond the competence of local courts. A similar arrangement is envisaged in Deut. 17: 8–13, and something on these lines may well have been in operation in the Chronicler's own day. It may be that he is appealing for loyalty to this Levite-dominated judicial system by claiming its antiquity.

11. *Amariah the chief priest...Zebediah son of Ishmael, the prince of the house of Judah:* both names are common in the Chronicler, though there is no reason for identifying these men with others of the same name mentioned elsewhere. More striking is the similarity of the governmental structure

implied with that found in Haggai and Zechariah, where a
member of the Davidic line (Zerubbabel) is found alongside
a priestly figure (Joshua). ✳

THE LORD GIVES JEHOSHAPHAT VICTORY

It happened some time afterwards that the Moabites, **20**
the Ammonites, and some of the Meunites*ᵃ* made war on
Jehoshaphat. News was brought to him that a great horde ²
of them was attacking him from beyond the Dead Sea,
from Edom,*ᵇ* and was already at Hazazon-tamar, which
is En-gedi. Jehoshaphat in his alarm resolved to seek ³
guidance of the LORD and proclaimed a fast for all Judah.
Judah gathered together to ask counsel of the LORD; from ⁴
every city of the land they came to consult him. Jehosha- ⁵
phat stood up in the assembly of Judah and Jerusalem in
the house of the LORD, in front of the New Court, and ⁶
said, 'O LORD God of our fathers, art not thou God in
heaven? Thou rulest over all the kingdoms of the nations;
in thy hand are strength and power, and there is none who
can withstand thee. Didst not thou, O God our God, ⁷
dispossess the inhabitants of this land in favour of thy
people Israel, and give it for ever to the descendants of
Abraham thy friend? So they lived in it and have built a ⁸
sanctuary in it in honour of thy name and said, "Should ⁹
evil come upon us, war or flood,*ᶜ* pestilence or famine,
we will stand before this house and before thee, for in this
house is thy Name, and we will cry to thee in our distress
and thou wilt hear and save." Thou didst not allow Israel, ¹⁰
when they came out of Egypt, to enter the land of the

[a] *Prob. rdg., cp. Sept.; Heb.* Ammonites.   [b] *So one MS.; others*
Aram.   [c] *Prob. rdg.; Heb.* judgement.

Ammonites, the Moabites, and the people of the hill-country of Seir, so they turned aside and left them alone
11 and did not destroy them. Now see how these people repay us: they are coming to drive us out of thy posses-
12 sion which thou didst give to us. Judge them, O God our God, for we have no strength to face this great horde which is invading our land; we know not what we ought to do; we lift our eyes to thee.'

13 So all Judah stood there before the LORD, with their
14 dependants, their wives and their children. Then, in the midst of the assembly, the spirit of the LORD came upon Jahaziel son of Zechariah, son of Benaiah, son of Jeiel,
15 son of Mattaniah, a Levite of the line of Asaph, and he said, 'Attend, all Judah, all inhabitants of Jerusalem, and King Jehoshaphat; this is the word of the LORD to you: "Have no fear; do not be dismayed by this great horde,
16 for the battle is in God's hands, not yours. Go down to meet them tomorrow; they will come up by the Ascent of Ziz. You will find them at the end of the valley, east of
17 the wilderness of Jeruel. It is not you who will fight this battle; stand firm and wait, and you will see the deliverance worked by the LORD: he is on your side, O Judah and Jerusalem. Do not fear or be dismayed; go out to-morrow to face them; for the LORD is on your side."'
18 Jehoshaphat bowed his face to the ground, and all Judah and the inhabitants of Jerusalem fell down before the
19 LORD to make obeisance to him. Then the Levites of the lines of Kohath and Korah stood up and praised the LORD the God of Israel with a mighty shout.

20 So they rose early in the morning and went out to the wilderness of Tekoa; and, as they were starting, Jehosha-

phat took his stand and said, 'Hear me, O Judah and inhabitants of Jerusalem: hold firmly to your faith in the
LORD your God and you will be upheld; have faith in his
prophets and you will prosper.' After consulting with the   21
people, he appointed men to sing to the LORD and praise
the splendour of his holiness[a] as they went before the
armed troops, and they sang:

> Give thanks to the LORD,
>   for his love endures for ever.

As soon as their loud shouts of praise were heard, the   22
LORD deluded the Ammonites and Moabites and the men
of the hill-country of Seir, who were invading Judah, and
they were defeated. It turned out that the Ammonites   23
and Moabites had taken up a position against the men of
the hill-country of Seir, and set themselves to annihilate
and destroy them; and when they had exterminated the
men of Seir, they savagely attacked one another. So when   24
Judah came to the watch-tower in the wilderness and
looked towards the enemy horde, there they were all
lying dead upon the ground; none had escaped. When   25
Jehoshaphat and his men came to collect the booty, they
found a large number of cattle,[b] goods, clothing,[c] and
precious things, which they plundered until they could
carry away no more. They spent three days collecting the
booty, there was so much of it. On the fourth day they   26
assembled in the Valley of Berakah,[d] the name that it
bears to this day because they blessed the LORD there.
Then all the men of Judah and Jerusalem, with Jehosha-   27

[a] *Or* singers in sacred vestments to praise the LORD.   [b] of cattle: *so
Sept.; Heb.* among them.   [c] *So some MSS.; others* effigies.   [d] *That
is* Valley of Blessing.

phat at their head, returned home to the city in triumph;
for the LORD had given them cause to triumph over their
28 enemies. They entered Jerusalem with lutes, harps, and
trumpets playing, and went into the house of the LORD.
29 So the dread of God fell upon the rulers of every country
when they heard that the LORD had fought against the
30 enemies of Israel; and the realm of Jehoshaphat was at
peace, God giving him security on all sides.

✻ A further section unparalleled in Kings gives an opportunity to show how the appropriate response of faith will
ensure divine intervention. Again there is sharp disagreement
whether a genuine historical reminiscence is embedded in
this story, and again in the absence of any supporting evidence
and the strongly sermonic character of much of this chapter, a
cautious attitude seems justified. This sermonic element is of
particular interest, for it affords an opportunity to the
Chronicler to use what may well have been the style of
preaching of the Levites of his own time, with allusions to
sacred writings applied to new situations so as to enable his
readers to see more of their significance. Such brief sermons
are found all through the work of the Chronicler, but this
chapter provides some particularly striking examples of his
method.

1. *Meunites:* this is a conjectural, but likely, emendation,
since the Hebrew text refers to the Ammonites twice. The
Meunites (mentioned in 1 Chron. 4: 41) lived south-east of
Judah, near Petra. All the adversaries mentioned are therefore
groups settled south and east of Judah, which makes the
correction 'Edom' for Hebrew 'Aram' in verse 2 a very
probable one.

2. *Hazazon-tamar:* the site is unknown, but it seems that a
deliberate link is being made here with the great battle of the
nations in Gen. 14: 7, where the LORD had protected Abraham.

En-gedi: near the Dead Sea, where Saul had pursued David (1 Sam. 24: 1).

3–5. The appropriate response to these threats is to *fast*, to *ask counsel of the LORD*, and to pray to him. Further, all this is done by the *assembly of Judah* (the *qahal*; see note on 10: 3), and takes place at Jerusalem *in the house of the LORD*, nowhere near the battle-front.

6–12. Jehoshaphat's prayer is reminiscent of Moses' speech to Israel in Deut. 4; there he had warned that various evils would afflict the people, and now they are seen to be offering the right response through prayer.

7. *dispossess the inhabitants:* a constant theme of the book of Joshua is here alluded to, that it is the LORD himself who had driven out the inhabitants of Canaan before the Israelites. Similarly the reference to *Abraham thy friend* links Jehoshaphat to an even more ancient tradition, though the way it is here expressed seems to be dependent on Isa. 41: 8, where the theme is the LORD's choosing Israel and bringing her from the ends of the earth.

9. Here Jehoshaphat is represented as quoting Solomon's prayer at the dedication of the temple (2 Chron. 6).

10. *Thou didst not allow Israel...the hill-country of Seir:* again, continuity between ancient Israel, Jehoshaphat's people, and, by implication, the people of the Chronicler's own time, is asserted. There is a variety of ancient traditions explaining the very circuitous journey which the Israelites made from Egypt to Palestine; here the tradition found in Deut. 2: 4–20 is used, according to which this détour was due to the LORD's kindness in not dispossessing these peoples.

12. The prayer ends with a lament of the type found in many Psalms of national or communal lament (e.g. Ps. 44).

13–17. This section is really a sermon preached by a Levite under the guidance of God's spirit rather than an account of the progress of a war. Thus two references are made which allude to earlier texts describing God's support of those who are loyal to him: 'the battle is in God's hands, not yours'

223

(verse 15) is a reference to David's words to the Philistine giant (1 Sam. 17: 47), and the whole of verse 17 is reminiscent of Moses' words of encouragement at the parting of the Red Sea (Exod. 14: 13f.). In this way once again the Chronicler brings out the theme of continuity and identity between the Israel of old and of his own time.

16. *the Ascent of Ziz:* unknown, and probably only a variant of 'Hazazon' in verse 2.

20. *hold firmly to your faith in the LORD your God and you will be upheld:* another sermon is preached before the battle, this time by the king himself. The allusion is to Isa. 7: 9: 'Have firm faith, or you will not stand firm.' (The word translated here *be upheld* might be better rendered 'stand firm' – it is the same word as in Isaiah.) Those words had been addressed to the impious king Ahaz; here the people show faith by believing the prophetic word in the mouth of the king, and will be rewarded appropriately.

21. *he appointed men to sing to the LORD:* this is less a battle than a liturgy, in which ceremonial requirements are of the first importance. The chorus is found frequently in the Psalms and has already been used by the Chronicler (1 Chron. 16: 34).

22. *the LORD deluded:* other English versions have seen a reference to setting an ambush in the somewhat rare Hebrew word here used; this may be intended as a reference to the only other occasion when the same form is found (Judg. 9: 25), but in any case the battle is won, not by skill in war but by relying on the LORD to fight for his people.

26. *the Valley of Berakah:* again this is likely to be a site chosen for the significance of the name, which means 'Blessing'.

The account of this battle has been dealt with in somewhat greater detail than has been possible in every case; but the principles which have been indicated here are the same as are found in the other similar stories, especially in 2 Chronicles. Always it is the LORD who is really fighting the war; always the opportunity is taken to stress the continuity of Israel at every age – provided she is faithful to her God. ✻

JEHOSHAPHAT FALLS AWAY

Thus Jehoshaphat reigned over Judah. He was thirty- 31[a]
five years old when he came to the throne, and he reigned
in Jerusalem for twenty-five years; his mother was Azubah daughter of Shilhi. He followed in the footsteps of 32
Asa his father and did not swerve from them; he did what
was right in the eyes of the LORD. But the hill-shrines 33
were allowed to remain, and the people did not set their
hearts upon the God of their fathers. The other events of 34
Jehoshaphat's reign, from first to last, are recorded in the
history of Jehu son of Hanani, which is included in the
annals of the kings of Israel.

Later Jehoshaphat king of Judah allied himself with 35
Ahaziah king of Israel; he did wrong in joining with him 36
to build ships for trade with Tarshish; these were built in
Ezion-geber. But Eliezer son of Dodavahu of Mareshah 37
denounced Jehoshaphat with this prophecy: 'Because you
have joined with Ahaziah, the LORD will bring your
work to nothing.' So the ships were wrecked and could
not make the voyage to Tarshish.

* The last part of the account is largely derived from 1 Kings,
but as so often the Chronicler arranges his material in such a
way as to bring out his own distinctive viewpoint. Just as in
other instances wicked kings have repented and been for-
given, so good kings may fall from grace and be punished.
We see the Chronicler pointing an important lesson for the
people of his own day.

34. *the history of Jehu son of Hanani*: Jehu has been mentioned
already (19: 2), but nothing else is known of his history, which

[a] *Verses 31–3: cp. 1 Kgs. 22: 41–3.*

may once again be the Chronicler's way of referring to the
books of Kings.

35–7. These verses appear to be based on I Kings 22: 47–9,
though with major changes in detail. The point is the folly of
Jehoshaphat when he *allied himself with Ahaziah*, rather than
trusting in the LORD as he had previously done. Eliezer is
otherwise unknown, but his words express an important
theme for the Chronicler – the uselessness of human alliances.
It may be that there were those in his own day who wished
to pursue a more active political policy than the quietism
which seems to have characterized the Jewish community. *

THE REIGN OF JORAM

21 Jehoshaphat rested with his forefathers and was buried
with them in the city of David. He was succeeded by his
2 son Joram, whose brothers were Azariah, Jehiel, Zechariah, Azariah, Michael, and Shephatiah, sons of Jehoshaphat. All of them were sons of Jehoshaphat king of
3 Judah,*a* and their father gave them many gifts, silver and
gold and other costly things, as well as fortified cities in
Judah; but the kingship he gave to Joram because he was
the eldest.

4 When Joram was firmly established on his father's
throne, he put to the sword all his brothers and also some
5*b* of the princes of Israel. He was thirty-two years old when
he came to the throne, and he reigned in Jerusalem for
6 eight years. He followed the practices of the kings of
Israel as the house of Ahab had done, for he had married
Ahab's daughter; and he did what was wrong in the eyes
7 of the LORD. But for the sake of the covenant which he

[a] *So many MSS.; others* Israel.   [b] *Verses 5–10: cp. 2 Kgs. 8: 17–22.*

had made with David, the LORD was unwilling to destroy the house of David, since he had promised to give him and his sons a flame, to burn for all time.

During his reign Edom revolted against Judah and set 8 up its own king. Joram, with his commanders and all his 9 chariots, advanced into Edom. He and his chariot-commanders set out by night, but they were surrounded by the Edomites and defeated.[a] So Edom has remained 10 independent of Judah to this day. Libnah revolted against him at the same time, because he had forsaken the LORD the God of his fathers, and because he had built hill- 11 shrines in the hill-country of Judah and had seduced the inhabitants of Jerusalem into idolatrous practices and corrupted Judah.

A letter reached Joram from Elijah the prophet, which 12 ran thus: 'This is the word of the LORD the God of David your father: "You have not followed in the footsteps of Jehoshaphat your father and of Asa king of Judah, but 13 have followed the kings of Israel and have seduced Judah and the inhabitants of Jerusalem, as the house of Ahab did; and you have put to death your own brothers, sons of your father's house, men better than yourself. Because 14 of all this, the LORD is about to strike a heavy blow at your people, your children, your wives, and all your posses-sions, and you yourself will suffer from a chronic disease 15 of the bowels, until they prolapse and become severely ulcerated."' Then the LORD aroused against Joram the 16 anger of the Philistines and of the Arabs who live near the Cushites, and they invaded Judah and made their way 17 right through it, carrying off all the property which they

[a] and defeated: *prob. rdg.; Heb.* and he defeated them.

found in the king's palace, as well as his sons and wives;
not a son was left to him except the youngest, Jehoahaz.
18 It was after all this that the LORD struck down the king
19 with an incurable disease of the bowels. It continued for
some time, and towards the end of the second year the
disease caused his bowels to prolapse, and the painful
ulceration brought on his death. But his people kindled
20 no fire in his honour as they had done for his fathers. He
was thirty-two years old when he became king, and he
reigned in Jerusalem for eight years. His passing went unsung, and he was buried in the city of David, but not in
the burial-place of the kings.

* By contrast with Jehoshaphat, whose admirable reign had
been almost free from blemishes, the verdict on Joram, his
son and successor, is extremely unfavourable. This condemnation is shown by the convergence of a variety of circumstances: defeat in battle, loss of territory, destruction of his
family, and incurable disease. There is a similarity with the
afflictions of Job; the way in which Joram's troubles were
seen as signifying God's displeasure makes the attitude of the
friends to Job easier to understand. It is assumed that the
main characters from the story of the northern kingdom
(Ahab, Elijah) will be known, even though the Chronicler
himself has not mentioned them.

3. *the kingship he gave to Joram because he was the eldest:* our
knowledge of succession-arrangements in ancient Israel is very
limited, but it appears likely that the oldest son usually
succeeded, as in this case. This episode is unique in that
nowhere else after the time of David are we given an extended
list of members of the royal family. It seems clearly to be
implied that the king designated his own successor – a custom
known from other parts of the ancient Near East.

9. *surrounded by the Edomites and defeated:* the N.E.B.

228

emendation (see footnote) certainly makes better sense, but it is doubtful whether it represents the point originally intended, which may have been an illustration of verse 7: Edom's rebellion was successful in gaining independence, but the LORD continued to look after the house of David by sparing them the ignominy of defeat.

10. *because he had forsaken the LORD:* this section and the following verse are an addition to the text in 2 Kings 8: 16–24 which provides the source for this material, though the condemnations are entirely in line with the judgements passed in 2 Kings.

12. *A letter reached Joram from Elijah the prophet:* though described as a *letter*, what follows is really a prophetic oracle introduced by the authentication of the prophet as messenger (*This is the word of the LORD*), followed by the accusation of wrong-doing (verses 12*b*–13) and leading into an announcement of judgement (verses 14–15). The idea of a letter may suggest that by the Chronicler's day prophecy had come to be written down. Though attributed to Elijah – knowledge of whom is assumed, for he is not mentioned by the Chronicler – this can scarcely be authentic, if the time of his death in 2 Kings 2 is accurate. More probably, he is introduced here as a voice from the northern kingdom condemning Joram's wrong associations with that kingdom.

14. *strike a heavy blow at your people, your children, your wives, and all your possessions:* the corporate solidarity of the people is here well illustrated. The wickedness of the king must inevitably affect them all.

16. *the Arabs who live near the Cushites:* it is difficult to know who is meant here, for the Cushites are Ethiopians, and we know nothing of any such people as are here described, still less of an alliance with the Philistines, or of an invasion of Judah.

19. *the disease caused his bowels to prolapse:* the N.E.B. translation makes the description of the disease a good deal more

precise and technical than in fact it is; the Hebrew description is very vague.

20. *His passing went unsung:* the N.E.B. translation is a free rendering of the Hebrew which is literally 'without desire'. An alternative understanding would be to see a contrast between Joram's rejection and the picture of Saul at his choice as 'the desire of Israel' (N.E.B. 'that all Israel is wanting', 1 Sam. 9: 20). *

AHAZIAH: THE KINGDOM USURPED

22 1[a] Then the inhabitants of Jerusalem made Ahaziah, his youngest son, king in his place, for the raiders who had joined the Arabs in the campaign[b] had killed all the elder 2 sons. So Ahaziah son of Joram became king of Judah. He was forty-two years old when he came to the throne, and he reigned in Jerusalem for one year; his mother was 3 Athaliah granddaughter[c] of Omri. He too followed the practices of the house of Ahab, for his mother was his 4 counsellor in wickedness. He did what was wrong in the eyes of the LORD like the house of Ahab, for they had been his counsellors after his father's death, to his undoing. 5 He followed their counsel also in the alliance he made with Jehoram son of Ahab king of Israel, to fight against Hazael king of Aram at Ramoth-gilead. But Jehoram was 6 wounded by the Aramaeans, and returned to Jezreel to recover from[d] the wounds which were inflicted on him at Ramoth[e] in battle with Hazael king of Aram.

Because of Jehoram's illness Ahaziah[f] son of Joram king

[a] *Verses 1–6: cp. 2 Kgs. 8: 25–9.*   [b] *Lit.* camp.   [c] *Lit.* daughter˙
[d] *So some MSS.; others* because...   [e] *So Luc. Sept.; Heb.* Ramah˙
[f] *So some MSS., cp. 2 Kgs. 8:29; others* Azariah.

of Judah went down to Jezreel to visit him. It was God's 7
will that the visit of Ahaziah to Jehoram should be the
occasion of his downfall. During the visit he went out
with Jehoram to meet Jehu son of Nimshi, whom the
LORD had anointed to bring the house of Ahab to an end.
So it came about that Jehu, who was then at variance with 8
the house of Ahab, found the officers of Judah and*a* the
kinsmen of Ahaziah who were his attendants, and killed
them. Then he searched out Ahaziah himself, and his men 9
captured him in Samaria, where he had gone into hiding.
They brought him to Jehu and put him to death; they
gave him burial, for they said, 'He was a son of Jehoshaphat who sought the guidance of the LORD with his
whole heart.' Then the house of Ahaziah had no one
strong enough to rule.

As soon as Athaliah mother of Ahaziah saw that her son 10*b*
was dead, she set out to extirpate the royal line of the
house of Judah. But Jehosheba*c* daughter of King Joram 11
took Ahaziah's son Joash and stole him away from among
the princes who were being murdered; she put him and
his nurse in a bedchamber. Thus Jehosheba*c* daughter of
King Joram and wife of Jehoiada the priest, because she
was Ahaziah's sister, hid Joash from Athaliah so that she
did not put him to death. He remained concealed with 12
them in the house of God for six years, while Athaliah
ruled the country.

✻ This chapter describes the only break in the Davidic
succession in Jerusalem during a period of about four centuries.

[*a*] *So Sept.; Heb. adds* the sons of.   [*b*] *22: 10 – 23: 21: cp. 2 Kgs. 11:
1–20.*   [*c*] *So Sept., cp. 2 Kgs. 11: 2; Heb.* Jehoshabeath.

In both Kings and Chronicles it provides a clear opportunity for sermonic reflection upon the perils of unfaithfulness.

1. *Ahaziah:* called 'Jehoahaz' in 21: 17. The names are different versions of the same, one with the Yahweh element as a suffix, the other as a prefix. Both mean 'Yahweh grasps' or 'maintains'. He is described as the *youngest son* in contrast with his father (21: 3): as this verse makes clear he was the only surviving son.

2. *forty-two years old:* clearly an error, since this would have made him older than his father. In 2 Kings 8: 26 Ahaziah is twenty-two, though even this would scarcely fit with the Chronicler's assertion that he was the 'youngest son' of Joram (verse 1). *Athaliah granddaughter of Omri:* Omri was the first king to set up a lasting dynasty in the northern kingdom, had established Samaria as the capital city, and is generally regarded as an extremely able ruler, though the Old Testament pays him little attention. Though there are some obscurities about his family, it seems probable that the N.E.B. correction is right and that Athaliah was his granddaughter. In the following verses the Chronicler stresses the extent and depravity of her influence.

5–6. This incident looks like an alternative version of the story told at much greater length in ch. 18, and there associated with Ahab and Jehoshaphat. The uncertainties of identification in stories of this kind are illustrated by the variation between *Ahaziah* and 'Azariah' in verse 6 (see N.E.B. footnote).

7. *the occasion of his downfall:* the word translated *downfall* is a strong one, which really means 'trampling down'; this is seen as the invitable divine response to Ahaziah's association with the northern kingdom.

7b–9. These verses outline in very summary form the story told at length in 2 Kings 9.

9. *they gave him burial:* but not even in Jerusalem. He had fallen away from the true succession of David, and so was not buried with the true Davidic line.

10–12. The Chronicler here follows his source in 2 Kings 11

very closely; the slightly more elaborate form may be due to the fact that his version of 2 Kings differed somewhat from that which is available to us. The repugnance which Athaliah's action had for the editor of 2 Kings is fully shared by the Chronicler who is therefore content to let his source tell the story. *

THE DAVIDIC LINE RESTORED

In the seventh year Jehoiada felt himself strong enough **23** to make an agreement with Azariah son of Jeroham, Ishmael son of Jehohanan, Azariah son of Obed, Maaseiah son of Adaiah, and Elishaphat son of Zichri, all captains of units of a hundred. They went all through Judah and 2 gathered to Jerusalem the Levites from the cities of Judah and the heads of clans in Israel, and they came to Jerusalem. All the assembly made a compact with the king in 3 the house of God, and Jehoiada said to them, 'Here is the king's son! He shall be king, as the LORD promised that the sons of David should be. This is what you must do: a 4 third of you, priests and Levites, as you come on duty on the sabbath, are to be on guard at the threshold gates, another third are to be in the royal palace, and another 5 third are to be at the Foundation Gate, while all the people will be in the courts of the house of the LORD. Let no one 6 enter the house of the LORD except the priests and the attendant Levites; they may enter, for they are holy, but all the people shall continue to keep the LORD's charge. The Levites shall mount guard round the king, each with 7 his weapons at the ready; anyone who tries to enter the house is to be put to death. They shall stay with the king wherever he goes.'

8 The Levites and all Judah carried out the orders of Jehoiada the priest to the letter. Each captain took his men, both those who came on duty on the sabbath and those who came off, for Jehoiada the priest had not
9 released the outgoing divisions. And Jehoiada the priest handed out to the captains King David's spears, shields,
10 and bucklers,[a] which were in the house of God; and he posted all the people, each man carrying his weapon at the ready, from corner to corner of the house to north and
11 south,[b] surrounding the king. Then they brought out the king's son, put the crown on his head, handed him the warrant and proclaimed him king, and Jehoiada and his sons anointed him; and a shout went up: 'Long live the
12 king.' When Athaliah heard the noise of the people as they ran about cheering for the king, she came into the
13 house of the LORD where the people were and found the king standing on the dais[c] at the entrance, amidst outbursts of song and fanfares of trumpets in his honour; all the populace were rejoicing and blowing trumpets, and singers with musical instruments were leading the celebrations. Athaliah rent her clothes and cried, 'Treason!
14 Treason!' Jehoiada the priest gave orders to[d] the captains in command of the troops: 'Bring her outside the precincts and let anyone in attendance on her be put to the sword'; for the priest said, 'Do not kill her in the house
15 of the LORD.' So they laid hands on her and took her to the royal palace and killed her there at the passage to the Horse Gate.

[a] *Mng. of Heb. word uncertain.*
[b] *Prob. rdg.; Heb. adds* of the altar and the house.
[c] *Prob. rdg., cp. 2 Kgs. 11: 14; Heb.* by his pillar.
[d] gave orders to: *prob. rdg., cp. 2 Kgs. 11: 15; Heb.* brought out.

Then Jehoiada made a covenant between the LORD[a] 16 and the whole people and the king, that they should be the LORD's people. And all the people went into the 17 temple of Baal and pulled it down; they smashed its altars and images, and they slew Mattan the priest of Baal before the altars. Then Jehoiada committed the super- 18 vision of the house of the LORD to the charge of the priests and[b] the Levites whom David had allocated to the house of the LORD, to offer whole-offerings to the LORD as prescribed in the law of Moses, with the singing and rejoicing as handed down from David. He stationed the 19 door-keepers at the gates of the house of the LORD, to prevent anyone entering who was in any way unclean. Then he took the captains of units of a hundred, the 20 nobles, and the governors of the people, and all the people of the land, and they escorted the king from the house of the LORD through the Upper Gate to the royal palace, and seated him on the royal throne. The whole people re- 21 joiced and the city was tranquil. That is how Athaliah was put to the sword.

---

* As in the last verses of ch. 22, the source in 2 Kings 11 is here followed very closely, with only minor emendations which give somewhat greater emphasis to the part played by the religious leaders in overthrowing Athaliah.

1. The names of the *captains* are found only here; this tendency to elaborate details by including names is characteristic of the Chronicler's method.

2. *gathered to Jerusalem the Levites:* a small but significant addition by the Chronicler both emphasizes the loyalty of the

[a] the LORD: *prob. rdg., cp. 2 Kgs. 11: 17; Heb.* him.
[b] and: *so some MSS.; others om.*

Levites and underlines the propriety of what is about to take place.

3. *All the assembly:* again an addition by the Chronicler which denotes the religious nature of what is taking place.

6. Again a marked shift of emphasis from the Kings account, where the main role is played by the royal bodyguard; here all is entrusted to *priests and...Levites.* We should not dismiss this as falsification; the Chronicler is concerned to tell the story in terms that would be appropriate for his own day, when there was no closer equivalent to a royal bodyguard than the religious leaders of Jerusalem, and also to stress the religious significance of the restoration of the right authority.

11–13. These verses, together with their equivalent in 2 Kings 11: 12–14, give us the clearest picture we have of the actual accession-ceremony of a king of Judah. The most obscure feature is the 'warrant' (verse 11); a slight change in the Hebrew to give the meaning 'bracelets', as part of the royal insignia, has often been suggested, but it may be better to see the warrant as a kind of decree setting out the duties of kingship (cp. Ps. 2: 7).

13. *on the dais at the entrance:* this gives us further detail concerning the lay-out of the temple. The dais – more satisfactory than the 'pillar' of the older English versions – appears to be an area set apart specially for the king.

16–21. The story of restoration closely follows 2 Kings 11: 17–20, with characteristic elaborations stressing the role of the priests and Levites and the importance of maintaining the purity of the temple. *

JOASH UNDER DIVINE FAVOUR

24 1[a] Joash was seven years old when he became king, and he reigned in Jerusalem for forty years; his mother was Zibiah of Beersheba. He did what was right in the eyes of

[a] *Verses 1–14: cp. 2 Kgs. 11: 21 – 12: 15.*

the LORD as long as Jehoiada the priest was alive. Jehoiada 3
chose him two wives, and he had a family of sons and
daughters.

Some time after this, Joash decided to repair the house 4
of the LORD. So he assembled the priests and the Levites 5
and said to them, 'Go through the cities of Judah and
collect the annual tax from all the Israelites for the restoration of the house of your God, and do it quickly.' But the
Levites did not act quickly. The king then called for 6
Jehoiada the chief priest and said to him, 'Why have you
not required the Levites to bring in from Judah and
Jerusalem the tax imposed by Moses the servant of the
LORD and by the assembly of Israel for the Tent of the
Tokens?' For the wicked Athaliah and*a* her adherents*b* 7
had broken into the house of God and had devoted all its
holy things to the service of the Baalim. So the king 8
ordered them to make a chest and to put it outside the
gate of the house of the LORD; and proclamation was 9
made throughout Judah and Jerusalem that the people
should bring to the LORD the tax imposed on Israel in the
wilderness by Moses the servant of God. And all the 10
leaders and all the people gladly brought their taxes and
cast them into the chest until it was full. Whenever the 11
chest was brought to the king's officers by the Levites and
they saw that it was well filled, the king's secretary and
the chief priest's officer would come to empty it, after
which it was carried back to its place. This they did daily,
and they collected a great sum of money. The king and 12
Jehoiada gave it to those responsible for carrying out the
work in the house of the LORD, and they hired masons

[a] and: *so Sept.; Heb. om.*　[b] her adherents: *lit.* her sons.

and carpenters to do the repairs, as well as craftsmen in
13 iron and copper[a] to restore the house. So the workmen
proceeded with their task and the new work progressed
under their hands; they restored the house of God accord-
14 ing to its original design and strengthened it. When they
had finished, they brought what was left of the money to
the king and to Jehoiada, and it was made into vessels for
the house of the LORD, both for service and for sacrificing, saucers and other vessels of gold and silver. While
Jehoiada lived, whole-offerings were offered in the house
of the LORD continually.

* The reign of Joash provides another example of the
Chronicler's method of showing how even a good king may
fall from grace. In his early years all is well and a great
reform is carried out; but later he falls away. In the account
of the reform the Chronicler uses 2 Kings 11: 21 – 12: 15 as
his main source, but in many detailed points he interprets the
story according to his own characteristic interests.

5. *collect the annual tax:* such a tax was almost certainly
unknown in Joash's time, and the Kings version speaks of
voluntary contribution (though the Hebrew is obscure, as
the N.E.B. notes on 2 Kings 12: 4). Such a tax was an important matter in later Judaism, and therefore the Chronicler
stresses its significance with his own readers in mind.

But the Levites did not act quickly: one of the very rare
occasions when the Chronicler is critical of the Levites. Does
this reflect some lack of diligence in the Chronicler's own day?

6. *the tax imposed by Moses:* this addition to the Kings text
links the requirement of a tax with the requirements of the
Pentateuch (Exod. 30: 12–16).

7. It is stressed that the need for reform is due to the
depravity of Athaliah.

[a] *Or* bronze.

11. *a great sum of money:* the Chronicler clearly envisages coin, as was usual in his day. The Kings text implies silver that had to be 'melted down' (2 Kings 12: 10).

14. *vessels for the house of the LORD:* the importance of the right vessels for service in the temple is a theme which the Chronicler stresses throughout his work. *While Jehoiada lived:* great stress is laid on the good influence of the priest upon Joash, and the disasters which inevitably followed his death. ✻

JOASH FALLS FROM FAVOUR

Jehoiada, now old and weighed down with years, died 15 at the age of a hundred and thirty and was buried with 16 the kings in the city of David, because he had done good in Israel and served God and his house.

After the death of Jehoiada the leading men of Judah 17 came and made obeisance to the king. He listened to them, and they forsook the house of the LORD the God of 18 their fathers and worshipped sacred poles and idols. And 19 Judah and Jerusalem suffered for this wickedness. But the LORD sent prophets to bring them back to himself, prophets who denounced them and were not heeded. Then the spirit of God took possession of[a] Zechariah son 20 of Jehoiada the priest, and he stood looking down on the people and said to them, 'This is the word of God: "Why do you disobey the commands of the LORD and court disaster? Because you have forsaken the LORD, he has forsaken you."' But they made common cause against 21 him, and on orders from the king they stoned him to death in the court of the house of the LORD. King Joash 22 did not remember the loyalty of Zechariah's father

[a] took possession of: *lit.* clothed itself with.

Jehoiada but killed his son, who said as he was dying,
'May the LORD see this and exact the penalty.'

23   At the turn of the year an Aramaean army advanced
against Joash; they invaded Judah and Jerusalem and
massacred all the officers, so that the army ceased to exist,
24 and sent all their spoil to the king of Damascus. Although
the Aramaeans had invaded with a small force, the LORD
delivered a very great army into their hands, because the
people had forsaken the LORD the God of their fathers;
and Joash suffered just punishment.

25*a*   When the Aramaeans had withdrawn, leaving the king
severely wounded, his servants conspired against him to
avenge the death of the son*b* of Jehoiada the priest; and
they killed him on his bed. Thus he died and was buried
in the city of David, but not in the burial-place of the
26 kings. The conspirators were Zabad son of Shimeath an
Ammonite woman and Jehozabad son of Shimrith a
27 Moabite woman. His children, the many oracles about
him, and his reconstruction of the house of God are all on
record in the story given in the annals of the kings. He
was succeeded by his son Amaziah.

⁂ In 2 Kings Joash did what was right 'all his days' (12: 2);
the Chronicler however makes a sharp distinction between
his behaviour while under Jehoiada's influence and what
happened after the priest died. The Aramaean wars, noted
without further comment in 2 Kings, are here seen as the
means of divine punishment.

15. *died at the age of a hundred and thirty and was buried with
the kings:* two ways of expressing the honour due to Jehoiada:
his great age, rivalling that of the patriarchs, and his royal

[a] *Verses 25–7: cp. 2 Kgs. 12: 20, 21.*   [b] *So Sept.; Heb.* sons.

burial-place. The honours he was accorded resemble those given to the high priest in the Chronicler's own day.

18–19. The offences listed here are a further indication that the Chronicler stood in the tradition represented by the book of Deuteronomy; both the *poles and idols*, symbolic of Canaanite worship of Baal, and the sending of *prophets* are characteristic Deuteronomic themes, the first of condemnation, the second of the continuing concern of the LORD for his people.

20. Zechariah's sermon consists of an allusion to Moses' warning to the Israelites in Num. 14: 41 (the correspondence is much closer than the N.E.B. translation suggests) and that already used by Azariah against Asa in 15: 2.

21. *they stoned him to death:* 2 Chronicles is the last book of the Hebrew Bible, and this is the last murder recorded in it. This explains the phrase in Luke 11: 51, 'from the blood of Abel to the blood of Zechariah'. In the parallel passage, Matt. 23: 35, the words 'son of Berachiah' have been added through a confusion of this Zechariah with the prophet of the same name.

22. *May the LORD see this and exact the penalty:* the dying man is pictured as invoking the principle of 'life for life' laid down in Gen. 9.

24. *Although the Aramaeans had invaded with a small force, the LORD delivered a very great army into their hands:* this is the exact reversal of what had happened to earlier kings such as Asa and Jehoshaphat who had been loyal, and had seen the LORD defeat much larger enemy armies. The account of this war is not based in any of its details on that in 2 Kings.

25. *his servants conspired against him:* Joash suffers the double indignity of wounding by the enemy and disloyalty from his own entourage. But this disloyalty is really part of a greater loyalty to God by Joash's servants.

not in the burial place of the kings: the disgrace of Joash is complete. This contradicts 2 Kings 12: 21.

26. *Zabad:* there is some variation in the form of the con-

spirators' names, and this form is found only here, as is the information concerning their foreign origin. Again the picture
is of the LORD using foreigners to punish the disloyal Israelite.

27. *many oracles about him:* a better translation would be
'against him'. *oracles* is a technical term for the words of
prophets, and the allusion here is probably to the prophets
mentioned in verse 19 whose words were unheeded. *story:
midrash,* as in 13: 22. See the note there. ✳

THE REIGN OF AMAZIAH

25 1 ᵃ Amaziah was twenty-five years old when he came to the
throne, and he reigned in Jerusalem for twenty-nine years;
2 his mother was Jehoaddan of Jerusalem. He did what was
right in the eyes of the LORD, but not whole-heartedly.
3 When the royal power was firmly in his grasp, he put to
death those of his servants who had murdered the king
4 his father; but he spared their children, in obedience to
the LORD's command written in the law of Moses:
'Fathers shall not die for their children, nor children for
their fathers; a man shall die only for his own sin.'

5   Then Amaziah assembled the men of Judah and drew
them up by families, all Judah and Benjamin as well,
under officers over units of a thousand and a hundred.
He mustered those of twenty years old and upwards and
found their number to be three hundred thousand, all
picked troops ready for service, able to handle spear and
6 shield. He also hired a hundred thousand seasoned troops
7 from Israel for a hundred talents of silver. But a man of
God came to him and said, 'My lord king, do not let the
Israelite army march with you; the LORD is not with

[a] *Verses 1–4: cp. 2 Kgs. 14: 1–6.*

Israel – all these Ephraimites! For, if you make these 8
people[a] your allies in the war, God will overthrow you
in battle; he has power to help or to overthrow.' Then 9
Amaziah said to the man of God, 'What am I to do about
the hundred talents which I have spent on the Israelite
army?' The man of God answered, 'It is in the LORD's
power to give you much more than that.' So Amaziah 10
detached the troops which had come to him from
Ephraim and sent them home; that infuriated them
against Judah and they went home in a rage.

Then Amaziah took heart and led his men to the Valley 11
of Salt and there killed ten thousand men of Seir. The 12
men of Judah captured another ten thousand men alive,
brought them to the top of a cliff[b] and hurled them over
so that they were all dashed to pieces. Meanwhile the 13
troops which Amaziah had sent home without allowing
them to take part in the battle raided the cities of Judah
from Samaria to Beth-horon, massacred three thousand
people in them and carried off quantities of booty.

After Amaziah had returned from the defeat of the 14
Edomites, he brought the gods of the people of Seir and,
setting them up as his own gods, worshipped them and
burnt sacrifices to them. The LORD was angry with 15
Amaziah for this and sent a prophet who said to him,
'Why have you resorted to gods who could not save
their own people from you?' But while he was speaking, 16
the king said to him, 'Have we appointed you counsellor
to the king? Stop! Why risk your life?' The prophet did
stop, but first he said, 'I know that God has determined

[a] these people: *prob. rdg.; Heb. obscure.*
[b] a cliff: *or Sela.*

to destroy you because you have done this and have not listened to my counsel.'

17[a] Then Amaziah king of Judah, after consultation, sent messengers to Jehoash son of Jehoahaz, son of Jehu, king

18 of Israel, to propose a meeting. But Jehoash king of Israel sent this answer to Amaziah king of Judah: 'A thistle in Lebanon sent to a cedar in Lebanon to say, "Give your daughter in marriage to my son." But a wild beast in

19 Lebanon, passing by, trampled on the thistle. You have defeated Edom, you say, but it has gone to your head. Enjoy your glory at home and stay there. Why should you involve yourself in disaster and bring yourself to the ground, and Judah with you?'

20 But Amaziah would not listen; and this was God's doing in order to give Judah into the power of Jehoash,[b]

21 because they had resorted to the gods of Edom. So Jehoash king of Israel marched out, and he and Amaziah king of Judah met one another at Beth-shemesh in Judah.

22 The men of Judah were routed by Israel and fled to their

23 homes. But Jehoash king of Israel captured Amaziah king of Judah, son of Joash, son of Jehoahaz, at Beth-shemesh, and brought him to Jerusalem. There he broke down the city wall from the Gate of Ephraim to the Corner Gate,

24 a distance of four hundred cubits; he also took[c] all the gold and silver and all the vessels found in the house of God, in the care of Obed-edom, and the treasures of the royal palace, as well as hostages, and returned to Samaria.

25[d] Amaziah son of Joash, king of Judah, outlived Jehoash

[a] *Verses 17–24: cp. 2 Kgs. 14: 8–14.*   [b] of Jehoash: *so Luc. Sept.;*
Heb. om.   [c] he also took: *prob. rdg., cp. 2 Kgs. 14: 14; Heb. om.*
[d] *25: 25 – 26: 2: cp. 2 Kgs. 14: 17–22.*

son of Jehoahaz, king of Israel, by fifteen years. The other 26
events of Amaziah's reign, from first to last, are recorded
in the annals of the kings of Judah and Israel. From the 27
time when he turned away from the LORD, there was
conspiracy against him in Jerusalem and he fled to
Lachish; but they sent after him to Lachish and put him
to death there. Then his body was conveyed on horseback 28
to Jerusalem, and there he was buried with his forefathers
in the city of David.[a]

✱ The account of Joash's reign made a sharp division between
an initial period of favour and then a fall from grace. Amaziah
is differently treated, with an intermingling of periods of
acceptance of the divine will and of rejection. Such variations
should be borne in mind against any tendency to stereotype
the Chronicler's presentation of his people's history. Again,
the basic source of the material is clearly to be found in 2 Kings
(ch. 14), but there are extensive modifications.

1. *his mother:* the queen-mother often played an important
role in the monarchical period, but the Chronicler probably
was unaware of this and only rarely incorporates such notes
from Kings.

2. *but not whole-heartedly:* a warning of likely weakness is
already given.

4. *in obedience to the LORD's command:* the reference is to
Deut. 24: 16, which probably modified earlier and harsher
practice.

7. *the LORD is not with Israel:* the reference here is, of
course, to the northern kingdom, as the explanatory note, *all
these Ephraimites,* makes clear. The Chronicler emphasizes
both that it is only with the people of the south that the
divine presence is assured, and that to make an alliance with

[a] *So some MSS.; others* the city of Judah.

245

the north is to reject that presence. The episode has no parallel in Kings.

12. *hurled them over so that they were all dashed to pieces:* the fact that such an appalling massacre is almost certainly no more than an invention of the Chronicler's, at least as involving the numbers here mentioned, only removes by one step the problem that is created for a modern reader. It is one of many examples of the bitter hostility which existed between Judah and Edom (here represented by *Seir*, its chief mountain-range) in the later Old Testament period. Psalm 137 and the book of Obadiah are other examples of comparable bitterness. We are forcibly reminded that the Bible has as much to tell us about attitudes to avoid as of behaviour to be imitated.

13. This verse is the sequel to verse 10, but is very unexpected in that Amaziah's faith leads to this reversal. The suggestion has been made that there should be a change of subject before *massacred*, so that it is the northern mercenaries who are killed. This eases the sense, though the meaning of the Hebrew is more naturally conveyed by the N.E.B. translation.

14. *worshipped them:* the alternation of faith and unfaith in Amaziah continues. There is no other evidence for the worship of Edomite gods in Judah, and it seems very unusual for the victor to worship the gods of those whom he has defeated.

15–16. The prophetic condemnation echoes a theme found frequently in the prophetic books: the folly of resorting to gods who are powerless to save even those who are their worshippers. It is found in the taunts against idolatry in the second part of Isaiah (e.g. 44: 9–20) and is used against the people of Judah by the Rabshakeh (N.E.B. 'chief officer') of the Assyrian army (2 Kings 18: 33–5). That scene is also recalled here by the requirement to *Stop!* – which the prophet does, but not before he has delivered the gist of his message (cp. 2 Kings 18: 26).

17. *to propose a meeting:* the phrase in itself is neutral, as the translation suggests, but since the same phrase is used in

verse 21 (there translated 'met one another') in the context of a battle, it may have been a technical term denoting a declaration of war. The section to verse 24 closely follows 2 Kings 14: 8–14, but both the allusion to Edom and the discomfiture of Amaziah make it very appropriate in its context.

20. *and this was God's doing…gods of Edom:* this addition by the Chronicler serves to link this episode specifically to what has gone before.

23. *and brought him to Jerusalem:* a further addition, stressing the humiliation brought upon Amaziah. The destruction of Jerusalem underlines the hostility that existed at many periods between the two kingdoms.

24. *in the care of Obed-edom:* a further, and somewhat puzzling, addition. The intention is presumably to supply a link back to the earlier references to Obed-edom (cp. 1 Chron. 13: 13f. and 26: 15) and there may be an allusion also to the other references to Edom in this chapter. If this is so, it has not been preserved very clearly.

25–8. The same alternation of judgement and reprieve continues through Amaziah's reign. He is granted fifteen years more of rule; he is nevertheless murdered, yet in the end he receives honourable burial.

27. *From the time when he turned away from the LORD:* by this addition the Chronicler not only makes a more coherent story, but also indicates that there was a remnant in Judah loyal to the LORD who would not accept a faithless ruler. ✷

UZZIAH UNDER DIVINE FAVOUR

All the people of Judah took Uzziah, now sixteen years **26** old, and made him king in succession to his father Amaziah. It was he who built Eloth and restored it to 2 Judah after the king rested with his forefathers.

Uzziah was sixteen years old when he came to the 3[a]

[a] *Verses 3, 4: cp. 2 Kgs. 15: 2, 3.*

throne, and he reigned in Jerusalem for fifty-two years;
4 his mother was Jecoliah of Jerusalem. He did what was
right in the eyes of the LORD, as Amaziah his father had
5 done. He set himself to seek the guidance of God in the
days of Zechariah, who instructed him in the fear of[a]
God; as long as he sought guidance of the LORD, God
caused him to prosper.

6   He took the field against the Philistines and broke down
the walls of Gath, Jabneh, and Ashdod; and he built cities
7 in the territory of Ashdod and among the Philistines. God
aided him against them, against the Arabs who lived in
8 Gur-baal, and against the Meunites. The Ammonites
brought gifts to Uzziah and his fame spread to the bor-
9 ders of Egypt, for he had become very powerful. Besides,
he built towers in Jerusalem at the Corner Gate, at the
Valley Gate, and at the escarpment, and fortified them.
10 He built other towers in the wilderness and dug many
cisterns, for he had large herds of cattle both in the
Shephelah and in the plain. He also had farmers and vine-
dressers in the hill-country and in the fertile lands, for he
loved the soil.

11   Uzziah had an army of soldiers trained and ready for
service, grouped according to the census made by Jeiel
the adjutant-general and Maaseiah the clerk under the
direction of Hananiah, one of the king's commanders.
12 The total number of heads of families which supplied
13 seasoned warriors was two thousand six hundred. Under
their command was an army of three hundred and seven
thousand five hundred, a powerful fighting force to aid
14 the king against his enemies. Uzziah prepared for the

[a] in the fear of: *so some MSS.; others* on seeing.

whole army shields, spears, helmets, coats of mail, bows, and[a] sling-stones. In Jerusalem he had machines designed 15 by engineers for use upon towers and bastions, made to discharge arrows and large stones. His fame spread far and wide, for he was so wonderfully gifted that he became very powerful.

* The account of Uzziah's reign is structured in a way closely resembling that of Joash in ch. 24: a period when 'He set himself to seek the guidance of God' (verse 5), followed by a time when 'he offended against the LORD' (verse 16). The account of his reign in 2 Kings 15 is extremely brief and each part of the Chronicler's account has been considerably expanded. It seems likely that during his reign, which lasted approximately for the first half of the eighth century B.C., Judah enjoyed considerable prosperity, but there is no independent evidence for the campaigns here described.

1. *Uzziah:* so named throughout this chapter, and in the introductory verses to several prophetic books (Isaiah, Hosea, Amos). In 1 Chron. 3: 12 he is called 'Azariah', and in 2 Kings 15 both names are found. The most satisfactory explanation of this variation is that one was a birth-name, the other a name given on accession to the throne. This may be right, but, if so, there is no agreement which was which!

2. *Eloth:* modern Eilat on the Red Sea. For ancient Israel, as for the modern state, this provided an important commercial outlet. An unelaborated note of this kind may well reflect a genuinely historical tradition available to the Chronicler.

5. The parallel with Joash extends to the picture of a wise counsellor, whose *guidance* led to his good standing with God. This *Zechariah* is otherwise unknown – it is not clear whether any direct link with the Zechariah who was murdered at the instigation of Joash (24: 20) is intended.

[a] *Prob. rdg.; Heb. adds* for.

6–8. This picture of Uzziah's military success – likely in itself, though unsupported by any further evidence – is used by the Chronicler to illustrate the theme of divine favour giving strength. This is especially appropriate at this point, for the name *Uzziah* means 'Yahweh is my strength'. Of the places mentioned Gath and Ashdod are two of the Philistine cities; Jabneh is in the same district and under its later name 'Jamnia' was the meeting-place of those who did so much to establish Judaism after the destruction of the Jerusalem temple in the first century A.D.; Gur-baal is otherwise unknown, and there is some doubt whether the name has been correctly transmitted.

9–10. It is impossible to establish in detail the nature of Uzziah's building work in Jerusalem, because of the difficulty in excavating an inhabited site; but both this and the picture given in the following verses of an expansion of Judah's power and a reorganization of the state structure fit in with what archaeological investigation at a number of sites, especially in the far south of the country, has indicated. The suggestion has even been made that there might be a link between the *towers in the wilderness* and the later settlement at Qumran where the Dead Sea Scrolls were found.

13. *three hundred and seven thousand five hundred:* though we may accept the fact of a reorganization of an army, the numbers are once again clearly an exaggeration. An Assyrian annal from the latter part of this period claims a victory over the army of Azariah (Uzziah) of Judah, and it is possible that it was the increasing threat from Assyria that led to the reorganization. *

UZZIAH FALLS FROM FAVOUR

But when he grew powerful his pride led to his own 16
undoing:[a] he offended against the LORD his God by
entering the temple of the LORD to burn incense on the
altar of incense. Azariah the priest and eighty others of the 17
LORD's priests, courageous men, went in after King
Uzziah, confronted him and said, 'It is not for you, 18
Uzziah, to burn incense to the LORD, but for the Aaronite
priests who have been consecrated for that office. Leave
the sanctuary; for you have offended, and that will certainly bring you no honour from the LORD God.' The 19
king, who had a censer in his hand ready to burn incense,
was indignant; and because of his indignation at the
priests, leprosy broke out on his forehead in the presence
of the priests, there in the house of the LORD, beside the
altar of incense. When Azariah the chief priest and the 20
other priests looked towards him, they saw that he had
leprosy on his forehead and they hurried him out of the
temple, and indeed he himself hastened to leave, because
the LORD had struck him with the disease. And King 21[b]
Uzziah remained a leper till the day of his death; he lived
in his own house as a leper, relieved of all duties and excluded from the house of the LORD, while his son Jotham
was comptroller of the household and regent. The other 22
events of Uzziah's reign, from first to last, are recorded by
the prophet Isaiah son of Amoz. So he rested with his 23
forefathers and was buried in a burial-ground, but not

[a] his pride...undoing: *or* he became so proud that he acted corruptly.
[b] *Verses 21–3: cp. 2 Kgs. 15: 5–7.*

that of the kings;[a] for they said, 'He is a leper'; and he was succeeded by his son Jotham.

✶ In 2 Kings 15: 5 it is simply stated that 'The LORD struck the king with leprosy', no further detail being given. Upon this source the Chronicler constructs a story of a midrashic type (see the note on 13: 22) accounting for this manifestation of divine displeasure.

16. *by entering the temple of the LORD to burn incense:* this is contrary to the regulations in the Pentateuch limiting ritual actions of this kind to the priesthood. See in particular the story of Korah in Num. 16, and the regulations laid down in Num. 18. But these requirements – though they would have been understood by the Chronicler's own readers – come from the latest parts of the Pentateuch, and were almost certainly not operative at Uzziah's time. Indeed the books of Samuel and Kings have many examples of kings playing a prominent part in the ritual, from David onwards. This story must therefore be seen as an illustrative one presenting the Chronicler's own interpretation of divine favour and disfavour.

17. *Azariah the priest:* not otherwise mentioned, since neither he nor the other priests mentioned in 2 Chronicles seem to appear in the Levitical genealogies in 1 Chron. 6. It may be coincidence that his name is the same as the alternative form of Uzziah, but it is also possible that this name is given him deliberately as part of the story.

19. *because of his indignation at the priests:* it is noteworthy that the actual cause of Uzziah's affliction is said to be his *indignation* (perhaps better 'rage') rather than the action itself. In the Chronicler's time the priests were the leaders of society, and part of his concern for the maintenance of the existing state of affairs involved proper reverence for those in authority. *leprosy:* not Hansen's disease, as true leprosy is now called,

[a] in a...kings: *so Pesh.; Heb.* with his forefathers in the burial-ground belonging to the kings.

but some form of skin disease. The N.E.B. has a footnote to indicate this fact in 2 Kings 15, but not here, where the same word is used.

20. *he himself hastened to leave:* there were strict rules for excluding anyone afflicted with this disease from the community (Lev. 13), which would of course apply with the greatest force to the temple itself, regarded as the most holy place.

21. *his son Jotham was...regent:* the period from Uzziah until the reign of Manasseh (2 Chron. 33) is one of the most confused chronologically in the history of Judah, and one of the unknown factors is the length of time that Jotham acted as regent for his father. ✷

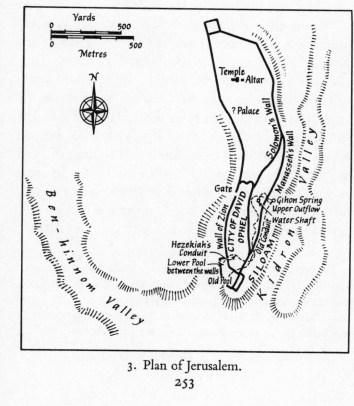

3. Plan of Jerusalem.

THE REIGN OF JOTHAM

27 1[a] Jotham was twenty-five years old when he came to the throne, and he reigned in Jerusalem for sixteen years; his
2 mother was Jerushah daughter of Zadok. He did what was right in the eyes of the LORD, as his father Uzziah had done, but unlike him he did not enter the temple of the LORD; the people, however, continued their corrupt
3 practices. He constructed the upper gate of the house of
4 the LORD and built extensively on the wall at Ophel. He built cities in the hill-country of Judah, and forts and
5 towers on the wooded hills. He made war on the king of the Ammonites and defeated him; and that year the Ammonites gave him a hundred talents of silver, ten thousand kor of wheat and ten thousand of barley. They paid him the same tribute in the second and third years.
6 Jotham became very powerful because he maintained a
7 steady course of obedience to the LORD his God. The other events of Jotham's reign, all that he did in war and in peace, are recorded in the annals of the kings of Israel
8 and Judah. He was twenty-five years old when he came to the throne, and he reigned in Jerusalem for sixteen
9 years. He rested with his forefathers and was buried in the city of David; and he was succeeded by his son Ahaz.

* By contrast with the considerable detail that is provided both for Uzziah and for those kings who succeeded Jotham, Jotham's own reign is treated very cursorily both in Kings and Chronicles. It may well be that his period as sole ruler was brief; the 'sixteen years' of verse 1 probably includes the

[a] *Verses 1–3: cp. 2 Kgs. 15: 33–5.*

time when he was regent for his father, and his sole reign may not have lasted longer than seven years (about 742–735 B.C.).

2. *but unlike him he did not enter the temple of the LORD:* the point being stressed is that Jotham continued in divine favour, unlike his father who had forfeited it through his presumptuous behaviour.

3. *and built extensively on the wall at Ophel:* this addition to the material in 2 Kings 15 refers to an area which appears to have caused concern in the fortification of Jerusalem (cp. 33: 14). The exact site of the *Ophel* (the word means 'mound') is unknown, but it was south of the temple-site, in the city of David, overlooking the Kidron Valley.

4–6. These verses are not found in 2 Kings. Historically the events recorded here appear to be a continuation of Uzziah's policy of strengthening his kingdom against possible external attack; theologically they are understood by the Chronicler as symbolic of the security which God gives to those who are faithful to him.

8. This verse duplicates information already given in verse 1, and may imply that more than one source was being used by the Chronicler. ✳

THE APOSTASY OF AHAZ

Ahaz was twenty years old when he came to the throne, **28** 1[a] and he reigned in Jerusalem for sixteen years. He did not do what was right in the eyes of the LORD like his forefather David, but followed in the footsteps of the kings of 2 Israel, and cast metal images for the Baalim. He also burnt 3 sacrifices in the Valley of Ben-hinnom; he even burnt his sons in[b] the fire according to the abominable practice of

[a] *Verses 1–4: cp. 2 Kgs. 16: 2–4.*
[b] burnt his sons in: *or, with one MS.,* passed his sons through.

the nations whom the LORD had dispossessed in favour of
4 the Israelites. He slaughtered and burnt sacrifices at the
hill-shrines and on the hill-tops and under every spreading
tree.

5   The LORD his God let him suffer at the hands of the
king of Aram, and the Aramaeans defeated him, took
many captives and brought them to Damascus; he was
also made to suffer at the hands of the king of Israel, who
6 inflicted a severe defeat on him. This was Pekah son of
Remaliah, who killed in one day a hundred and twenty
thousand men of Judah, seasoned troops, because they had
7 forsaken the LORD the God of their fathers. And Zichri,
an Ephraimite hero, killed Maaseiah the king's son[a] and
Azrikam the comptroller of the household and Elkanah
8 the king's chief minister. The Israelites took captive from
their kinsmen two hundred thousand women and children; they also took a large amount of booty and brought
it to Samaria.

9   A prophet of the LORD was there, Oded by name; he
went out to meet the army as it returned to Samaria and
said to them, 'It is because the LORD the God of your
fathers is angry with Judah that he has given them into
your power; and you have massacred them in a rage that
10 has towered up to heaven. Now you propose to force the
people of Judah and Jerusalem, male and female, into
slavery. Are not you also guilty men before the LORD
11 your God? Now, listen to me. Send back those you have
taken captive from your kinsmen, for the anger of the
12 LORD is roused against you.' Next, some Ephraimite
chiefs, Azariah son of Jehohanan, Berechiah son of

[a] son: *or* deputy.

Meshillemoth, Hezekiah[a] son of Shallum, and Amasa son
of Hadlai, met those who were returning from the war
and said to them, 'You must not bring these captives into   13
our country; what you are proposing would make us
guilty before the LORD and add to our sins and trans-
gressions. We are guilty enough already, and there is
fierce anger against Israel.' So the armed men left the   14
captives and the spoil with the officers and the assembled
people. The captives were put in charge of men nomi-   15
nated for this duty, who found clothes from the spoil for
all who were naked. They clothed them and shod them,
gave them food and drink, and anointed them; those who
were tottering from exhaustion they conveyed on the
backs of asses, and so brought them to their kinsmen in
Jericho, in the Vale of Palm Trees. Then they themselves
returned to Samaria.

* We have noted on several occasions that the Chronicler's
judgement upon a particular king is likely to be more
balanced than the verdict found in Kings, where condemnation is frequently unqualified. Ahaz, however, is an exception;
in his case, the Chronicler sees no redeeming features. Much
of his material is drawn from 2 Kings 16, where the judgement
is already a severe one, but he also has fresh stories of his own.
It is in the light of this complete condemnation of Ahaz that
we may best understand the unexpected episode in verses 9–
15; the wickedness of Ahaz even serves to put the northerners
in a favourable light.

1. *Ahaz was twenty years old…reigned in Jerusalem for
sixteen years:* the chronological difficulties already noted under
Jotham become more acute here, for on this reckoning Ahaz
died at the age of thirty-six; yet 29: 1 tells us that his son

[a] Or Jehizkiah.

257

Hezekiah was then already twenty-five. In 2 Kings the matter is still further complicated by the presence of data correlating the southern and northern kingdoms, and no entirely satisfactory solution of these problems has ever been put forward. The events that are certainly to be associated with Ahaz' reign took place in the years following 735, but we have no means of telling whether they came at the beginning or end of his reign.

2. *cast metal images for the Baalim:* a double offence is involved here. Not only is the making of such images forbidden in the Pentateuch (Exod. 34: 17), but that they should be for Canaanite gods was to compound the offence.

3. *the Valley of Ben-hinnom:* the valley south of Jerusalem, where idolatrous practices condemned by the prophets were carried out (cp. Jer. 7: 31). Later it apparently became a continually smouldering rubbish-pit and gave its name (*Ge* is the Hebrew for 'valley') to the word 'Gehenna' as a name for a place of torment after death. *he even burnt his sons in the fire:* the Chronicler has made two small but important changes in the text of 2 Kings 16: 3, which was his source. He has altered 'son' to *sons*, thereby changing a single incident into a regular practice; and he has made a text which may originally have referred to some sort of ritual ordeal into a specific statement of human sacrifice.

5. *The LORD his God let him suffer at the hands of the king of Aram:* in the years following 735, the kings of Aram (Syria) and northern Israel tried to establish a coalition of the small states of Syria and Palestine against the increasing threat from Assyria. This episode is described in Isa. 7, 2 Kings 16 and the present chapter, and each tradition presents the story in a different way in accordance with its own understanding of God's dealings with his people. The presentation here is noteworthy in that it emphasizes the success of the kings against Ahaz, whereas 2 Kings and Isaiah both stress their ineffectiveness; and in the way in which the threat from Aram and from Israel is treated separately, rather than as part

of one coalition. *brought them to Damascus:* this event is other-wise unknown, and may be introduced by the Chronicler as a fulfilment of the prophecy of Amos 5: 27.

6. *seasoned troops:* this they may have been, but it was of no avail since *they had forsaken the LORD.*

7. *Zichri, an Ephraimite hero:* nothing is known of him from early traditions, but at a later date Samaritan legend fastened on him and pictured him as a Samaritan, while the whole following episode is also claimed as an example of Samaritan magnanimity. The details of the leading men killed serve to emphasize the gravity of the situation brought about by apostasy; nothing is known of any of those here mentioned. *the king's chief minister:* literally 'second to the king', a title found also in Esther 10: 3. It may correspond to a rank well known in the Chronicler's day.

9–15. This episode is one of the most unexpected (and attractive) in the whole of the Chronicler's work. It is clearly one of the formative influences underlying Jesus' story of the good Samaritan in Luke 10: 30–7. Elsewhere in the Chroni-cler's work he can find no good thing to say about the northerners. In understanding this story we need to remember, first, that it is told as a means of emphasizing that the LORD was *angry with Judah* (verse 9), and secondly, that, though the Chronicler rejected the northerners for having forsaken worship at Jerusalem, he still hoped for their return, and this story may therefore be seen as an appeal, in the hope that there would in his own day be those who were large-hearted like the *Ephraimite chiefs* of verse 12 and would either them-selves return to Jerusalem or at least put no obstacle in the way of those who wished to do so. We should also notice that no attempt is made to hide the guilt of the north (*We are guilty enough already, and there is fierce anger against Israel*) (verse 13), but this does not exclude the possibility of faithful prophets and others being found there who will appeal to the people to return to a better way. (Why such prophets did not themselves return to Jerusalem seems not to be asked.) ✳

THE PUNISHMENT FOR APOSTASY

16 At that time King Ahaz sent to the king[a] of Assyria for
17 help. The Edomites had invaded again and defeated Judah
18 and taken away prisoners; and the Philistines had raided
the cities of the Shephelah and of the Negeb of Judah and
had captured Beth-shemesh, Aijalon, and Gederoth, as
well as Soco, Timnah, and Gimzo with their villages, and
19 occupied them. The LORD had reduced Judah to submission because of Ahaz king of Judah;[b] for his actions
in Judah had been unbridled and he had been grossly
20 unfaithful to the LORD. Then Tiglath-pileser[c] king of
Assyria marched against him and, so far from assisting
21 him, pressed him hard. Ahaz stripped the house of the
LORD, the king's palace and the houses of his officers, and
gave the plunder to the king of Assyria; but all to no
purpose.

22   This King Ahaz, when hard pressed, became more and
23 more unfaithful to the LORD; he sacrificed to the gods of
Damascus who had defeated him and said, 'The gods of
the kings of Aram helped them; I will sacrifice to them so
that they may help me.' But in fact they caused his down-
24 fall and that of all Israel. Then Ahaz gathered together the
vessels of the house of God and broke them up, and shut
the doors of the house of the LORD; he made himself
25 altars at every corner in Jerusalem, and at every single city
of Judah he made hill-shrines to burn sacrifices to other
gods and provoked the anger of the LORD the God of his
fathers.

[a] *So Sept.; Heb.* kings.   [b] *So some MSS.; others* Israel.
[c] *So Pesh.; Heb.* Tilgath-pilneser.

The other acts and all the events of his reign, from first 26^a to last, are recorded in the annals of the kings of Judah and Israel. So Ahaz rested with his forefathers and was 27 buried in the city of Jerusalem, but was not given burial with the kings of Judah.^{b} He was succeeded by his son Hezekiah.

* By the time that the Chronicler wrote, Assyria had become an almost legendary symbol of the forces of wickedness to whom those who forsook the way of God might be delivered (cp. the picture in Jonah). To be delivered into Assyrian power was therefore seen as the inevitable punishment of Ahaz' apostasy. Again the main source is 2 Kings, but as in the first half of the chapter, the Chronicler has added further material and also drawn the existing source into a story which gives a somewhat different picture from that found in the earlier book.

16. *Ahaz sent to the king of Assyria for help:* in Kings, this is related to the attacks of Aram and Israel, rather than, as here, that of Edomites and Philistines. The Hebrew text 'kings' (see footnote) may reflect the Chronicler's belief, noted already at the commentary on 1 Chron. 5: 26, that Pul and Tiglath-pileser were separate kings.

20. *so far from assisting him, pressed him hard:* this tradition is peculiar to the Chronicler, and seems to imply that Ahaz' wickedness was doubly repaid to him.

23. *he sacrificed to the gods of Damascus:* this episode appears to be based on the account in 2 Kings 16: 10–14 of the new altar built in the temple on the model of one Ahaz had seen at Damascus. It is disputed whether in the Kings version this should be understood as an Assyrian or an Aramaean altar, but the Chronicler clearly takes it in the latter sense.

they caused his downfall: the N.E.B. rendering, like the

[a] *Verses 26, 27: cp. 2 Kgs. 16: 19, 20.*   [b] *So Pesh.; Heb.* Israel.

Hebrew, is somewhat ambiguous, but the general sense clearly is that Ahaz' downfall was brought about by his worship of these gods, rather than that they were effective in bringing it about.

24. So impious a king cannot be associated with the temple, and so it stated that its doors were shut; true worship ceased.

27. *but was not given burial with the kings of Judah*: the Chronicler clearly attached great importance to the appropriate funerary ceremonies, and notes what took place in the case of each king. The wickedness of Ahaz had led him astray from the true line of kings; therefore he cannot have been buried with them. This directly contradicts 2 Kings 16: 20. ✶

The kings of Judah from Hezekiah to the exile

HEZEKIAH: TRUE RELIGION RESTORED

29 1[a] HEZEKIAH WAS TWENTY-FIVE YEARS OLD when he came to the throne, and he reigned in Jerusalem for twenty-nine years; his mother was Abijah daughter of
2 Zechariah. He did what was right in the eyes of the LORD, as David his forefather had done.

3 In the first year of his reign, in the first month, he opened the gates of the house of the LORD and repaired
4 them. He brought in the priests and the Levites and gathered them together in the square on the east side, and
5 said to them, 'Levites, listen to me. Hallow yourselves

[a] *Verses 1, 2: cp. 2 Kgs. 18: 1-3.*

now, hallow the house of the LORD the God of your
fathers, and remove the pollution from the sanctuary. For 6
our forefathers were unfaithful and did what was wrong
in the eyes of the LORD our God; they forsook him, they
would have nothing to do with his dwelling-place, they
turned their backs on it. They shut the doors of the porch 7
and extinguished the lamps, they ceased to burn incense
and offer whole-offerings in the sanctuary to the God of
Israel. Therefore the anger of the LORD fell upon Judah 8
and Jerusalem and he made them repugnant, an object of
horror and derision, as you see for yourselves. Hence it is 9
that our fathers have fallen by the sword, our sons and
daughters and our wives are in captivity. Now I intend 10
that we should pledge ourselves to the LORD the God of
Israel, in order that his anger may be averted from us. So, 11
my sons, let no time be lost; for the LORD has chosen you
to serve him and to minister to him, to be his ministers
and to burn sacrifices.'

Then the Levites set to work – Mahath son of Amasai 12
and Joel son of Azariah of the family of Kohath; of the
family of Merari, Kish son of Abdi and Azariah son of
Jehalelel; of the family of Gershon, Joah son of Zimmah
and Eden son of Joah; of the family of Elizaphan, Shimri 13
and Jeiel; of the family of Asaph, Zechariah and Mattaniah; of the family of Heman, Jehiel and Shimei; and of 14
the family of Jeduthun, Shemaiah and Uzziel. They 15
assembled their kinsmen and hallowed themselves, and
then went in, as the king had instructed them at the
LORD's command, to purify the house of the LORD. The 16
priests went inside to purify the house of the LORD; they
removed all the pollution which they found in the temple

into the court of the house of the LORD, and the Levites took it from them and carried it outside to the gorge of

17 the Kidron. They began the rites on the first day of the first month, and on the eighth day they reached the porch; then for eight days they consecrated the house of the LORD, and on the sixteenth day of the first month they

18 finished. Then they went into the palace*a* and said to King Hezekiah, 'We have purified the whole of the house of the LORD, the altar of whole-offering with all its vessels, and the table for the Bread of the Presence arranged in

19 rows with all its vessels; and we have put in order and consecrated all the vessels which King Ahaz cast aside during his reign, when he was unfaithful. They are now in place before the altar of the LORD.'

20   Then King Hezekiah rose early, assembled the officers
21 of the city and went up to the house of the LORD. They brought seven bulls, seven rams, and seven lambs for the whole-offering,*b* and seven he-goats as a sin-offering for the kingdom, for the sanctuary, and for Judah; these he commanded the priests of Aaron's line to offer on the

22 altar of the LORD. So the bulls were slaughtered, and the priests took their blood and flung it against the altar; the rams were slaughtered, and their blood was flung against the altar; the lambs were slaughtered, and their blood was

23 flung against the altar. Then the he-goats for the sin-offering were brought before the king and the assembly,
24 who laid their hands on them; and the priests slaughtered them and used their blood as a sin-offering on the altar to make expiation for all Israel. For the king had com-

[a] into the palace: *lit.* within.
[b] for the whole-offering: *prob. rdg.; Heb. om.*

manded that the whole-offering and the sin-offering should
be made for all Israel.

He posted the Levites in the house of the LORD with 25
cymbals, lutes, and harps, according to the rule prescribed
by David, by Gad the king's seer and Nathan the prophet;
for this rule had come from the LORD through his prophets. The Levites stood ready with the instruments of 26
David, and the priests with the trumpets. Hezekiah gave 27
the order that the whole-offering should be offered on the
altar. At the moment when the whole-offering began, the
song to the LORD began too, with the trumpets, led by the
instruments of David king of Israel. The whole assembly 28
prostrated themselves, the singers sang and the trumpeters sounded; all this continued until the whole-offering
was complete. When the offering was complete, the king 29
and all his company bowed down and prostrated themselves. And King Hezekiah and his officers commanded 30
the Levites to praise the LORD in the words of David and
of Asaph the seer. So they praised him most joyfully and
bowed down and prostrated themselves.

Then Hezekiah said, 'You have now given to the LORD 31
with open hands; approach with your sacrifices and thank-
offerings for the house of the LORD.' So the assembly
brought sacrifices and thank-offerings; and every man of
willing spirit brought whole-offerings. The number of 32
whole-offerings which the assembly brought was seventy
bulls, a hundred rams, and two hundred lambs; all these
made a whole-offering to the LORD. And the consecrated 33
offerings were six hundred bulls and three thousand
sheep. But the priests were too few and could not flay all 34
the whole-offerings; so their colleagues the Levites helped

them until the work was completed and all the priests had hallowed themselves – for the Levites had been more
35 scrupulous than the priests in hallowing themselves. There were indeed whole-offerings in abundance, besides the fat of the shared-offerings and the drink-offerings for the whole-offerings. In this way the service of the house of
36 the LORD was restored; and Hezekiah and all the people rejoiced over what God had done for the people and because it had come about so suddenly.

* For the editor of the books of Kings, the climax of Judah's history under the monarchy was reached with Josiah; for the Chronicler, by contrast, it was Hezekiah who – though not faultless – most nearly approached the perfect response to God's will. It is not surprising, therefore, to find in the chapters dealing with Hezekiah a considerable elaboration on the earlier source, nor that – as with David – this elaboration is mainly concerned with religious reforms: the purification of the temple after the disasters of Ahaz' reign, and the re-establishment of the correct ritual.

1. *Twenty-five years old...reigned...for twenty-nine years:* we have noted already that the reigns of Jotham and Ahaz presented chronological problems. These continue with Hezekiah, whose accession-date has been variously calculated at either 727 or 715 B.C.

3. *In the first year of his reign, in the first month:* of all those whom the Chronicler especially praises – David, Hezekiah, the returning exiles – it is stressed that they began their good work at the first opportunity. What follows is peculiar to the Chronicler; the Kings material on Hezekiah is almost entirely concerned with his political struggles.

5–11. Hezekiah here preaches a sermon, in the manner found elsewhere in the mouths of Levites (cp. ch. 20). As with such sermons elsewhere, this one is characterized by the application of prophetic and other scriptural passages – in this case notably the curses of Deut. 28 and the warnings of the prophets (e.g. Jer. 19: 8, which is alluded to in verse 8). The other striking feature of this sermon is its universality of application; it is not concerned simply with Hezekiah's own day, for which some of the allusions would be inappropriate, but with the constant threat under which Judah lived. Thus the picture of slaughter and of the derision of other nations, though both motifs are common in earlier writings, would most readily apply to the exile.

12–14. The Levite families named here are those listed in 1 Chron. 6, though the individuals are not otherwise known.

16. *to the gorge of the Kidron:* the Chronicler is here drawing a deliberate parallel between his account of Hezekiah's reform and the account of Josiah's reform in 2 Kings 23, where similarly the remnants of the pagan altars were thrown 'into the gorge of the Kidron' (verse 12); similar action had also been reported of Asa (2 Chron. 15: 16).

17. *the first day of the first month:* again this is probably a note of the urgency with which the task was taken up rather than an exact calendrical detail.

19. *consecrated all the vessels which King Ahaz cast aside:* an important theme for the Chronicler is that, though the temple itself might be polluted (as by Ahaz) or destroyed (as by the Babylonian army) yet the vessels remained inviolate, and the proper continuity of worship could therefore be ensured when the temple was once again fit for worship (cp. Ezra 1: 6–10).

20–4. The offerings made correspond with the requirements for the 'sin-offering' in Lev. 4. The N.E.B., probably rightly, adds a reference to 'the whole-offering', where bulls, rams and lambs (regarded as alternative forms of offering in Lev. 1) are here all offered to the perfect number of seven.

24. *all Israel:* the Chronicler regarded the southern kingdom as the true Israel, but this now gains added point because the northern kingdom had by this time been destroyed by Assyrian power.

25. The ordinances laid down by David under divine guidance, as recorded in 1 Chron. 25, are here resumed. The whole ceremony is pictured as an equivalent to the original work of David in preparing the temple.

34. *But the priests were too few:* the point is not simply lack of numbers, as the last part of the verse makes clear. *the Levites had been more scrupulous:* a judgement which is more likely to reflect a difference from the Chronicler's own time than a historical record, since in Hezekiah's time the later distinction between priests and Levites was probably unknown. We need not necessarily conclude that the Chronicler and his circle were themselves Levites, but the whole work evinces a favourable attitude toward them.

35. The regular ritual of the temple built after the exile is here described. ✶

HEZEKIAH'S APPEAL TO THE NORTH

30 Then Hezekiah sent word to all Israel and Judah, and also wrote letters to Ephraim and Manasseh, inviting them to come to the house of the LORD in Jerusalem to
2 keep the Passover of the LORD the God of Israel. The king and his officers and all the assembly in Jerusalem had
3 agreed to keep the Passover in the second month, but they had not been able to keep it at that time, because not enough priests had hallowed themselves and the people
4 had not assembled in Jerusalem. The proposal was accept-
5 able to the king and the whole assembly. So they resolved to make a proclamation throughout all Israel, from Beer-sheba to Dan, that the people should come to Jerusalem to keep the Passover of the LORD the God of Israel. Never before had so many kept it according to the prescribed
6 form. Couriers went throughout all Israel and Judah with letters from the king and his officers, proclaiming the

royal command: 'Turn back, men of Israel, to the LORD the God of Abraham, Isaac, and Israel, so that he may turn back to those of you who escaped capture by the kings of Assyria. Do not be like your forefathers and your 7 kinsmen, who were unfaithful to the LORD the God of their fathers, so that he made them an object of horror, as you yourselves saw. Do not be stubborn as your fore- 8 fathers were; submit yourselves to the LORD and enter his sanctuary which he has sanctified for ever, and worship the LORD your God, so that his anger may be averted from you. For when you turn back to the LORD, your 9 kinsmen and your children will win compassion from their captors and return to this land. The LORD your God is gracious and compassionate, and he will not turn away from you if you turn back to him.'

So the couriers passed from city to city through the 10 land of Ephraim and Manasseh and as far as Zebulun, but they were treated with scorn and ridicule. However, a 11 few men of Asher, Manasseh, and Zebulun submitted and came to Jerusalem. Further, the hand of God moved the 12 people in Judah with one accord to carry out what the king and his officers had ordered at the LORD's command.

* In 722 or 721 the already much reduced northern kingdom of Israel was finally overrun by the Assyrians and the territory incorporated in the Assyrian provincial system. The Chronicler does not describe this event, but he assumes knowledge of it in his readers. As we have seen (cp. note on 29: 1) it is doubtful whether Hezekiah was already king when this took place, but the events described in this chapter clearly assume that the northern kingdom had already lost its independent existence. But the Chronicler has already shown his awareness

that even in the apostate northern kingdom might be found some loyal servants of God (cp. 28: 9–15), and so here Hezekiah is pictured as appealing to any such, that they would return to true worship in Jerusalem. Again, a parallel appears to be drawn between Hezekiah as he appeared to the Chronicler and the portrait of Josiah in 2 Kings (especially 23: 21–3), which makes it difficult to determine how far this action has its roots in historical fact and how far it is simply the product of a parallelism drawn out by the Chronicler for his own purposes. If any historical basis is to be traced, it is likely to be in the setting of Hezekiah's rising against Sennacherib rather than at the very beginning of his reign, as suggested here.

1. *Ephraim and Manasseh:* these were the leading tribes of the old northern kingdom.

2. *in the second month:* the account of the inauguration of the Passover in Exod. 12 stresses that it is to be observed in the first month, but provision is also made for an individual to keep the festival in the second month as here (Num. 9: 11). In addition to the reasons listed here for the delay, it has been suggested that just as the Numbers passage indicates ritual impurity as the cause of such postponement, so here the ritual impurity of those who had been worshipping away from Jerusalem may have been in mind.

5. *from Beersheba to Dan:* traditional boundaries of Israel, though elsewhere always listed in the reverse order.

Never before...prescribed form: two characteristic emphases of the Chronicler are here brought out – the idea of an observance outdoing all that had previously taken place, and the importance of the correct ritual. In Exod. 12 the Passover is a family festival; here, as in Deut. 16, it is a national celebration.

6. *those of you who escaped capture by the kings of Assyria:* this clearly presupposes that the fall of Samaria in 722/1 had already taken place. The number of those actually carried away captive was only a small percentage of the total population

(the Assyrians themselves claimed a total of 27,290 people), but later tradition enlarged these numbers until eventually the legend of the 'ten lost tribes' grew up. This passage already suggests a large number of captives. The whole passage to verse 9 is in effect another sermon.

8. *Do not be stubborn as your forefathers were:* this is an allusion to the passages in the Pentateuch which describe Israel during the wilderness wandering as a 'stubborn people' (literally: 'stiff of neck', Exod. 32: 9; Deut. 9: 6). Similarly in verse 9 the description of the LORD as 'gracious and compassionate' would call to mind the description in Exod. 34: 6.

10–12. Three attitudes are set out here. Most of the northerners show *scorn and ridicule*; a few, from the most distant parts, *submitted and came to Jerusalem*; the *people in Judah with one accord* were obedient. It is possible that something like this actually took place – we know little of the detail of Assyrian provincial administration, or of the amount of freedom of movement that was allowed – but it seems at least as likely that the reactions represented here are in reality reflections of the situation in the Chronicler's own time. ✳

THE PASSOVER CELEBRATED

Many people, a very great assembly, came together in 13 Jerusalem to keep the pilgrim-feast of Unleavened Bread in the second month. They began by removing the altars 14 in Jerusalem; they removed the altars for burning sacrifices and threw them into the gorge of the Kidron. They 15 killed the passover lamb on the fourteenth day of the second month; and the priests and the Levites were bitterly ashamed. They hallowed themselves and brought whole-offerings to the house of the LORD. They took their 16 accustomed places, according to the direction laid down for them in the law of Moses the man of God; the priests

flung against the altar the blood which they received from
17 the Levites. But many in the assembly had not hallowed
themselves; therefore the Levites had to kill the passover
lamb for every one who was unclean, in order to hallow
18 him to the LORD. For a majority of the people, many
from Ephraim, Manasseh, Issachar, and Zebulun, had not
kept themselves ritually clean, and therefore kept the
Passover irregularly. But Hezekiah prayed for them, say-
19 ing, 'May the good LORD grant pardon to every one who
makes a practice of seeking guidance of God, the LORD
the God of his fathers, even if he has not observed the
20 rules for the purification of the sanctuary.' The LORD
21 heard Hezekiah and healed the people. And the Israelites
who were present in Jerusalem kept the feast of Unleavened Bread for seven days with great rejoicing, and
the Levites and the priests praised the LORD every day
22 with unrestrained fervour.[a] Hezekiah spoke encouragingly
to all the Levites who had shown true understanding in
the service of the LORD. So they spent the seven days of
the festival sacrificing shared-offerings and making confession to[b] the LORD the God of their fathers.

23 Then the whole assembly agreed to keep the feast for
another seven days; so they kept it for another seven days
24 with general rejoicing. For Hezekiah king of Judah set
aside for the assembly a thousand bulls and seven thousand sheep, and his officers set aside for the assembly
a thousand bulls and ten thousand sheep; and priests
25 hallowed themselves in great numbers. So the whole
assembly of Judah, including the priests and the Levites,

[a] with unrestrained fervour: *prob. rdg.; Heb.* with powerful instruments.   [b] making confession to: *or* confessing.

rejoiced, together with all the assembly which came out
of Israel, and the resident aliens from Israel and those who
lived in Judah. There was great rejoicing in Jerusalem, the 26
like of which had not been known there since the days of
Solomon son of David king of Israel. Then the priests 27
and[a] the Levites stood to bless the people; the LORD
listened to their cry,[b] and their prayer came to God's holy
dwelling-place in heaven.

When this was over, all the Israelites present went out **31**
to the cities of Judah and smashed the sacred pillars,
hacked down the sacred poles and broke up the hill-
shrines and the altars throughout Judah and Benjamin,
Ephraim and Manasseh, until they had made an end of
them. That done, the Israelites returned, each to his own
patrimony in his own city.

✶ In the days before the exile the main festival of the year was
Tabernacles, held in the Autumn. By the time that the
Chronicler wrote, however, the Feast of Passover or Unleavened Bread (two observances which were probably
originally distinct, but had come to be merged together so
that both names are found in this section) had become the
chief festival, and so it was appropriate that a great celebration
of the Passover should be the high-point of Hezekiah's reform.
Again there is a parallel with the account of Josiah's reform
in 2 Kings, which culminated in a celebration of the Passover
(2 Kings 23: 21–4).

14. This verse is somewhat unexpected after the full
account of purification already given in ch. 29. It appears as
if this is a summary of the reforms which had already taken
place.

[a] and: *so many MSS.; others om.*
[b] the LORD...cry: *so Pesh.; Heb.* their cry was heard.

15. *the priests and the Levites were bitterly ashamed:* no reason can be given for this unexpected statement unless it is that the worship had for so long been contaminated. The Chronicler does from time to time criticize the priests (cp. 29: 34), but nowhere is he so critical of the Levites.

18. *kept the Passover irregularly:* the Chronicler does not see in this irregularity grounds for exclusion, but rather uses it as an illustration of the efficacy of prayer. There is so much stress on correct ritual in the Chronicler's work that it is important to bear in mind that he did not regard it as all-important. True prayer could override the non-observance of rules for purification.

22. *the Levites who had shown true understanding:* this is a much more characteristic attitude to the Levites than the criticism of verse 15.

23. *another seven days:* this double period of observance is reminiscent of the account of the dedication festival under Solomon (1 Kings 8: 65; see N.E.B. footnote).

25. This is an important description of the true community: not only *the whole assembly of Judah,* with its religious leaders, but also those from Israel (here of course the northern area) who were willing to join themselves to the true community. There is no spirit of exclusivism here.

27. A summary of an important aspect of the Chronicler's theology: the people blessed by their religious leaders, the gracious willingness of the LORD in heaven to listen to prayer duly offered.

31: 1. *throughout Judah and Benjamin, Ephraim and Manasseh:* the extension of Hezekiah's religious reform in this way is an idealization for which there is little historical justification. The territory of Ephraim and Manasseh, in particular, was under Assyrian control, and there is no indication that Hezekiah's moves for political independence ever reached thus far. ✳

HEZEKIAH: FURTHER RELIGIOUS REFORMS

Then Hezekiah installed the priests and the Levites in 2
office, division by division, allotting to each priest or
Levite his own particular duty, for whole-offerings or
shared-offerings, to give thanks or to sing praise, or to
serve*a* in the gates of the several quarters in the LORD's
house.*b*

The king provided from his own resources, as the share 3
due from him, the whole-offerings for both morning and
evening, and for sabbaths, new moons, and appointed
seasons, as prescribed in the law of the LORD. He ordered 4
the people living in Jerusalem to provide the share due
from the priests and the Levites, so that they might devote
themselves entirely to the law of the LORD. As soon as the 5
king's order was issued to the Israelites, they gave
generously from the firstfruits of their corn and new wine,
oil and honey, all the produce of their land; they brought
a full tithe of everything. The Israelites and the Judaeans 6
living in the cities of Judah also brought a tithe of cattle
and sheep, and a tithe of all produce as offerings*c* dedicated to the LORD their God, and they stacked the produce
in heaps. They began to deposit the heaps in the third 7
month and completed them in the seventh. When Heze- 8
kiah and his officers came and saw the heaps, they blessed
the LORD and his people Israel. Hezekiah asked the priests 9
and the Levites about these heaps, and Azariah the chief 10
priest, who was of the line of Zadok, answered, 'From
the time when the people began to bring their contribu-

[*a*] to serve: *transposed from before* to give thanks.
[*b*] in the LORD's house: *so Sept.; Heb.* of the LORD.
[*c*] tithe of all produce as offerings: *lit.* tithe of offerings.

tion into the house of the LORD, they have had enough to eat, enough and to spare; indeed, the LORD has so greatly blessed them that they have this great store left over.'

11 Then Hezekiah ordered store-rooms to be prepared in
12 the house of the LORD, and this was done; and the people honestly brought in their contributions, the tithe, and their dedicated gifts. The overseer in charge of them was Conaniah the Levite, with Shimei his brother as his
13 deputy; Jehiel, Azaziah, Nahath, Asahel, Jerimoth, Jozabad, Eliel, Ismachiah, Mahath, and Benaiah were appointed by King Hezekiah and Azariah, the chief overseer of the house of God, to assist Conaniah and Shimei his
14 brother. And Kore son of Imnah the Levite, keeper of the East Gate, was in charge of the freewill offerings to God, to apportion the contributions made to the LORD and the
15 most sacred offerings. Eden, Miniamin, Jeshua, Shemaiah, Amariah, and Shecaniah in the priestly cities assisted him in the fair distribution of portions to their kinsmen, young
16 and old[a] alike, by divisions. Irrespective of their registration, shares were distributed to all males three years of age and upwards who entered the house of the LORD to take their daily part in the service, according to their divisions,
17 as their office demanded. The priests were registered by families, the Levites from twenty years of age and up-
18 wards by their offices in their divisions. They were registered with all their dependants, their wives, their sons, and their daughters, the whole company of them, because in virtue of their permanent standing they had
19 to keep themselves duly hallowed. As for the priests of Aaron's line in the common lands attached to their cities,

[a] *Or* high and low.

in every city men were nominated to distribute portions to every male among the priests and to every one who was registered by the Levites.

Such was the action taken by Hezekiah throughout 20 Judah; he did what was good and right and loyal in the sight of the LORD his God. Whatever he undertook in the 21 service of the house of God and in obedience to the law and the commandment to seek guidance of his God, he did with all his heart, and he prospered.

* This section describes the way in which Hezekiah restored to its proper order all the religious ritual of the temple and its priesthood. Like the preceding two chapters it has no parallel in Kings, and is a further example of the way in which the Chronicler presents Hezekiah as the ideal successor of David. Once again much debate has raged over the historical basis of what is here described; in the absence of any supporting evidence, the question must probably be left open, though it should always be borne in mind that the Chronicler's main purpose is not the recording of history but the edification of the people of his own day.

2. The restoration of the temple is now complete, with the personnel carrying out their allotted duties. As so often, it is the temple of the Chronicler's own day which is here envisaged.

6. *The Israelites and the Judaeans living in the cities of Judah:* the phrase is ambiguous in Hebrew as in English. It may be read as if there were a comma after *Israelites*, in which case two distinct groups would be meant; more probably it is simply a rather extended description of the inhabitants of the cities of Judah other than Jerusalem itself, who were acting in full harmony with the inhabitants of the capital, and whose generosity is stressed.

10. The abundance of blessing on those who are loyal to

the Law is stressed. It is difficult to identify the Azariah here mentioned with any of the priests in the list in 1 Chron. 6: 1–15.

12–15. It is a characteristic of the Chronicler's method to insert lists of names at points where he wishes to stress the especial importance and solemnity of what is being undertaken.

16. *three years of age:* this reference is without parallel in the Old Testament, and an amendment, perhaps to 'thirty', has often been suggested.

17. *twenty years of age:* as already noted (cp. 1 Chron. 23: 3), differing ages are given for the point at which Levitical service might first be undertaken.

18. *with all their dependants:* in the Jewish community of New Testament times, and possibly already by the time of the Chronicler, strict regulations were in existence as to whom a priest and a Levite might marry. This was an important manner of keeping themselves *duly hallowed.*

21. *and he prospered:* emphasis is again placed upon the reward given to loyal and devoted service. ✳

HEZEKIAH AND THE ASSYRIAN CRISIS

32 1[a] After these events and this example of loyal conduct, Sennacherib king of Assyria invaded Judah and encamped against the fortified cities, believing that he could attach 2 them to himself. When Hezekiah saw that he had come 3 and was determined to attack Jerusalem, he consulted his civil and military officers about blocking up the springs 4 outside the city; and they encouraged him. They gathered together a large number of people and blocked up all the springs and the stream which flowed through the land. 'Why', they said, 'should Assyrian kings come here and 5 find plenty of water?' Then the king acted boldly; he

[a] *Verses 1–19: cp. 2 Kgs. 18: 13–37; Isa. 36: 1–22.*

made good every breach in the city wall and erected towers on it;[a] he built another wall outside it and strengthened the Millo of the city of David; he also collected a great quantity of weapons and shields. He ap- 6 pointed military commanders over the people and assembled them in the square by the city gate and spoke encouragingly to them in these words: 'Be strong; be 7 brave. Do not let the king of Assyria or the rabble he has brought with him strike terror or panic into your hearts. We have more on our side than he has. He has human 8 strength; but we have the LORD our God to help us and to fight our battles.' So spoke Hezekiah king of Judah, and the people were buoyed up by his words.

After this, Sennacherib king of Assyria, while he and 9 his high command were at Lachish, sent envoys to Jerusalem to deliver this message to Hezekiah king of Judah and to all the Judaeans in Jerusalem: 'Sennacherib king 10 of Assyria says, "What gives you confidence to stay in Jerusalem under siege? Hezekiah is misleading you into 11 risking death by famine or thirst where you are, when he tells you that the LORD your God will save you from the grip of the Assyrian king. Was it not Hezekiah himself 12 who suppressed the LORD's hill-shrines and altars and told the people of Judah and Jerusalem that they must prostrate themselves before one altar only and burn sacrifices there? You know very well what I and my forefathers 13 have done to all the peoples of the lands. Were the gods of these nations able to save their lands from me? Not one 14 of the gods of these nations, which my forefathers exterminated, was able to save his people from me. Much less

[a] towers on it: *so Targ.; Heb.* on the towers.

15 will your god save you! How, then, can Hezekiah deceive you or mislead you like this? How can you believe him, for no god of any nation or kingdom has been able to save his people from me or my forefathers? Much less will your gods save you*[a]*!'''

16 The envoys of Sennacherib spoke still more against the
17 LORD God and against his servant Hezekiah. And the king himself wrote a letter to defy the LORD the God of Israel, in these terms: 'Just as the gods of other nations could not save their people from me, so the god of Hezekiah will
18 not save his people from me.' Then they shouted in Hebrew at the top of their voices at the people of Jerusalem on the wall, to strike them with fear and terror,
19 hoping thus to capture the city. They described the god*[b]* of Jerusalem as being like the gods of the other peoples of the earth – things made by the hands of men.

20*[c]*   In this plight King Hezekiah and the prophet Isaiah son
21 of Amoz cried to heaven in prayer. So the LORD sent an angel who cut down all the fighting men, as well as the leaders and the commanders, in the camp of the king of Assyria, so that he went home disgraced to his own land. When he entered the temple of his god, certain of his own sons struck him down with their swords.

22 Thus the LORD saved Hezekiah and the inhabitants of Jerusalem from Sennacherib king of Assyria and all their
23 enemies; and he gave them respite on every side. Many people brought to Jerusalem offerings for the LORD and costly gifts for Hezekiah king of Judah. From then on he was held in high honour by all the nations.

[a] Or, *with some MSS.*, will your god save you.   [b] Or gods.   [c] *Verses 20–2: cp. 2 Kgs. 19: 1–37; Isa. 37: 1–38.*

* It has already been noted (cp. p. 266) that the account of
Hezekiah's religious reforms has been much extended by the
Chronicler in comparison with earlier accounts of his reign.
By contrast the extended description in 2 Kings 18 and 19 of
Sennacherib's siege of Jerusalem in 701 B.C. is reduced very
drastically. The whole episode raises considerable literary and
historical problems (see the commentary on 2 Kings for a full
discussion); the Chronicler's account may provide some
independent information about the period, but is for the most
part better understood as a commentary upon the earlier
account, some knowledge of which is really presupposed here.
Once again, it may be appropriate to regard this story as a
midrash (cp. 13: 22).

1. *After these events:* it has often been supposed that
Hezekiah's religious reform and his bid for political independence were part and parcel of one another historically; the
Chronicler, however, presents the link in theological rather
than historical or political terms. *Sennacherib:* king of Assyria
from 705 to 681 B.C. His own annals give a full account of
his capture of the *fortified cities* of Judah and historically there is
no reason to doubt his claim (cp. 2 Kings 18: 13); the Chronicler does not in fact mention or even imply their capture.

3. *blocking up the springs:* possibly underlying this comment
is the knowledge that at this time the Siloam Tunnel was
built, which linked the perennial spring of Gihon outside the
walls of Jerusalem to the merely seasonal spring of Siloam
inside the city, but that is not the main point of the narrative
in its present form, which shows how the water-supply is
denied to the invader.

4–5. The military preparations made here are commended;
the same preparations had been severely condemned by Isaiah,
for whom they represented insufficient trust in the LORD
(cp. Isa. 22: 8a–14).

5. *strengthened the Millo:* cp. 1 Chron. 11: 8. Here as elsewhere it appears as if a deliberate comparison is being made
between Hezekiah and David.

7–8. Again there is a marked contrast between the pious sentiments expressed by Hezekiah here, in complete confidence in God, with the anxiety expressed in his prayer in 2 Kings 19. Each phrase of his speech here is an allusion to some other biblical passage, which would have been familiar to the Chronicler's readers and would have allowed them to draw appropriate parallels.

9. *he and his high command were at Lachish:* Lachish, modern Tell ed-Duweir, south-west of Jerusalem, is frequently mentioned both in biblical and Assyrian records. Here the Chronicler appears to be harmonizing the rather confused references to the site in 2 Kings 18 and 19 rather than using independent traditions.

10–15. The *envoys'* speech has some similarities with those found in 2 Kings, but is clearly an independent composition by the Chronicler, the overall effect of which is to stress Hezekiah's religious policy as wholly acceptable, and to show the blasphemy of the Assyrians.

16–19. These verses underline the point already made – that to the Assyrians the LORD is no more effective than *the gods of the other peoples of the earth*.

20. In 2 Kings, Hezekiah and Isaiah had their own distinctive roles to play, and in the book of Isaiah, the prophet had been critical of the king (cp. especially Isa. 22). Here they are joined together in prayer.

21. Again the different emphases of the earlier accounts are smoothed out by the Chronicler. The earlier accounts gave two pictures of the end of Sennacherib's threat; according to one, he withdrew to his own land because of the danger from an Egyptian army (2 Kings 19: 9, 36); according to the other 'the angel of the LORD' brought about the sudden and mysterious death of the Assyrian army (2 Kings 19: 35). In addition to combining these two themes, the Chronicler has shifted the scene from Jerusalem to the Assyrian camp, presumably at Lachish; this change may well have been motivated by the promise in 2 Kings 19: 32–4, that Jerusalem

would not even be besieged. Sennacherib's death did not in fact take place for another twenty years, but the foreshortening of the time perspective, already apparent in 2 Kings 19: 37, is carried a stage further here, so that it appears as if his death followed immediately.

22–3. The Chronicler adds a summary stressing that the deliverance had been due to the LORD's own intervention, but that it had been occasioned by Hezekiah's loyalty, and that Hezekiah was duly rewarded by the honour in which all now held him. ✳

CONCLUDING SUMMARY ON HEZEKIAH

About this time Hezekiah fell dangerously ill and prayed 24 to the LORD; the LORD said, 'I will heal you',[a] and granted him a sign. But, being a proud man, he was not grate- 25 ful for the good done to him, and Judah and Jerusalem suffered for it. Then, proud as he was, Hezekiah submitted, 26 and the people of Jerusalem with him, and the LORD's anger did not fall on them again in Hezekiah's time.

Hezekiah enjoyed great wealth and fame.[b] He built for 27 himself treasuries for silver and gold, precious stones and spices, shields and other costly things; and barns for the 28 harvests of corn, new wine, and oil; and stalls for every kind of cattle, as well as sheepfolds.[c] He amassed[d] a great 29 many flocks and herds; God had indeed given him vast riches. It was this same Hezekiah who blocked the upper 30 outflow of the waters of Gihon and directed them down-wards and westwards to the city of David. In fact, Heze-kiah was successful in everything he attempted, even in 31

[a] I will heal you: *prob. rdg., cp. 2 Kgs. 20: 5; Heb. om.*
[b] *Or* riches.
[c] sheepfolds: *so Sept.; Heb.* sheep for the folds.
[d] *Prob. rdg.; Heb. adds* cities.

the affair of the envoys sent by the king*a* of Babylon – the envoys who came to inquire about the portent which had been seen in the land at the time when God left him to himself, to test him and to discover all that was in his heart.

32 The other events of Hezekiah's reign, and his works of piety, are recorded in the vision of the prophet Isaiah son of Amoz and*b* in the annals of the kings of Judah and
33 Israel. So Hezekiah rested with his forefathers and was buried in the uppermost of the graves of David's sons; all Judah and the people of Jerusalem paid him honour when he died, and he was succeeded by his son Manasseh.

* The extended account of Hezekiah's reign is concluded by a brief allusion to the other traditions about him found in the other sources, one of which shows a not uncritical attitude toward him, but the overall impression, in line with what has gone before, is to stress the way in which all Hezekiah's behaviour was that of an ideal ruler.

24–6. The tradition concerning Hezekiah's illness is not elaborated here as it is in 2 Kings 20 and still more in Isa. 38. Here the allusions already well known about the illness are used by the Chronicler in a way which shows Hezekiah as liable to the same pride as that of Uzziah of whom a similar phrase is used in 26: 16. Hezekiah, however, *submitted*, and all was well. The nature of the suffering undergone by Judah and Jerusalem is not specified; again a link with the falling-away of previously good kings seems to be intended (cp. 24: 18, where a similar phrase is used of Joash) rather than some specific historical event.

27–9. These verses provide an instructive summary of the Chronicler's view of the outward signs of *great wealth and*

[a] Prob. rdg., cp. 2 Kgs. 20: 12; Heb. officers.
[b] and: so Sept.; Heb. om.

fame. This phrase is also used to describe Solomon in 1 Kings
3: 13 (the N.E.B. there translates 'wealth and honour'), and
it is likely that a deliberate comparison is intended.

30. This description clearly refers to the construction of the
Siloam Tunnel (cp. on verse 3 above).

31. *even in the affair of the envoys sent by the king of Babylon:*
this passage affords a remarkable example of the way in which
the Chronicler is prepared to reinterpret earlier traditions.
In 2 Kings 20, Hezekiah is condemned by Isaiah for his
co-operation with the Babylonian envoys, who were probably hoping for his assistance in rebellion against Assyria.
Here, by contrast, their purpose is quite different; their story
is linked with the 'sign' of verse 24 (the word here translated
portent is the same Hebrew word), that is, the tradition that
the sun had gone back ten steps on the stairway of Ahaz
(2 Kings 20: 11) – the Chronicler does not state explicitly
what the sign was. Further, Hezekiah's attitude here is praise-
worthy: he did not succumb to their temptation.

32. *the vision of the prophet Isaiah:* this appears to be an
allusion to Isa. 1: 1, whereas the *annals* are probably the books
of Kings.

33. *in the uppermost of the graves:* this is more likely to be
a note of special honour than a geographical indication. ✶

THE WICKEDNESS OF MANASSEH

Manasseh was twelve years old when he came to the [a] 33
throne, and he reigned in Jerusalem for fifty-five years.
He did what was wrong in the eyes of the LORD, in fol- 2
lowing the abominable practices of the nations which the
LORD had dispossessed in favour of the Israelites. He 3
rebuilt the hill-shrines which his father Hezekiah had
dismantled, he erected altars to the Baalim and made
sacred poles, he prostrated himself before all the host of

[a] *Verses 1–9: cp. 2 Kgs. 21: 1–9.*

4 heaven and worshipped them. He built altars in the house
of the LORD, that house of which the LORD had said, 'In
5 Jerusalem shall my Name be for ever.' He built altars for
all the host of heaven in the two courts of the house of the
6 LORD; he made his sons pass through the fire in the Valley
of Ben-hinnom, he practised soothsaying, divination, and
sorcery, and dealt with ghosts and spirits. He did much
wrong in the eyes of the LORD and provoked his anger;
7 and the image that he had had carved in relief he put in
the house of God, the place of which God had said to
David and Solomon his son, 'This house and Jerusalem,
which I chose out of all the tribes of Israel, shall receive
8 my Name for all time. I will not again displace Israel from
the land which I assigned to their forefathers, if only they
will be careful to observe all that I commanded them
through Moses, all the law, the statutes, and the rules.'
9 But Manasseh misled Judah and the inhabitants of Jerusalem into wickedness far worse than that of the nations
which the LORD had exterminated in favour of the
Israelites.

* For the deuteronomic editors of 2 Kings, Manasseh was
the most wicked among many wicked kings, and it was his
sin which, in their view, finally led to the LORD abandoning
his people and to the destruction of Jerusalem and the exile
(cp. 2 Kings 21: 10–15). In this first section, the Chronicler
follows the account in 2 Kings 21 almost word for word, and
it seems as if his verdict is going to be substantially similar to
that of 2 Kings.

1. *for fifty-five years:* the period covered was approximately
696–642 B.C., and if the later dating of Hezekiah is accepted
(cp. on 29: 1), during part of that time he will have shared

the throne with his father. One of the factors in the Chronicler's change of emphasis in the account of Manasseh may be the thought that so long a reign must have implied a measure of divine favour.

2–9. The account of Manasseh's wrong-doings follows very closely that in 2 Kings 21: 2–9. Such minor differences as there are may point to the fact that the Chronicler had before him a text of 2 Kings which differed slightly from that which has come down to us. ✳

THE REPENTANCE OF MANASSEH

The LORD spoke to Manasseh and to his people, but 10 they paid no heed. So the Lord brought against them the 11 commanders of the army of the king of Assyria; they captured Manasseh with spiked weapons, and bound him with fetters, and bought him to Babylon. In his distress 12 he prayed to the LORD his God and sought to placate him and made his humble submission before the God of his fathers. He prayed, and God accepted his petition and 13 heard his supplication. He brought him back to Jerusalem and restored him to the throne; and thus Manasseh learnt that the LORD was God.

After this he built an outer wall for the city of David, 14 west of Gihon in the gorge, and extended it to the entrance by the Fish Gate, enclosing Ophel; and he raised it to a great height. He also put military commanders in all the fortified cities of Judah. He removed the foreign 15 gods and the carved image from the house of the LORD and all the altars which he had built on the temple mount[a] and in Jerusalem, and threw them out of the city. More- 16 over, he repaired the altar of the LORD and sacrificed at it

[a] temple mount: *lit.* mount of the house of the LORD.

shared-offerings and thank-offerings, and commanded
17 Judah to serve the LORD the God of Israel. But the people
still continued to sacrifice at the hill-shrines, though only
to the LORD their God.

18 The rest of the acts of Manasseh, his prayer to his God,
and the discourses of the seers who spoke to him in the
name of the LORD the God of Israel, are recorded in
19 the chronicles of the kings of Israel. His prayer and the
answer he received to it, and all his sin and unfaithfulness,
and the places where he built hill-shrines and set up sacred
poles and carved idols, before he submitted, are recorded
20 in the chronicles of the seers.[a] So Manasseh rested with
his forefathers and was buried in the garden-tomb of[b] his
family; he was succeeded by his son Amon.

✶ There have been numerous occasions already when the
Chronicler has felt quite free to make significant changes in
the tradition which had come down to him in the books of
Kings. Perhaps the most striking such change is that which is
depicted in these verses. Whereas 2 Kings stresses the continuing wickedness of the king, the Chronicler pictures the
punishment inflicted upon him by the Assyrian kings as
leading to repentance. Very different opinions have been
expressed by scholars concerning the historicity of this repentance, but since there is no mention of it in any source closer
to the time of Manasseh, it is most probably unhistorical. The
length of his reign, and the aversion of the Chronicler from
all-or-nothing judgements, may be two of the contributory
factors that brought about this new assessment. Once under
way, the tradition grew, and gave rise to a number of legends
describing his repentance in more detail; one such is preserved

[a] *So one MS.; others* my seers.
[b] the garden-tomb of: *prob. rdg., cp. 2 Kgs. 21: 18; Heb. om.*

in the Apocrypha under the title *The Prayer of Manasseh* (cp. the commentary on *The Shorter Books of the Apocrypha*, in this series).

10–11. There is no other biblical evidence for this bringing of Manasseh to Babylon, though his name has been found in Assyrian inscriptions among a list of those vassals who remained loyal to the Assyrian ruler at a time of widespread rebellion. But it is surprising that he should have been taken *to Babylon*, rather than to the Assyrian capital Nineveh, and it may be that the origin of this story lies less in historical reminiscences than in the tradition of exile leading to repentance which is to be set out in more elaborate fashion in 2 Chron. 36 and Ezra 1.

12–13. The expressions used here to denote Manasseh's repentance are all found frequently in the Old Testament to express the turning of sinners from their wickedness; there is nothing here which indicates the particular circumstances of Manasseh.

14. Again it is possible that a historical core underlies this picture of the strengthening of the defences of Jerusalem, though it is used by the Chronicler as part of his overall picture of security being a concomitant of piety. The area here designated appears to have been on the eastern side of the city, but it is impossible to identify it with confidence. If he did indeed put *commanders in all the fortified cities of Judah*, this would be an indication of the breakdown of Assyrian power, but of this there is no evidence before the time of Josiah.

15–17. Manasseh's reform is otherwise unknown, and appears to be the Chronicler's deduction from the portrait of repentance which has just been given.

18. *his prayer:* this reference probably provides the origin for the speculation which led to such works as 'The Prayer of Manasseh', already mentioned.

20. The Hebrew of this verse has been slightly altered (cp. the N.E.B. footnote) to make it correspond more closely with 2 Kings 21: 18. ✳

THE REIGN OF AMON

21*a* Amon was twenty-two years old when he came to the
22 throne, and he reigned in Jerusalem for two years. He did
what was wrong in the eyes of the LORD as his father
Manasseh had done. He sacrificed to all the images that
his father Manasseh had made, and worshipped them.
23 He was not submissive before the LORD like his father
24 Manasseh; his guilt was much greater. His courtiers con-
25 spired against him and murdered him in his house; but
the people of the land killed all the conspirators and made
his son Josiah king in his place.

* Of Amon we know almost nothing, for both 2 Kings and
2 Chronicles dismiss his reign in a few disapproving verses.
It has been disputed whether Amon's murder was due to
his subservience to Assyria, or to his anti-Assyrian policy.
Though the description of his reign here substantially follows
that in 2 Kings (cp. the N.E.B. footnote), a significantly
different impression is created because he here follows a
repentant Manasseh, and therefore undoes all the good of his
father's reform, whereas in Kings, Manasseh's wickedness is
simply continued by Amon. Save for the note of Manasseh's
repentance in verse 23, the Chronicler here follows the earlier
source, with some abbreviations. *

JOSIAH AND RELIGIOUS REFORM

34 1*a* Josiah was eight years old when he came to the throne,
2 and he reigned in Jerusalem for thirty-one years. He did
what was right in the eyes of the LORD; he followed in the
footsteps of his forefather David, swerving neither right

[a] *Verses 21–5: cp. 2 Kgs. 21: 19–24.*
[b] *Verses 1, 2: cp. 2 Kgs. 22: 1, 2.*

nor left. In the eighth year of his reign, when he was still 3
a boy, he began to seek guidance of the God of his forefather David; and in the twelfth year he began to purge
Judah and Jerusalem of the hill-shrines and the sacred
poles, and the carved idols and the images of metal. He 4
saw to it that the altars for the Baalim were destroyed and
he hacked down the incense-altars which stood above
them; he broke in pieces the sacred poles and the carved
and metal images, grinding them to powder and scattering
it on the graves of those who had sacrificed to them. He 5
also burnt the bones of the priests on their altars and
purged Judah and Jerusalem. In the cities of Manasseh, 6
Ephraim, and Simeon, and as far as Naphtali, he burnt
down their houses wherever he found them; he destroyed 7
the altars and the sacred poles, ground the idols to powder, and hacked down the incense-altars throughout the
land of Israel. Then he returned to Jerusalem.

✳ For the author of 2 Kings, Josiah was second only to David
as a perfect embodiment of his ideals of kingship. As we have
seen, for the Chronicler, those ideals were to a greater extent
embodied in Hezekiah, and so there is a corresponding reduc-
tion, both in extent and enthusiasm, in his picture of Josiah.
Nevertheless, on any showing, this reign was of major
importance in the history of Judah, at a time when after
more than a century, a bid for independence from Assyrian
control was being made.

In one important respect the Chronicler's portrait differs
from that of 2 Kings with regard to the interrelation of the
various events in Josiah's reign. In 2 Kings nothing is said of
events before the eighteenth year of his reign (622–1 B.C.: see
22: 3); the Chronicler, by contrast, sets out details of a reform
which began in the eighth year, that is, around 632 B.C. Many

scholars who are in general cautious about accepting unsupported statements of the Chronicler as historical, have felt that there might be a solid basis of fact underlying this presentation, both because of what we know of the decline of Assyrian power, which may well have contributed to Josiah's religious policy, and also because of the fact that the author of 2 Kings wished to stress the role of the 'book of the law' (22: 8) above all else in his presentation of Josiah.

1. *he reigned in Jerusalem for thirty-one years:* most of the chronological problems of the earlier period are no longer present, and Josiah's reign can be dated with fair confidence at 640–609 B.C.

3. *in the twelfth year:* that is, around 629 B.C. It was at about this period that Assyrian power began seriously to weaken, and it is at least a possibility that Josiah's religious reform was part of a bid for independence from Assyrian political control – certainly political and religious subservience often went together in the ancient world. But the actual reforms listed do not appear to have any direct link with Assyrian practices.

6. *In the cities of Manasseh, Ephraim, and Simeon, and as far as Naphtali:* like so many of the Chronicler's statements, this has caused much dispute as to its historical accuracy. What seems to be pictured is a claim by Josiah to rule the old northern kingdom's territory, and in a state of affairs of political confusion, we may feel that such a bid was inherently probable. At the same time, there must be some doubt about the reliability of the Chronicler's report, since Simeon, linked with the northern tribes as in 15: 9, was in fact the southernmost of the tribal groups, and there is a suspicion that the Chronicler knew little of the historical reality of the situation being described. *

THE FINDING OF THE LAW-BOOK

In the eighteenth year of his reign, after he had purified 8*a* the land and the house, he sent Shaphan son of Azaliah and Maaseiah the governor of the city and Joah son of Joahaz the secretary of state to repair the house of the LORD his God. They came to Hilkiah the high priest and 9 gave him the silver that had been brought to the house of God, the silver which the Levites, on duty at the threshold, had gathered from Manasseh, Ephraim, and all the rest of Israel, as well as from Judah and Benjamin and the inhabitants of Jerusalem. It was then handed over to the 10 foremen in charge of the work in the house of the LORD, and these men, working in the house, used it for repairing and strengthening the fabric; they gave it also to the car- 11 penters and builders to buy hewn stone, and timber for rafters and beams, for the buildings which the kings of Judah had allowed to fall into ruin. The men did their 12-13 work honestly under the direction of Jahath and Obadiah, Levites of the line of Merari, and Zechariah and Meshullam, members of the family of Kohath. These also had control of the porters and directed the workmen of every trade. The Levites were all skilled musicians, and some of them were secretaries, clerks, or door-keepers. When 14 they fetched the silver which had been brought to the house of the LORD, the priest Hilkiah discovered the book of the law of the LORD which had been given through Moses. Then Hilkiah told Shaphan the adjutant-general, 15 'I have discovered the book of the law in the house of the LORD.' Hilkiah gave the book to Shaphan, and he brought 16

[*a*] *Verses 8–32: cp. 2 Kgs. 22: 3 – 23: 3.*

it to the king and reported to him: 'Your servants are
17 doing all that was entrusted to them. They have melted
down the silver in the house of the LORD and have handed
18 it over to the foremen and the workmen.' Shaphan the
adjutant-general also told the king that the priest Hilkiah
had given him a book; and he read it out in the king's
19 presence. When the king heard what was in the book of
20 the law, he rent his clothes, and ordered Hilkiah, Ahikam
son of Shaphan, Abdon son of Micah, Shaphan the
21 adjutant-general, and Asaiah the king's attendant, to go
and seek guidance of the LORD, for himself and for all who
still remained in Israel and Judah, about the contents of
the book that had been discovered. 'Great is the wrath of
the LORD,' he said, 'and it has been poured out upon us
because our forefathers did not observe the command of
the LORD and do all that is written in this book.'

22   So Hilkiah and those whom the king had instructed[a]
went to Huldah the prophetess, wife of Shallum son of
Tikvah,[b] son of Hasrah, the keeper of the wardrobe, and
consulted her at her home in the second quarter of Jeru-
23 salem. 'This is the word of the LORD the God of Israel,'
she answered: 'Say to the man who sent you to me,
24 "This is the word of the LORD: I am bringing disaster on
this place and its inhabitants, fulfilling all the imprecations
recorded in the book which was read in the presence of
25 the king of Judah, because they have forsaken me and
burnt sacrifices to other gods, provoking my anger with
all the idols they have made with their own hands; therefore my wrath is poured out upon this place and will not

[a] had instructed: *so Sept.; Heb. om.*
[b] *Prob. rdg., cp. 2 Kgs. 22: 14; Heb.* Tokhath.

be quenched." This is what you shall say to the king of ²⁶
Judah who sent you to seek guidance of the LORD: "This
is the word of the LORD the God of Israel: You have
listened to my words and shown a willing heart, you ²⁷
humbled yourself before God when you heard what I
said about this place and its inhabitants, you humbled
yourself and rent your clothes and wept before me. Because of all this,*ᵃ* I for my part have heard you. This is the
very word of the LORD. Therefore, I will gather you to ²⁸
your forefathers, and you will be gathered to your grave
in peace; you will not live to see all the disaster which I
am bringing upon this place and upon its inhabitants.'"
So they brought back word to the king.

Then the king sent and called all the elders of Judah and ²⁹
Jerusalem together, and went up to the house of the LORD; ³⁰
he took with him all the men of Judah and the inhabitants
of Jerusalem, the priests and the Levites, the whole population, high and low. There he read them the whole book
of the covenant discovered in the house of the LORD; and ³¹
then, standing on the dais,*ᵇ* the king made a covenant
before the LORD to obey him and keep his commandments, his testimonies, and his statutes, with all his heart
and soul, and so fulfil the terms of the covenant written
in this book. Then he swore an oath with all who were ³²
present in Jerusalem to keep the covenant.*ᶜ* Thereafter the
inhabitants of Jerusalem did obey the covenant of God,
the God of their fathers. Josiah removed all abominable ³³
things from all the territories of the Israelites, so that

[a] Because of all this: *prob. rdg.; Heb. om.*   [b] on the dais: *so Sept.;
Heb.* in his place.   [c] to keep the covenant: *prob. rdg., cp. 2 Kgs.
23: 3; Heb.* and Benjamin.

everyone living in Israel might serve the LORD his God. As long as he lived they did not fail in their allegiance to the LORD the God of their fathers.

* In 2 Kings 22 and 23, the finding of the book of the law in the eighteenth year is clearly the climax of the whole narrative. Whatever the historical original underlying that episode, there can be no doubt that the editors of 2 Kings understood it, and wished their readers to understand it, as being the book of Deuteronomy. Since those editors are usually regarded, on account of their theological viewpoint, as 'deuteronomists', it is scarcely surprising that they regarded the book as important. The Chronicler, though he reproduces much of the material from 2 Kings, seems to regard the book as somewhat less significant. For him the reform was already under way when the book was found; and many of the phrases used by Kings to describe the reform brought about by the book are used by the Chronicler of what had already been achieved. It will be possible here only to comment on those points which are peculiar to the Chronicler; for a fuller discussion of the whole episode, see the commentary on 2 Kings.

8. *after he had purified the land and the house:* it is again stressed that the finding of the book of the law was the result, rather than the cause of the purification. No mention has in fact been made of any activity in *the house*, that is, the temple at Jerusalem. Of the names here listed, only Shaphan is found in 2 Kings 22, and according to 2 Kings 23: 8, the *governor of the city* at this time was 'Joshua'.

9. This verse stresses both the role of the Levites in the temple ritual and also that the collection came from all Israel.

10. *repairing and strengthening:* these words imply a more extensive renewal than is envisaged in 2 Kings.

14. *which had been given through Moses:* this link, implicit in 2 Kings, is here explicitly brought out.

14–32. The reaction to the finding of the book is described in terms which correspond very closely to those of 2 Kings

22: 8 – 23: 3, with a few of the Chronicler's characteristic modifications, such as the reference to *Levites* instead of 'prophets' in verse 30. No attempt is made to modify Huldah's prophecy concerning Josiah's peaceful death (verse 28) which might seem curious in view of the unhappy fate that he actually suffered; it is possible that the point is that he would die before the coming disaster struck the city. ✳

JOSIAH'S PASSOVER

Josiah kept a Passover to the LORD in Jerusalem, and the **35** passover lamb was killed on the fourteenth day of the first month. He appointed the priests to their offices and 2 encouraged them to perform the service of the house of the LORD. He said to the Levites, the teachers of Israel, 3 who were dedicated to the LORD, 'Put the holy Ark in the house which Solomon son of David king of Israel built; it is not to be carried about on your shoulders. Now is the time to serve the LORD your God and his people Israel: prepare yourselves by families according to your divisions, 4 following the written instructions of David king of Israel and those of Solomon his son; and stand in the 5 Holy Place as representatives of the family groups of the lay people, your brothers, one division of Levites to each family group. Kill the passover lamb and hallow your- 6 selves and prepare for your brothers to fulfil the word of the LORD given through Moses.'

Josiah contributed on behalf of all the lay people pre- 7 sent thirty thousand small cattle, that is young rams and goats, for the Passover, in addition to three thousand bulls; all these were from the king's own resources. And 8 his officers contributed willingly for the people, the priests, and the Levites. Hilkiah, Zechariah, and Jehiel, the

chief officers of the house of God, gave on behalf of the priests two thousand six hundred small cattle for the
9 Passover, in addition to three hundred bulls. And Conaniah, Shemaiah and Nethaneel his brothers, and Hashabiah, Jeiel, and Jozabad, the chiefs of the Levites, gave on behalf of the Levites for the Passover five thousand small cattle in addition to five hundred bulls.

10 When the service had been arranged, the priests stood in their places and the Levites in their divisions, according
11 to the king's command. They killed the passover victim, and the priests flung the blood[a] against the altar as the
12 Levites flayed the animals. Then they removed the fat flesh,[b] which they allocated to the people by groups of families for them to offer to the LORD, as prescribed in the
13 book of Moses; and so with the bulls. They cooked the passover victim over the fire according to custom, and boiled the holy offerings in pots, cauldrons, and pans, and
14 served them quickly to all the people. After that they made the necessary preparations for themselves and the priests, because the priests of Aaron's line were engaged till nightfall in offering whole-offerings and the fat portions; so the Levites made the necessary preparations for
15 themselves and for the priests of Aaron's line. The singers, the sons of Asaph, were in their places according to the rules laid down by David and by Asaph, Heman, and Jeduthun, the king's seers.[c] The door-keepers stood, each at his gate; there was no need for them to leave their posts, because their kinsmen the Levites had made the preparations for them.

[a] the blood: *so Pesh.; Heb.* from their hand.   [b] fat flesh: *or* whole-offering.   [c] *So some MSS.; others* seer.

In this manner all the service of the LORD was arranged 16
that day, to keep the Passover and to offer whole-
offerings on the altar of the LORD, according to the command of King Josiah. The people of Israel who were 17
present kept the Passover at that time and the pilgrim-
feast of Unleavened Bread for seven days. No Passover 18
like it had been kept in Israel since the days of the prophet
Samuel; none of the kings of Israel had ever kept such a
Passover as Josiah kept, with the priests and Levites and all
Judah and Israel who were present and the inhabitants of
Jerusalem. In the eighteenth year of Josiah's reign this 19
Passover was kept.

✳ At this point in the 2 Kings narrative there follows the
account of the religious purification carried out by Josiah,
some of the material from which has been used already in
2 Chron. 34: 1–7, and the Chronicler thus passes direct to
the account of the Passover which is the climax of the picture
of Josiah's action. Though there are some similarities with the
account of the Passover in 2 Kings 23: 21–3, the account
here is much elaborated, and probably owes a great deal in its
detail to the liturgical practice of the Chronicler's own day.

1. *the fourteenth day of the first month:* this is a specific allusion
to the establishment of the Passover in Exod. 12: 6, where
this is laid down as the correct date.

3. *the teachers of Israel:* an important function of the Levites,
several times referred to elsewhere, is here brought out
explicitly.

3–4. Stress is laid here, as in 1 Chronicles 10–29, on the
role of David as preparing everything necessary for the proper
sacrifices in the temple.

7. *Josiah contributed on behalf of all the lay people:* in early
days the Passover had essentially been a family festival (as it
is now), but from the time of Deut. 16 (probably seventh

century) it was celebrated in Jerusalem, and it was a custom
for pious Jews to go to Jerusalem to observe the festival, as
did Jesus and his disciples. This and the following verses
stress the generosity of all involved, but it is noteworthy here
that the king, as in the vision of Ezek. 40–8, is classed among
the lay people rather than as a sacral person.

10–12. The ceremonies described here are otherwise unknown, but it is most likely that they represent the liturgical
practice of the second temple.

13. *according to custom:* this may be right, but it is also
possible to translate it as in other English versions, 'according
to the ordinance', the reference being to the commands in the
Pentateuch (Exod. 12: 8).

17. The observances of *Passover* and *Unleavened Bread* had
probably differed in their origin, but long before the time of
the Chronicler they had been merged into one, so that the
picture given here is of the eating of the Passover meal as
the climax of the week-long festival of Unleavened Bread.

18. *since the days of the prophet Samuel:* this allusion is
unexpected and puzzling, since there is no reference in any
source known to us of the observance of Passover at the time
of Samuel. It may be intended to make more specific the
much vaguer reference to the uniqueness of this celebration
in 2 Kings. 23: 22. ✳

THE DEATH OF JOSIAH

20 After Josiah had thus organized all the service of the
house, Necho king of Egypt marched up to attack Carchemish on the Euphrates; and Josiah went out to con-
21 front him. But Necho sent envoys to him, saying, 'What
do you want with me, king of Judah? I have no quarrel
with you today, only with those with whom I am at war.
God has purposed to speed me on my way, and God is on
my side; do not stand in his way, or he will destroy you.'

Josiah would not be deflected from his purpose but in- 22
sisted on fighting; he refused to listen to Necho's words
spoken at God's command, and he sallied out to join
battle in the vale of Megiddo. The archers shot at him; he 23
was severely wounded and told his bodyguard to carry
him off. They lifted him out of his chariot and carried him 24
in his viceroy's chariot to Jerusalem. There he died and
was buried among the tombs of his ancestors, and all
Judah and Jerusalem mourned for him. Jeremiah also 25
made a lament for Josiah; and to this day the minstrels,
both men and women, commemorate Josiah in their
lamentations. Such laments have become traditional in
Israel, and they are found in the written collections.

The other events of Josiah's reign, and his works of 26
piety, all performed in accordance with what is laid down
in the law of the LORD, and his acts, from first to last, are 27
recorded in the annals of the kings of Israel and Judah.

* The Chronicler has on several occasions qualified the
condemnation of evil kings by setting out a pattern of their
subsequent repentance; here the process is to some extent
reversed. In his last days Josiah is disobedient to the word of
the LORD and his death in battle is seen as the inevitable
consequence.

20. The time-lag here is in fact of some twelve years, from
622/1 to 609 B.C., but here as elsewhere details of this kind are
not the Chronicler's primary concern. The Babylonian
Chronicle, a series of clay tablets describing this period (cp.
Old Testament Illustrations in this series, pp. 91f.) has greatly
clarified our picture of these events; *Necho* (Pharaoh of Egypt
from 609 to 593 B.C.) made it one of his first acts to attempt
to shore up the last remnants of Assyrian power against the
rising might of Babylon; Josiah, still conscious of Assyrian

threats in the past, or simply wishing to show his independence, opposed his passage. *Carchemish on the Euphrates,*
which may have been the main Egyptian army base, was to be
the scene of a great battle between Babylon and Egypt in
605 B.C., which put an end to Egypt's attempts to control
Palestine.

22. *Necho's words spoken at God's command:* this phrase
should warn us against any temptation to see the Chronicler
as interested only in correct ecclesiastical forms for the giving
of God's word to his people. Necho had been empowered to
speak as a prophet of God and Josiah had ignored his advice
at his own peril. *Megiddo:* the site of the battle is another
indication of Josiah's attempt to establish control over the
northern territory. It is an area commanding the main trade
route through Palestine and renowned for battles, from the
struggle against Sisera in Judg. 5 to the promise of the seer
in Revelation that the last battle would be fought there
(Armageddon in Rev. 16: 16).

24. *There he died:* in the Kings account (2 Kings 23: 29)
Josiah was killed on the field of battle. The Chronicler
regards it as more appropriate that such a king, whose unhappy
end was far outweighed by the good he had previously done,
should be presented as dying in his own city, and so he is
brought there ceremonially in the last act of his reign.

25. *Jeremiah also made a lament:* the Old Testament book
called Lamentations came to be attributed to the prophet
Jeremiah (this is obscured in the N.E.B. title). It seems
unlikely that the reference here could be to any of the poems
in that book, but the tradition linking Jeremiah with Lamentations may have given rise to this reference. The death of
Josiah was undoubtedly a shattering blow to the hopes of
Judah for a revival of her independent life, and this is expressed
very vividly by the Chronicler here. The custom of linking
liturgical observances with historical events was a normal
one in Judaism (e.g. the Passover), but nothing else is known
of the customs here referred to.

26–7. After the criticism implied in the account of his death, the final estimate of Josiah is once again wholly favourable. *

BABYLONIAN RULE ESTABLISHED

The people of the land took Josiah's son Jehoahaz and 36 1[a]
made him king in place of his father in Jerusalem. He was 2
twenty-three years old when he came to the throne, and
he reigned in Jerusalem for three months. Then Necho 3
king of Egypt deposed him and fined the country a hundred talents of silver and one talent of gold, and made his 4
brother Eliakim king over Judah and Jerusalem in his
place, changing his name to Jehoiakim; he also carried
away his brother Jehoahaz to Egypt. Jehoiakim was 5
twenty-five years old when he came to the throne, and
he reigned in Jerusalem for eleven years. He did what was
wrong in the eyes of the LORD his God. So Nebuchad- 6
nezzar king of Babylon marched against him and put him
in fetters and took him to Babylon. He also removed to 7
Babylon some of the vessels of the house of the LORD and
put them into his own palace there. The other events of 8
Jehoiakim's reign, including the abominations he committed, and everything of which he was held guilty, are
recorded in the annals of the kings of Israel and Judah. He
was succeeded by his son Jehoiachin.

Jehoiachin was eight years old when he came to the 9[b]
throne, and he reigned in Jerusalem for three months and
ten days. He did what was wrong in the eyes of the LORD.
At the turn of the year King Nebuchadnezzar sent and 10

[a] *Verses 1–4: cp. 2 Kgs. 23: 30–4.*
[b] *Verses 9, 10: cp. 2 Kgs. 24: 8–17.*

brought him to Babylon, together with the choicest vessels of the house of the LORD, and made his father's brother[a] Zedekiah king over Judah and Jerusalem.

✻ Our knowledge of the events in Judah from the death of Josiah to the fall of Jerusalem is unusually detailed, being based both on the Babylonian Chronicle and the material in 2 Kings. The Chronicler's treatment is much briefer, and it is doubtful if it provides any new information. Instead it appears as if he regards the punishment of exile as inevitable from this point on, and is anxious to reach it as soon as possible. So all the events of the period leading up to the exile are regarded as a unity, just as in the book of Ezra all the events of the century or so after the exile, when Judah was restored, were also regarded as a unity. In this section, the events described in 2 Kings 23: 30 – 24: 17 are dealt with in much briefer fashion, with only two important additions (see the notes on verses 6 and 7 below). The outline history of the period can be told simply: Egypt's control over Palestine was short-lived and power passed to the Neo-Babylonian Empire of Nebuchadnezzar; Jehoiakim was at first a loyal vassal, but when he rebelled the Babylonians laid siege to Jerusalem, captured it and ended the independent existence of Judah. A fuller account of the period will be found in the commentary on 2 Kings.

6. *put him in fetters and took him to Babylon:* there is no supporting evidence for this statement elsewhere, and it is difficult to fit such an episode into the historical outline which has come down to us. Some such tradition as this may underlie the story of a siege of Jerusalem referred to in Dan. 1: 1 – a book later in date than 2 Chronicles.

7. This verse, like the preceding statement, has no parallel in Kings, but here it is much easier to recognize the introduction of one of the Chronicler's most important concerns.

[a] father's brother: *so Sept.; Heb.* brother.

He wished to emphasize the continuity of the second temple with its predecessor. The actual building had been destroyed, but continuity could still be shown by stressing the fact that the vessels used in the temple were those of the first temple. So whereas 2 Kings 24: 13 speaks of the destruction of the vessels, this verse (and verse 10) emphasizes that they were not destroyed, and the restoration of these vessels is an important theme in Ezra 1. A similar tradition underlies the story of Belshazzar's feast in Dan. 5.

9. *eight years old:* 2 Kings 24: 8 has 'eighteen', a much more likely figure; *eight* here may simply be due to scribal error. ✶

THE DESTRUCTION OF THE TEMPLE AND THE EXILE OF THE PEOPLE

Zedekiah was twenty-one years old when he came to 11 the throne, and he reigned in Jerusalem for eleven years. He did what was wrong in the eyes of the LORD his God; 12 he did not defer to the guidance of the prophet Jeremiah, the spokesman of the LORD. He also rebelled against King 13 Nebuchadnezzar, who had laid on him a solemn oath of allegiance. He was obstinate and stubborn and refused to return to the LORD the God of Israel. All the chiefs of 14 Judah and[a] the priests and the people became more and more unfaithful, following all the abominable practices of the other nations; and they defiled the house of the LORD which he had hallowed in Jerusalem. The LORD 15 God of their fathers had warned them betimes through his messengers, for he took pity on his people and on his dwelling-place; but they never ceased to deride his mes- 16 sengers, scorn his words and scoff at his prophets, until the anger of the LORD burst out against his people and could

[a] Judah and: *so* Sept.; Heb. *om.*

17[a] not be appeased. So he brought against them the king of the Chaldaeans, who put their young men to the sword in the sanctuary and spared neither young man nor maiden, neither the old nor the weak; God gave them all into his

18 power. And he brought all the vessels of the house of God, great and small, and the treasures of the house of the LORD and of the king and his officers – all these he brought

19 to Babylon. And they burnt down the house of God, razed the city wall of Jerusalem and burnt down all its stately mansions and all their precious possessions until

20 everything was destroyed. Those who escaped the sword he took captive to Babylon, and they became slaves to him and his sons until the sovereignty passed to the

21 Persians, while the land of Israel ran the full term of its sabbaths. All the time that it lay desolate it kept the sabbath rest, to complete seventy years in fulfilment of the word of the LORD by the prophet Jeremiah.

✶ Zedekiah is regarded in both Kings and Chronicles as one of the line of kings in Jerusalem, though it is clear that he owed such power as he had to Babylonian policy (2 Kings 24: 17), and for many Israelites the true king was the exiled Jehoiachin. But this is not a concern for the Chronicler, who treats Zekediah as another in the succession of evil kings of the last days of Judah. His main concern here is with the destruction of city and temple in 587 or 586 B.C., and the exile of the inhabitants, which for him was total and complete, so that we are given a picture of the land left deserted. The greater part of this section is a condensation of the material in 2 Kings 24: 18 – 25: 21, but in a number of places the Chronicler adds his own distinctive interpretation of events.

12. *he did not defer to the guidance of the prophet Jeremiah:*

[a] *Verses 17–20: cp. 2 Kgs. 25: 1–17.*

there are two earlier accounts of the time of Zedekiah, one in
2 Kings which does not mention Jeremiah at all, and one in
the book of Jeremiah (Jer. 37–9), in which the role of the
prophet himself is stressed. This verse probably alludes to that
material.

13. Zedekiah's behaviour here is described in a way somewhat similar to that of Josiah when he failed to see God's
hand at work in Pharaoh Necho. For the Chronicler, probably
writing at a time of Persian rule, loyalty in one's duty to
foreign rulers was an important prerequisite so that true
worship could be offered without fear of persecution.

14. *they defiled the house of the LORD:* this comment
provides an explanation how it came about that the temple
could have been destroyed. God did not intervene to prevent
it because of this defilement.

15–16. These two verses are not found in 2 Kings, though
the summary of increasing wickedness here set out is very
much in line with the viewpoint of the deuteronomic editors
of K ngs.

17–19. Whereas the capture of the city in 597 B.C. is only
implied, its final fall in 587 or 586 B.C. is here described, in
a summary of the fuller account given in 2 Kings 25. Other
accounts do not suggest such wholesale slaughter, but the
picture of large-scale destruction is almost certainly correct.
Again the theme of the preservation of the remaining temple
vessels is stressed.

20. *Those who escaped the sword he took captive to Babylon:*
a characteristic feature of the different accounts of these events
in the Old Testament is that the completeness of the exile is
increasingly stressed. The account in Jer. 52: 28–30, perhaps
the earliest record we have, mentions 4600 exiles in all; by
the time of the Chronicler, the picture is of all who survived
being exiled, and the land of Judah left uninhabited. There is
no need to doubt the reality of the exile, as some scholars
have done, but it is important to bear in mind that the
Chronicler has probably exaggerated its extent. As the next

verse will show, he has modified the historical picture in order to express his theological convictions. *until the sovereignty passed to the Persians:* the Chronicler here brings out two further important points in his presentation of the exile: first, that it lasted for a specific and limited length of time, so that we may envisage both a mass exile and a mass return; secondly, the Persian rule is contrasted with that of the Babylonians, and thus the acceptable position of the Jews under Persian dominion in the Book of Ezra is prepared for.

21. The preceding picture has already suggested that the exile is a theological as well as a historical idea, and this is now further stressed. The N.E.B. translation has altered the order of the Hebrew original, which is somewhat obscure, but the idea underlying the phrase *ran the full term of its sabbaths* seems to be that of restitution for previous neglect. In any case the land is envisaged as totally deserted, keeping a *sabbath rest,* for *seventy years.* This might represent the time from the destruction of the temple in 587/6 until its restoration in 516/15 B.C., but is more likely to stand for a complete lifespan than for a specific period of time. The reference to Jeremiah concerns the seventy-year period (cp. Jer. 25: 11; 29: 10); there are also allusions to the sermonic passage in Lev. 26 dealing with the significance of the sabbath. ✳

THE DECREE OF CYRUS

22[a] Now in the first year of Cyrus king of Persia, so that the word of the LORD spoken through Jeremiah might be fulfilled, the LORD stirred up the heart of Cyrus king of Persia; and he issued a proclamation throughout his kingdom, both by word of mouth and in writing, to this effect:

23   This is the word of Cyrus king of Persia: The LORD the God of heaven has given me all the kingdoms of

[a] *Verses 22, 23: cp. Ezra 1: 1–3.*

the earth, and he himself has charged me to build him a house at Jerusalem in Judah. To every man of his people now among you I say, the LORD his God be[a] with him, and let him go up.

✶ These final verses form a kind of coda. They are substantially the same as the opening verses of Ezra, and fuller commentary upon them is given in the commentary on Ezra and Nehemiah. Here it may be noted that they provide a more hopeful ending to the books of Chronicles, the last books in the Hebrew Bible, and serve to link the story here told with that which is more fully unfolded in Ezra. The punishment which has been described is not the end; there is still a restoration to which the people, purged and purified by exile, might look forward. ✶

✶ ✶ ✶ ✶ ✶ ✶ ✶ ✶ ✶ ✶ ✶ ✶ ✶

THE CHRONICLER AS HISTORIAN AND INTERPRETER

What we have been studying in these books is the Chronicler's interpretation for his own day of events that had taken place hundreds of years earlier. The exact details of those original events are now lost to us, as they probably were to the Chronicler, who, like us, had to rely mainly on earlier interpretations, mostly in the books of Samuel and Kings. But this should not be a cause of anxiety or regret, for in all history it is not 'what actually happened' but the event together with the interpretation placed upon it that is significant. In that process of interpretation, the Chronicler played an important part, and his own work has in its turn become the subject of interpretation and comment, as it continues to speak to new situations. It is in this continuing process of interpretation that the justification of this and other modern commentaries is to be found.

[a] be: *prob. rdg., cp. Ezra 1: 3; Heb. om.*

A NOTE ON FURTHER READING

The reader of this volume may wish to read further either about the historical period covered or about the Chronicler and his own distinctive approach to that period. For the former, the commentaries in this series, on *1 Samuel* by P. R. Ackroyd and on *1 Kings* by J. Robinson, should be consulted. (Volumes on 2 Samuel and 2 Kings by the same authors are forthcoming.) Further information will be found in E. W. Heaton, *The Hebrew Kingdoms* (Oxford University Press, 1968), M. Noth, *The History of Israel* (A. & C. Black, 1960) and S. Herrmann, *A History of Israel in Old Testament Times* (S.C.M. Press, 1975).

For the Chronicler's own work, other commentaries on these books are: P. R. Ackroyd, *I & II Chronicles, Ezra, Nehemiah*, Torch Bible Commentaries (S.C.M. Press, 1973); J. M. Myers, *1 Chronicles* and *2 Chronicles* (separate volumes), Anchor Bible (Doubleday, New York, 1965). Further background material is to be found in the histories by Noth and Herrmann already mentioned, and in P. R. Ackroyd, *Israel under Babylon and Persia* (Oxford University Press, 1970).

APPENDIX

MEASURES OF LENGTH AND EXTENT

	span	cubit	rod[a]
span	1	...	...
cubit	2	1	...
rod[a]	12	6	1

The 'short cubit' (Judg. 3: 16) was traditionally the measure from the elbow to the knuckles of the closed fist; and what seems to be intended as a 'long cubit' measured a 'cubit and a hand-breadth', i.e. 7 instead of 6 hand-breadths (Ezek. 40: 5). What is meant by cubits 'according to the old standard of measurement' (2 Chr. 3: 3) is presumably this pre-exilic cubit of 7 hand-breadths. Modern estimates of the Hebrew cubit range from 12 to 25·2 inches, without allowing for varying local standards.

Area was measured by the 'yoke' (Isa. 5: 10), i.e. that ploughed by a pair of oxen in one day, said to be half an acre now in Palestine, though varying in different places with the nature of the land.

MEASURES OF CAPACITY

liquid measures	equivalences	dry measures
'log'	1 'log'	...
...	4 'log'	'kab'
...	7⅕ 'log'	'omer'
'hin'	12 'log'	...
...	24 'log'	'seah'
'bath'	72 'log'	'ephah'
'kor'	720 'log'	'homer' or 'kor'

According to ancient authorities the Hebrew 'log' was of the same capacity as the Roman *sextarius*; this according to the

[a] Hebrew literally 'reed', the length of Ezekiel's measuring-rod.

best available evidence was equivalent to 0·99 pint of the English standard.

WEIGHTS AND COINS

	heavy (Phoenician) standard			light (Babylonian) standard		
	shekel	mina	talent	shekel	mina	talent
shekel	1	...	...	1	...	...
mina	50	1	...	60	1	...
talent	3,000	60	1	3,600	60	1

The 'gerah' was $\frac{1}{20}$ of the sacred or heavy shekel and probably $\frac{1}{24}$ of the light shekel.

The 'sacred shekel' according to tradition was identical with the heavy shekel; while the 'shekel of the standard recognized by merchants' (Gen. 23: 16) was perhaps a weight stamped with its value as distinct from one not so stamped and requiring to be weighed on the spot.

Recent discoveries of hoards of objects stamped with their weights suggest that the shekel may have weighed approximately 11·5 grammes towards the end of the Hebrew monarchy, but nothing shows whether this is the light or the heavy shekel; and much variety, due partly to the worn or damaged state of the objects and partly to variations in local standards, increases the difficulty of giving a definite figure.

Coins are not mentioned before the Exile. Only the 'daric' (1 Chr. 29: 7) and the 'drachma' (Ezra 2: 69; Neh. 7: 70–2), if this is a distinct coin, are found in the Old Testament; the former is said to have been a month's pay for a soldier in the Persian army, while the latter will have been the Greek silver drachma, estimated at approximately 4·4 grammes. The 'shekel' of this period (Neh. 5: 15) as a coin was probably the Graeco-Persian *siglos* weighing 5·6 grammes.

INDEX

In this select Index only the most prominent proper names have been included. Readers requiring references to the many individuals listed in the Chronicler's work should refer to a biblical concordance or to such works as J. Comay, Who's Who in the Old Testament (Weidenfeld & Nicolson, 1971) or H. H. Rowley, Dictionary of Bible Personal Names (Nelson, 1968).

Aaron, as founder of priestly line 42, 45f., 122, 196

Abraham 14, 16f., 91, 111, 143, 155, 201, 222f.

Alexander the Great 4

'Amen', as liturgical response 92

angel of the LORD 109, 111, 282

ark: as symbol of divine presence 137, 148; brought to Jerusalem 77f., 84–6, 90, 92, 114, 163, 175

Assyria: conquest of northern kingdom 36f., 269, 271; attack on Judah 250, 258, 261, 281–3; decline of 289, 291f., 301f.

Baal: as place-name 32; as element in personal names 55, 81; condemnation of worship of 258

Babylonian Chronicle 301, 304

Babylonian Empire 301f., 304, 308

Bathsheba 10, 24f., 69f., 99, 104

Benjamin, tribe of 50, 54f., 62, 74, 108

breath of God *see* spirit

burial-practice 207, 232, 240f., 262, 285, 302

Calebite genealogies 21f., 29

canon: the Old Testament as 'scripture' 1, 79, 91, 188

census 31, 108, 134

cherubim 78, 156

coined money 142, 239

continuity, as theological theme 6, 8, 58, 152, 155, 162f., 223f., 305

David: his reign as Israel's true beginning 6, 64; secular achievement 66–82, 98–105; preparations for the temple 6, 10, 44, 61, 114–43, 156, 268, 299; promise of successors 11, 24, 94f.; 'a new David' 11, 26, 95, 97

deuteronomic writers 5, 94, 156, 162f., 241, 286, 296, 307

disease 207, 228f., 252f., 284

door-keepers 61, 92, 129f.

Edom 16f., 100, 228f., 246f.

Elijah 21, 228f.

exile 6, 36f., 43, 96, 167, 267, 304, 307f.

exodus from Egypt 96, 156, 172

Ezra, book of 3–6, 37, 114, 303, 308f.

genealogies, significance of 8–12, 16, 24–6, 42–4

Gibeon 30, 92, 112, 148

glory of the LORD, the 163, 171

Greek translation of the Old Testament 2

Hebron 22, 66, 75

high priest 9, 43, 241

hill-shrines, suppression of 200, 208

history, the Chronicler's understanding of 5f., 144, 191, 288f.

Israel: 'all Israel' as theological motif 58, 78, 85, 98, 134, 137, 183, 192, 267, 296; northern kingdom 183, 204, 208, 214–16, 245, 269f., 274

Jehoiachin (Jeconiah) 25f., 306

Jeremiah 50, 302, 306–8

Jerusalem: signficance for the Chronicler, 3, 6f., 78, 189, 195f., 247,